MARK DAVIES

Glad to have you
part of my home

Allen Hamer
2/24/2014

a home
OF THEIR OWN

a home
OF THEIR OWN

The story of Ohio's
Greatest
Orphanage

Edward Lentz

ORANGE FRAZER PRESS
Wilmington, Ohio

ISBN 978-1933197-722

Additional copies of *A Home of Their Own* may be ordered directly from:
Orange Frazer Press
P.O. Box 214
Wilmington, OH 45177

Telephone 1.800.852.9332 for price and shipping information.
Website: *www.orangefrazer.com*

Art direction & cover: Jeff Fulwiler
Formatting and additional text: John Baskin

Cover scene, courtesy Wright State University, *Dayton Daily News* Archives, as well as the photographs on pages 110-11, 198-199, 202, 250-251, 270, 313.
The photograph on page 316 is courtesy the *Columbus Dispatch*.

Second printing

Library of Congress Cataloging-in-Publication Data

Lentz, Edward R.
  A home of their own : the story of Ohio's greatest orphanage / Edward Lentz.
      p. cm.
  Includes bibliographical references and index.
  ISBN 978-1-933197-72-2
  1. Ohio Soldiers' and Sailors' Orphans' Home--History. 2. Orphanages--Ohio--Xenia--History. 3. Public welfare--Ohio--Xenia--History. 4. Orphans--Biography. I. Title.
  HV995.X462L46 2010
  362.73'2--dc22
                    2010013329

To the houseparents, teachers, administrators, and veterans groups—all those who helped raise the children of the Home.

Table of contents

The Rooney Fund Board

It was the campus of Never -A-Dull-Moment, and an activity for everyone: From top, the Boy Scouts; the Peter Pan 6 kids, circa 1942; a kid from the Class of 1954; a young lady from the 1940s; the Home band; and a lineup of Home cadets.

Introduction

We always just called it "the Home." Others may have known it as the Ohio Soldiers and Sailors Orphans Home from when it was founded in 1869 or—after 1978—as the Ohio Veterans' Children's Home. But for those who lived there, it was and is "the Home."

The Rooney Fund has sponsored this history of the OSSO/OVCH so that everyone can learn more about what the State of Ohio did for the children of its veterans, originally those Civil War veterans killed or disabled in defense of the Union, and then all Ohio veterans. We also want to show how progressive, unique, and innovative the Home was during its 125 years of caring for children. This book is one way we can honor the place of our childhood and say "thank you" to the family that raised us.

Over 13,500 children spent some or all of their childhood at the Home, located in Xenia, Ohio. It was created at the urging of the Grand Army of the Republic and of Governor Rutherford B. Hayes. The Home was a large place, growing from the original 100 acres of land and three cottages to encompass almost 500 acres and more than forty buildings. There were 125 children enrolled when it opened on August 25, 1870; at its peak, more than 900 children resided there. For most of the years, the average on-campus population was about 500 pupils.

The Home's size, its resources, and its long-term, dedicated staff of teachers, houseparents, and administrators were critical elements in the Home's success with the children who lived there, especially those who came at a young age and graduated from the high school. As a new student ("newkie"), it didn't take long to begin to meet other children and adults. A feeling of stability and security quickly developed—a belief that you belonged and that you could stay. It was your home and those around you were glad to know you and welcome you to the community. There was always someone to whom you could turn for advice or if you just wanted to talk about what was on your mind. The Home could not replace parents, but the many long-term employees did guide, direct, and encourage you to succeed. Most important, the Home provided us a place to grow to become adults.

It was largely a self-sufficient community. We had our own academic school, trades school, hospital, chapel, power plant for heating and electricity, water tower, laundry, shoe and tailor shops, farm, butcher shop, greenhouse, and housing for employees.

In addition to a full academic and vocational education, the Home provided numerous activities for the boys and girls to explore and gain a sense of achievement. Music, choir, and band were always a part of the Home and many times the programs earned superior ratings in state contests. The marching band traveled each summer around the state, and occasionally outside the state, to march in veteran parades. The drama program involved various grade levels and presented several shows each year. There were troops for Boy Scouts and Girl Scouts, along with rifle teams, photo clubs, and arts and craft activities.

The success of the Home's high school sports teams helped identify us to others and give us a sense of pride. In the early days, baseball was the principal sport; while there were no organized leagues, the Home regularly defeated local teams, including some college teams. When we competed in leagues in later years, we became a school to be respected in the three major sports—football, basketball, and track.

Calendar year 1941 was a sports year to remember at the Home. We were in the Final Four in basketball that winter; in the spring we won the state track championship for the second year in a row; and that fall the Home football team not only was undefeated—its opponents didn't score a single point (359–0)! The Home's second team came closest to scoring, as they got to the five-yard line in an intrasquad scrimmage.

In the years that followed, the Home's high school sports program continued to be successful, fielding some great basketball teams, some undefeated football teams, and winning six state track titles. Cross country and soccer were added to the sports program in the last years of the Home and also were quite successful. Success at the Home often led to success for students after they left the Home.

In 1978, the Home's name was changed to the Ohio Veterans' Children's Home. Admission standards also were changed and, in subsequent years, the population dropped below 200 students. Children came for shorter periods of time and many had behavioral problems. While many things previously done at the Home were no longer able to be done, the children still had many advantages they did not have before they came. The Home provided them with stability, security, and caring employees. Continued success came to many.

Two groups of people—veterans and ex-pupils—made the Home special and supported it throughout its 125-year history. Veterans, in the form of the Grand Army of the Republic, were there from the beginning. Many new veterans' groups formed during the 20th Century and all supported the Home. They sponsored parties for all holidays and were present on every Field Day, Veterans Day, and Memorial Day. They also sponsored cottages and provided "extras" for the cottages, such as radios and TV's, band uniforms, and birthday presents. They raised money to build a bandshell for summer concerts and buy movie equipment so we could have a movie each Saturday night. They helped with many other projects the state did not support, including providing cash awards to top seniors in the graduating class. They made Christmas special, spending many hours buying and wrapping presents so each child had a happy Christmas morning. They also used their considerable influence over the years to insure that the Home was financed by the state of Ohio. It was an expensive place to operate but they helped make sure we had good food, good clothes, good housing, and a good education.

In 1880, ten years after the Home opened, the Association of Ex-Pupils (AXP) was founded and became an integral leader of support for the Home and the children. They raised funds to build a library for the school (now the Home museum building), construct bleachers and lights for the football field, erect scoreboards for both football and basketball, and provide cash awards for outstanding graduating seniors, among many other projects. The commitment of the ex-pupils to their Home is perhaps best expressed by their return each Fourth of July for a three day reunion. And even though the last children left the Home in 1995, they still return. They also return to the Home grounds for a Christmas dinner and on Memorial Day to honor the children who died at the Home.

Two major projects led by ex-pupils were the 1963 book *Pride of Ohio* and the creation of the Rooney Fund. *The Pride of Ohio* was written by Edward W. Hughes (1880 graduate) and William C. McCracken (1877) and edited by McKinley Warth (1914) and Lloyd Brewster (1923). It is a history of the Home from its beginning until 1962. McCracken was one of the original 125 students to come to the Home in 1870.

The Rooney Fund was founded by Morrison Gilbert (1956) in honor of J. R. Rooney, an English and drama teacher who died in 1972 after more than thirty years giving to the children; it also honors all other employees who had been important to an ex-pupil. The Rooney Fund, in addition to sponsoring this book, has awarded more than one million dollars in financial aid to ex-pupils to attend college.

Finally, and perhaps most important, a Home museum was created during the 1980s by a handful of ex-pupils to display artifacts, pictures, and to maintain the available written material on the history of the Home. Leading the effort were Alfred (Abie) Reynolds (1935) and Janice Dawson Zahn (1948). Appropriately, the museum is housed in the building donated to the Home by the Association of Ex-Pupils in the 1920s. Without these efforts by former students of the Home, this history would have not been possible. The Rooney Fund would also like to thank the more than eighty ex-pupils who took the time to be interviewed and the ex-pupils who sent photographs.

—*William H. Chavanne,*
president of the Rooney Fund

Prefatory note

This is the story of a great American institution.

The Ohio Soldiers and Sailors Orphans Home was founded in 1870 and for more than a century, it provided thousands of young people a place to call home. From the time the Home was founded in Xenia, Ohio, after the American Civil War, it was not only a refuge for young children. It was also a place where innovations in the care and treatment of young people would soon be adopted by many other places in America.

The OSSO Home was not unique. There were a number of other institutions in several other states that were founded after the American Civil War to deal with the large number of young people left without parents after that extraordinary conflict. Some of them still exist as treatment centers for young people with emotional or other social problems.

But few of them were ever as important or ever as effective as this place in Ohio.

It is important to understand just how different this place was and even now —several years after its closing—still is.

Orphanages have existed as long as there have been orphans. And that is a very long time. For most of human history, people living in groups have made some arrangement or another for the children among them who have been left without parents. Some of the earliest known written records of people living groups deal with, among other things, how children will be cared for if they are without one or more parents.

After America ceased being a New World and became simply a home of many people from the Old World, it was not long before children without parents became an issue once again—as it had been for more than a millennium in the places the newcomers left behind.

It should not be too surprising that many of the ways of dealing with homeless children in Europe would be adopted in America as well—whether one was in New France, New Spain or New England.

Since the language America speaks is English, and the laws America obeys are largely English, it should also be understandable that much of the way America has treated its orphan children has derived from England as well.

Over much of the first two centuries of the American colonial and new national experience, how we dealt with orphan children was often a reflection of the systems that had been left behind.

This was after all a new country. And Americans often did things a bit differently.

For most of the early years of the American story, the new colonies tucked in along the Atlantic seaboard had not needed orphanages. There were simply not all that many people and families tended to take care of one another.

But by the early 1830's, the world had changed. There were a lot more people and they were living very closely together. As towns became cities and cities issued forth more and more homeless children, it soon became clear that some place to put them was definitely needed.

The result was the orphanage in its modern form.

Some people a hundred and fifty years ago thought that orphanages were a very good idea. Some people thought they were just plain wrong. That debate was not decided then and—to some extent— it still goes on today.

But whether the orphanage was the nightmare of Charles Dickens' "Oliver Twist" or whether it was the "Home" of pleasant recollection, it was nevertheless a needed place in a troubled time.

The place whose story is told here was not a common place in its time or in ours. Most orphanages—through most of human history—have not been public places. Sponsored by private donors, civic groups or local groups of private donors, orphanages came to be largely religious undertakings in this country after the American Revolution.

There were a number of reasons why this came to be the case. But the most important reason was that a lot of religious people did not want to have their orphans raised in another faith.

So they weren't.

This should remind us of a few other things about the people who were our forebears. First, they were generally very religious. Second, they were also quite patriotic. And third, they simply did not define the family—and what that family did with most of its time—in the same way we do today.

The debate over how society looked at its children and—for that matter— how they looked at themselves rages on even today among people who study such things in considerable detail.

Some of this debate will spill over into this story as well. Simply trying to understand why children behave the way they do is based on how we believe children are likely to behave.

In the interest of clarity of explanation, a few assumptions should be stated.

For more than forty years, a debate has raged about just how childlike children were a couple of hundred years ago. Were these folks little adults or were they little people who behaved mostly—like children.

I happen to believe that kids will be kids—then and now.

For an even longer time, an even more vigorous debate has raged about whether orphanages ever did or ever could do much good. The whole thrust of modern social work looks more to the family as the place for children than a building full of other children in need.

I believe that Children's Homes did some very good work in their time. And several of them still do. There were and are many problems with children's homes. But there are even more serious problems with the current foster care system that largely has taken its place.

In the next few years, America will once again revisit this issue as we look for the best way to help children who have no friends or family to help them along the way.

And this is the last and most important point. Orphanages, foster care and adoption are not options usually chosen by the most privileged among us. Children of people of means will find themselves cared for by other friends, relatives or acquaintances of means. It is the most vulnerable and defenseless of young people who have needed the help of public and private care. It is to aid them that we as a society are looked to for help. And we as a society should and will meet that need.

This is not a fully delineated scholarly history of the Ohio Soldiers and Sailors Orphans Home. It is in that more difficult to define middle-ground called popular history.

How we have responded to young people in need says a lot about who we have been and who we are. We can learn a lot about what to do and not do for young people without parents by simply looking back to what has failed and what has worked in the American story.

For more than 125 years, the Ohio Soldiers and Sailors Orphans Home worked and worked quite well.

Its buildings still stand south of Xenia, Ohio. And many of the thousands of people who lived there are with us still.

This is the story of that place and its people.

Generations of students passed between these pillars and at the end of the winding path found something that before had proven elusive to them —a home of their own.

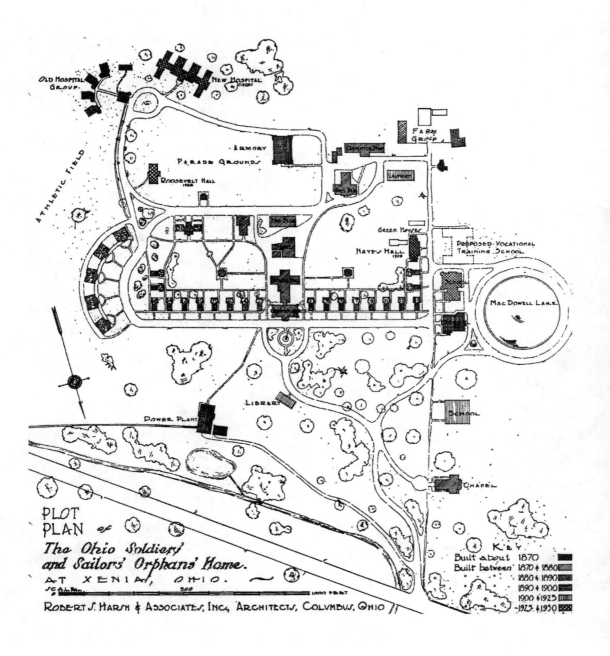

OLD HOSPITAL GROUP.

NEW HOSPITAL 1928

ATHLETIC FIELD

ARMORY

PARADE GROUNDS

ROOSEVELT HALL 1928

FARM GROUP

GREEN HOUSE

HAYES HALL 1920

PROPOSED VOCATIONAL TRAINING SCHOOL

MAC DOWELL LAKE

LIBRARY

POWER PLANT

SCHOOL

CHAPEL

PLOT PLAN of
The Ohio Soldiers'
and Sailors' Orphans' Home.
AT XENIA, OHIO.
SCALE 500 1000 FEET

ROBERT S. HARSH & ASSOCIATES, INC, ARCHITECTS, COLUMBUS, OHIO

KEY
Built about 1870
Built between 1870 & 1880
1880 & 1890
1890 & 1900
1900 & 1925
1925 & 1950

a home
OF THEIR OWN

A place called

Poverty Knoll *(circa 1870)*

OHIO SOLDIERS' AND SAILORS' ORPHANS' HOME.

A walk in the woods

On August 25, in the year 1870, a procession of children from the Ohio Soldiers and Sailors Orphans Home moved through the streets of Xenia, Ohio. One hundred and twenty-four boys and girls—Civil War orphans living in the OSSO Home's rented quarters on Main Street—carried with them all their material possessions and, no doubt, their dreams of a better life as they made the move from downtown to the former Pelham farm, known as Poverty Knoll, on the south side of Xenia.

To reach their new home, the children walked along a lane to the Pelham cabin, then over a log bridge across a small creek and up a slope to the dirt road that led to the front door. Joining the procession was 13-year-old E. Howard Gilkey, whose father had died fighting for the Union side in the war.

"I wish you could see it with the eager eyes of childhood as we saw it on that summer day," Gilkey wrote many years later, recalling the 100-acre site where the Grand Army of the Republic, the country's most powerful veterans

The good doctor Griswold and his "rigorous regimen" helped set the Home's work.

group, had begun construction of the new soldiers and sailors orphanage. Actually, there was not all that much to see on the heavily forested ridge above the meandering branch of Shawnee Creek. Where several acres of forest had been cleared, there were huge tree stumps and big piles of brush. Only three of twenty-four brick cottages planned for the site had been built. The future administration building was just a foundation—still several years from completion.

For the time being, the children would call a two-story frame building their home.

"It stood alone on the little knoll at the edge of the clearing in the middle of the woods," remembered Gilkey. "Just one big frame structure, with its kitchen, laundry and storeroom huddled in the rear like an enormous hen with three or four small chickens in her wake. I think (that) of all the inanimate witnesses to the progress of events at the time, the old Main Building is most entitled to be preserved as it was when it opened its hospitable doors to the children (who) came out from Xenia with wagon loads of furniture and hands full of personal belongings on the 25th day of August, 1870."

Nevertheless, there was nothing on the grounds to give the place "a sense of habitation," as Gilkey put it. No walkways. No driveways. No lawns. To get to their new home, he and the other children walked through piles of carpenter and plaster sweepings spread across the road and the path in front of the building. "It was like moving into a new house by the front door, just as the workmen left through the back door."

The boys and girls took separate staircases to the segregated dormitory and their bunks filled with straw on the second floor. For supper that first night, they had bread and milk, served in the first-floor dining room. "There was no attempt to cook a regular meal," wrote Gilkey. "It was sufficient that we had a wholesome supper, and that the bedding was in order by bedtime. Everyone capable of helping in moving was expected to lend a hand, and without the slightest discomfort to anyone, we were established in our new quarters comfortably."

Coal stoves provided warmth, and oil lamps lit the children's way through the building. Despite the somewhat primitive utilities and the lack of modern comforts, including inside plumbing, the matrons, teachers and staff of the Orphans Home were thrilled, too, by the prospect of a place they could call their own. Leading the procession from downtown was the Home's new superintendent, Dr. Luther Dwight Griswold. Dr. L.D. Griswold, as he was usually referred to, had assumed leadership of the orphanage three months earlier, riding into town, recalled Gilkey, with "his good wife in a closed physician's buggy, driving his little bay mare Fannie, bringing also his pet terrier dog Gyp."

Dr. Griswold knew what it was like to be one of many children. There were eleven in his family. He grew up on the family farm in Connecticut, the son of a veteran of the Revolutionary War, and began teaching in rural schools. By the age of 21, he had saved a small fortune—twenty dollars—and decided to head west to seek his destiny. He made it as far as Elyria, Ohio, visiting two of his sisters and staying on as a school teacher in the village. After studying medicine with a local doctor, Luther moved back east to Massachusetts to finish his studies, then returned to Ohio and married Jerusha Smith in 1835. Though suffering from poor health for most of the rest of her life, Mrs. Griswold was a strong supporter of her husband's work throughout the forty years of their marriage and became the chief matron of the Orphans Home.

Prior to coming to Xenia, Dr. Griswold practiced medicine in several Ohio communities and served as a trustee of the Northern Ohio Lunatic Asylum for ten years. During the Civil War, he was a surgeon in the Union Army. Following the conflict, he served two terms in the Ohio Senate and was instrumental in establishing the Reform and Industrial School for Girls in Delaware, Ohio, in 1868, where he first became aware of the OSSO Home in Xenia.

Drawing on his military experience, as well as his experience in institutions, Dr. Griswold set out a rigorous regimen for his young charges—a regimen that began every morning with the Home's clerk, Albert French, a one-armed veteran of the Civil War and an accomplished bugler, blowing reveille. With his horn, French also called the children to lunch and school. One morning, though, he blew reveille but failed to call the children to breakfast. French simply left the grounds and never returned, his whereabouts forever a mystery. His bugle was replaced with a large bell in a tower in front of the main building. In 1873, a large steam whistle took the place of the bell and remained in service for the rest of the history of the Home.

Dr. Griswold faced an extraordinary number of challenges as the Orphans Home began operations in its new location, not the least of which was the care and protection of 124 children (and more arriving seemingly every day) on what was still an active construction site. Not only had most of the buildings needed for the Home's growing population yet to be built, the money to build them had not yet been guaranteed by the Ohio legislature. Also, much of the area was not fully cleared. Years later, the children who were present at the beginning would remember watching the crew of the horse-drawn "stump puller" removing more than 400 tree stumps and the huge bonfires fueled by the large piles of brush left behind by the felling of trees. "No one, except (on) a lark, ever wandered as far away as the east woods," Gilkey wrote in his recollection. "The field to the east was grown waist- and shoulder-high, even head-high, with weeds."

To maintain order and discipline, to ensure that everyone was fed, clothed and educated, to make the Home "work," in other words, required rules. "Every morning at breakfast, Dr. Griswold would come into the dining room while the children were still at the tables and, rapping for order, announce that certain boys would report to the office for police duty," wrote Gilkey. The superintendent called out a dozen names or more so that the matrons, the teachers, the children—everyone— knew who the "officers" were each day. "In such cases," asserted Gilkey, "there could be no misunderstanding."

Matrons, of course, took care of the children, while teachers were responsible for their education. Over the years, the Home would add staff to provide job training until residents spent approximately half of each day in class and the other half learning a trade. In the beginning, though, Dr. Griswold implemented three separate sets of rules to make sure that all parties knew what was expected of them. His "general regulations," as well as the rules to be observed by cottage and dormitory managers and the rules to be followed by the children, reflected the expectations of the Board of Managers.

"The class of persons who are the recipients of its care, although now helpless, have a future which it is hoped the Home will thoroughly prepare them to meet," stated the board in its first annual report to the Governor of Ohio. "This unfortunate class are to be reclaimed, in many instances, from almshouses, from the streets and squalid places, and often from a life of vice and crime, and furnished a comfortable home, food, clothing, education and moral, mental and physical training. They are to be prepared to successfully run the race of life, and to cope with those children who have not been so unfortunate as to lose their father in their country's battles."

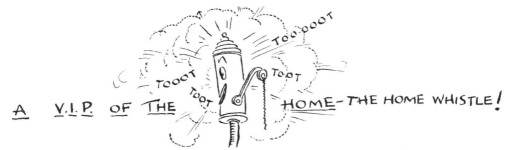

A V.I.P. OF THE HOME—THE HOME WHISTLE!

YOU COULD PUT YOUR TIME PIECES AWAY—EVERY THING STARTS AND STOPS BY WHISTLE.

The Home's original building was no harbinger of what Poverty Knoll—in only a few years—would really become.

The OSSO Home would be open for visitors on all days, except Saturdays and Sundays, from 10 a.m. to noon and 2 to 5 p.m. *"Persons not employed in the Institution will not be allowed in the dormitory rooms, private rooms or work rooms, except during reception hours, nor will they be allowed at any time to stroll over the buildings unattended."* Nor would employees be allowed to leave the grounds during "business hours" without permission.

Cottage and dormitory managers were to *"discharge every duty and exercise every care with strict impartiality, taking the place of a mother as far as possible. . . . In correcting the children, great care should be taken to do it in kindness, and in no case should a child be struck about the head. . . . The children should be thoroughly bathed at least once a week. . . . Cottage and Dining Hall Managers are to go to the Dining Hall with their children at meal time, and give close attention to their conduct during the meal, and also to see that they do not talk in the dining hall. . . ."*

Dr. Griswold laid down eight rules for the children:

"The use of profane or vulgar language will not be tolerated.

"No child can use the filthy weed, tobacco, and remain in the Institution.

"All will observe a quiet and orderly deportment in and about the building.

"At bell ringing, all children must repair promptly to the hall, ready to go to their several school rooms.

"No one will be allowed in school rooms or school halls unless by permission, outside of school hours.

"Children belonging to cottages are expected to go immediately from school rooms and dining halls to their cottages, unless detailed for duty.

"Those detailed for duty will attend to those duties promptly without contention."

And lastly, *"There must be prompt and willing obedience to all orders."*

The children spent half the day in the three classrooms on the ground floor. They used *McGuffey Readers*, *Wilson's Union Speller*, *Ray's Arithmetic Series*, *Ray's Algebra*, *Guyot's Geographies*, *Wilson's U.S. Histories*, *Harvey's Grammar*, a text on physiology, and the *Spencerian Copy Book*. After school, they worked. The boys helped out on the farm, milking the cows and feeding the pigs. They cut wood, scrubbed and swept the schoolrooms, built fires in the morning and tended them during the day. The girls made the beds in the dormitories, washed the dishes, set the tables, and did most of their own mending. "They are taught habits of neatness and order," stated Dr. Griswold in the report to the Governor. "Both boys and girls are taught to be polite and considerate toward each other, and towards all persons they may meet at the Home and elsewhere. It is our object to fit them for respectable positions in society and for lives of usefulness."

But there was time for play and celebration, too. That first Christmas, the OSSO Home received a $200 organ from a Mr. Wright of Cincinnati and holiday presents from folks in Cleveland, Columbus, Cincinnati, Springfield, Elyria, Wilmington, and Xenia. Mr. Burr of Ashland sent $125. W.S. Furay of Columbus gave them $125 in cash. The Xenia Post of the Grand Army of the Republic presented the Home with two tenor drums, one bass drum, and two fifes—"all in good order," reported Dr. Griswold, "so our martial band was fully equipped."

At the end of the year, there were 219 children living in the soldiers and sailors orphanage—140 boys and seventy-nine girls.

From the outset, there was a distinct sense of order. Yet, it must be said that in addition to his firm belief in a disciplined approach to life for the young people in his charge, Dr. Griswold liked children. He liked working *with* them, and *for* them, as Joe Morris, the son of a Civil War veteran and mother who died in childbirth, discovered after being dropped off at the OSSO Home at age 5. An aunt, unknown to the child, took him from Dayton to Xenia, then on the long walk out to Poverty Knoll. They were both tired and stopped to rest at the chapel, where the boy fell asleep. The aunt, wanting to get back, awakened him, pointed out the cottages, and pushed him along. *Imagine the feelings of the child, hungry, torn from mother and home, thrust into a strange world, sick in heart.* When he held back, she slapped him. The first violence he ever received. Too young to understand. Again she pushed him from her and told him there would be food and drink up at the cottages.

Joe toddles along, small for his age, hungry, thirsty, then he falls. When he reaches the cottages, he crawls up the steps, pants torn, hands and knees bleeding. He bursts into uncontrollable sobs.

A woman comes, full of pity, picks him up, and carries him to the superintendent's office. The boy's face is streaked with dust, tears, and sweat. The woman explains how she found him on the steps. Then Dr. Griswold takes him in his arms, wipes his face, soothes him, and calls for milk.

The woman, Mrs. Burroughs, asks for the boy, but Dr. Griswold says, "Mary, you are full now, about thirty . . . ?"

"But doctor, I want him."

"So take him, Mary. Bathe him and feed him and put him to bed. I'll call later and look him over. Poor waif, just a derelict cast into the stream . . ."

And so, the boy would write years later, "The good OSSO Home plucked me out, and soon I fell into blessed sleep in Mrs. Burroughs's arms. O two of God's greatest creations, Mrs. Burroughs and Dr. Griswold!"

With Mrs. Burroughs's care, food, and rest, he quickly took his place among the other children, the baby of Cottage 12, looked after by the larger boys, John Osborne, Frank Bolton, and the Burroughs boys.

Soon, it seemed that it was the only home he had ever known.

The "Poor Laws"

On the early frontier, before Ohio achieved statehood in 1803, the only mention of assistance to minors in the laws governing the Northwest Territory was a provision that children whose parents were dead or unable to support them could be placed in homes, boys as apprentices and girls as indentured servants. This option, though, which required the consent of two justices, was rarely exercised. There were still relatively few people in the territory, and the bonds of family and acquaintance usually meant no child was truly alone.

The first significant "Poor Law," as early relief measures were called, was passed in 1795. Developed from the English model brought to America's shores in the early 17th century, the law established tests to qualify a person for "settlement" and public assistance due to illness, infirmity, disability, or loss of support, as was the case with widows and orphans left helpless in the wake of the Indian Wars. Detractors of this so-called "outdoor" delivery system believed, though, that only within the four walls of an institution could the destitute be adequately cared for and protected.

Thus, in 1816, Ohio lawmakers gave counties and townships the option of providing "indoor" relief to the needy. Sometimes called poorhouses or almshouses, these early 19th century establishments—ancestors, in some ways, of the modern-day homeless shelter—welcomed "the poor, the tired, the huddled masses" of poet Emma Lazarus's famous 1883 sonnet inscribed on the Statue of Liberty. Unfortunately, in doing so they became "loathsome places," to quote one written account, teeming with "the sick, the aged, the disabled, the able-bodied paupers and their children, the orphans, the idiots, and the insane."

To alleviate the overcrowded conditions, poorhouses could farm out minors as apprentices and indentured servants to local households. They also were allowed to discharge a person admitted for illness as soon he or she recovered, or maintain the sick and incapacitated elsewhere, in "county infirmaries," if they could not be treated on the premises or at home. Over time, the local institutions made alternate (and more suitable) arrangements for many of the needy people—young and old—in their communities. But by the early 1830s, the world had changed.

The new colonies tucked in along the Atlantic seaboard had not needed group homes and treatment facilities as life unfolded in America; there simply weren't the numbers of needy, and families tended to take care of one another. Now, with Ohio's population mushrooming and people coagulating in cities, the poorhouses, almshouses, and infirmaries could not treat all of the afflicted—especially those with "special" needs. Over the course of three decades, Ohio would build state facilities for the deaf (1829), the blind (1837), the mentally ill (1837), and the developmentally disabled (1857). It would take the passing of another decade however, and a crisis of colossal proportions, before the state assumed guardianship over orphaned children, providing them the same institutional care and protection afforded other special needs groups.

The Civil War sparked a great social transformation in America. Never had so many men been called from their homes for so long. Never had so many failed to return. At the outbreak of the conflict in 1860, the United States was a country of about thirty million people. When the war ended, more than 600,000 soldiers from the North and the South were dead, killed in the battles and sieges from Fort Sumter to Appomattox. Hundreds of thousands had been badly wounded, and an untold number of civilians killed or maimed.

As the state with the greatest percentage of its population involved in the fighting, Ohio suffered a heavy loss of life. Approximately 350,000 of its able-bodied men fought on the side of the North, prompting Abraham Lincoln to declare as the Civil War came to a conclusion that "Ohio has saved the Union"—but in doing so, more than 34,000 died of battle wounds or disease. Another 30,000 were so badly wounded they were either partially or totally disabled for the rest of their lives. Many of the soldiers who came marching home, returned emotionally scarred, unable to continue the lives they once led. Among the groups desperately in need of help were the sons and daughters of the war-torn families.

In the beginning

The first public orphanage in America was established by the city fathers of Charleston, South Carolina, in 1790. The Charleston Orphan House admitted children from dislocated and distressed families unable to support and maintain them following the Revolutionary War. Charleston had originally tried to place its orphans with local families after the war. But the numbers were too great and it was decided to build an institution and keep all of the children at one place. The Charleston Orphan House served as a model for other institutions across the country, most of which would not be publicly managed.

A private group was formed to care for orphans in New York City in 1797. Another was formed in Philadelphia in the same year by a Catholic priest after a massive yellow fever epidemic destroyed many families. And in 1799 an institution for the care of homeless girls was established in Baltimore. A similar group for orphan girls was founded in Boston the following year. By 1800, these few orphanages were operating in America largely as a result of the distress and dislocation caused by the American Revolution. But most people still relied on locally delivered public and private assistance to meet the needs of their communities. And such would be the case for a number of years in the Ohio Country as well.

The building of at least a few new orphanages in Ohio was something of a reflection both of the reform spirit of the times and also a recognition that the system of poor relief then in operation in the state was not working all that well. In Cincinnati, the Catholic Sisters of Charity founded St. Peters in 1828, which was followed in 1832 by the ominous-sounding Protestant Cincinnati Orphans "Asylum." A businessman by the name of Joseph Hare opened Columbus's first home for orphans, also in 1832. It would be almost another twenty years before Cleveland had an orphanage.

In 1857, Katherine Fay Ewing founded Ohio's first "Children's Home" in Marietta. Saddened by the conditions that children endured in the county poorhouse, Ewing located her home on a ten-acre farm she bought with borrowed funds ($200) and her modest inheritance ($150). The county paid her $1 a week per resident, provided each child with a suit of clothes, and paid one-half of the medical bills and funeral expenses if needed.

By 1862, two-thirds of Katherine Fay Ewing's boarders were soldiers' orphans. Meanwhile, the number of private orphanages in Cincinnati had grown to six. In Columbus, children found refuge in the Hare Orphan House, the Female Benevolent Society and the Hannah Neil Mission and Home for the Friendless. Cleveland, which still had just one orphanage, operated a city infirmary that sent homeless kids to the City Industrial School, known as "The Ragged School," and a non-residential shelter called the House of Refuge, for their education.

On March 4, 1865, one month before Lee surrendered at Appomattox, President Lincoln delivered his second inaugural address to a divided nation, calling on all Americans to care not only for "him who shall have borne the battle" but for "his widow and his orphan" as well. Lincoln's message would resonate through the small southwestern Ohio community of Xenia, where citizens already had begun discussing a proposal to build a home for the orphans of the war.

Benevolence apparently was a Xenia tradition. In 1803—the year Ohio became a state—a local surveyor, Joseph Vance, had been appointed to lay out a town as the county seat for newly-formed Greene County, after selecting a tract along an old buffalo trace known as the Bullskin Trail (now U.S. Route 68), where two branches of Shawnee Creek joined and flowed west to the Little Miami River. To choose its name, Vance invited local residents and landowners to meet him in the middle of what would soon be the town. As the story goes, a well-dressed gentleman stepped forward and identified himself as Reverend Robert Armstrong. "In view of the kindly and hospitable manner in which I have been treated while a stranger to most of you," Reverend Armstrong told the gathering, "allow me to suggest the name of *Xenia*, taken from the Greek, and signifying hospitality."

History would recognize another Xenia pastor, the Reverend P.C. Prugh, as the "father" of the OSSO Home. Reverend Prugh started the discussion as he collected food, clothing, and provisions for the Union troops in the early months of the Civil War. The sanctuary he wanted to build for soldiers' and sailors' orphans had many supporters, but none would be more important in making his dream a bricks-and-mortar reality than a fledgling organization of Union veterans and an orphan, elected Governor of Ohio, who one day would become the 19th U.S. president.

Several veterans groups were established in the years immediately following the Civil War, including the Union Veterans League, the Soldiers and Sailors League, and the Boys in Blue, but few survived. Only the Grand Army of the Republic would become a national organization. America has never seen anything quite like the Grand Army. In its time and in its own way, the GAR was one of the country's most powerful groups, an army *without* arms that helped elect U.S. presidents from within its own ranks, founded hospitals for its sick and disabled members, and in Ohio, mobilized state officials and local citizens to build a one-of-a-kind, much-needed institution for its orphans.

The year 1869 saw a flurry of activity, much of it generated by the Ohio Department of the Grand Army, as momentum began to build for what very soon would be the ground-breaking OSSO Home in Xenia.

In January, at the Ohio GAR's third annual encampment and convention in Dayton, delegates from the 303 veteran posts around the state saw for themselves how an earlier pet project—the Dayton Soldiers' Home—had become an operational success. The sprawling physical plant encompassed 627 acres, and included a hospital, library, and chapel. It was run as a military institution. Men admitted and discharged themselves. They wore uniforms and were assigned to companies. They were called to daily events by bugles, cannons, and whistles.

Convention delegates visited all departments of the institution, according to a report of the proceedings, "the magnitude of which was surprising to all." The Soldier's Home was a shining example of how a grateful government could care for its defenders. By 1884, almost two thirds of the disabled veterans in America were being treated in Dayton. Chaplain George C. Collier, of Fremont, told the assembled delegates that "every battlefield of the late war" and "every prison pen" was represented in the facility. But Collier reminded the veterans of another group that still needed their help: the more than 2,000 Ohio orphans whose fathers had died or been disabled by their service to the Union Army. What the chaplain did not mention, but some of the visitors to the Soldiers' Home may have seen for themselves, was a small group of these children living in the facility. One of them, 10-year-old Thomas Molloy, showed up looking for his father and was allowed to stay because he had nowhere else to go. Molloy would be among the first children admitted to the OSSO Home in Xenia.

After receiving a committee report that paid eloquent lip service to the problem, urging the GAR "to seek promptly and earnestly by every just and

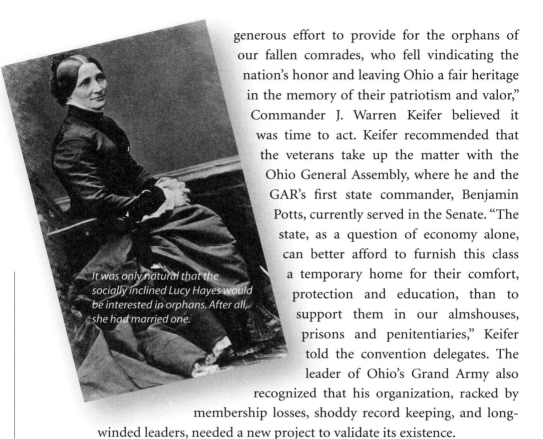

It was only natural that the socially inclined Lucy Hayes would be interested in orphans. After all, she had married one.

generous effort to provide for the orphans of our fallen comrades, who fell vindicating the nation's honor and leaving Ohio a fair heritage in the memory of their patriotism and valor," Commander J. Warren Keifer believed it was time to act. Keifer recommended that the veterans take up the matter with the Ohio General Assembly, where he and the GAR's first state commander, Benjamin Potts, currently served in the Senate. "The state, as a question of economy alone, can better afford to furnish this class a temporary home for their comfort, protection and education, than to support them in our almshouses, prisons and penitentiaries," Keifer told the convention delegates. The leader of Ohio's Grand Army also recognized that his organization, racked by membership losses, shoddy record keeping, and long-winded leaders, needed a new project to validate its existence.

On February 12—Lincoln's birthday—a bill was introduced in the Ohio Senate seeking to establish a state home. To supporters, it seemed like an opportune time; the GAR, after all, was still a force to be reckoned with, and two of its commanders had votes, if not influence, in the General Assembly. The bill, however, never made it to the Senate floor. Members of the standing committee on Benevolent Institutions tabled it indefinitely, citing what panel members believed to be the adequacy of existing facilities for the poor and orphans.

In late June, on his way to a meeting at Commander Keifer's home in Springfield to discuss the GAR's next move, Chaplain Collier stopped in Xenia and struck a deal with Reverend Prugh. The two men agreed that the pastor and his committee would seek private donations to purchase a site for the proposed orphans home, while the GAR would continue lobbying the legislature to construct the buildings and operate the institution.

The GAR leadership went a step further at the Springfield meeting, deciding that an effort should be made to open the home privately, on a temporary basis, until the state saw the wisdom of managing and maintaining a permanent facility for its growing orphan population. Their decision to move forward was no doubt influenced by a very interested observer of the deliberations that day at Commander Keifer's house.

In one sense, it was rather remarkable that the Governor of Ohio would drop in on a meeting of veterans in a private home to discuss the care of soldiers' orphans. But for Rutherford B. Hayes, it was not at all unusual. Hayes never forgot where he came from and the hard road to his success.

He was born in Delaware, Ohio, in 1822, ten days after his father—a storekeeper, farmer, and entrepreneur—died of a fever at age 35. His mother and sister became his protectors, and there were frequent visits from an uncle.

In Hayes, the Home had a powerful advocate, and being an orphan, he brought an emotional response.

After graduating from Kenyon College and Harvard Law School, "Ruddy," as he was known, eventually settled in Cincinnati in 1850. During the War Between the States, Hayes rose to the rank of major-general in the Union Army. He returned from the war, as many others did, in a state of virtual exhaustion, having had at least four horses shot out from under him and been wounded four times. But he quickly recovered and took a seat in the U.S. House of Representatives.

Hayes resigned from his congressional post to run for governor in 1867 and won a close election. He had a notably strong cohort in his wife, Lucy Webb Hayes. Ohio's new first lady was vitally interested in the social reforms sweeping across America at the time, including efforts to improve schools, prisons, and facilities for the needy, and was not shy about voicing her opinions to her husband. She shared his special interest in the plight of the poor, the weak, and the abandoned in American society. A project like Reverend Prugh's, helping orphans of the war that her husband had just endured, was especially appealing to her as well.

On July 13, one month after showing up on the GAR's doorstep, Governor Hayes traveled to Xenia to attend the third of three public meetings on Reverend

The Millen Building on Xenia's Main Street was, in 1869, the temporary home for orphans. The Home used the upstairs, and the lower part of the building indicated by the Central Market sign.

Prugh's proposal. He must have impressed the large turnout at City Hall, for by evening's end, organizers had secured $16,500 in pledges. More money would be raised in the coming days. The total came to $30,000. And the governor wasn't finished making appearances.

At its semi-annual meeting in Sandusky, the GAR agreed to establish a board of control to select a site, construct buildings, and oversee operation of the orphans home. Commander Keifer told the members that Xenia had raised the funds necessary to bring the home to that town. A number of other speakers, including Governor Hayes, suggested that the state would likely support the project as well.

On August 10, the newly-constituted board of control toured William Pelham's farm in Xenia. There was not much to see on "Poverty Knoll"—just a cabin in a clearing. Yet despite the lack of improvements and the site's less-than-inspiring name, the ground was high and dry and reasonably well drained. Reverend Prugh's fund-raising committee purchased 100 acres of the hilltop land from Pelham for $20,000 and presented the deed to the GAR board.

As autumn approached, the GAR found itself with a number of tasks to perform. It had to open a temporary home while hiring contractors and other professionals to begin the long process of building a permanent facility. It also had to persuade a reluctant legislature to fund a home sponsored by a group whose membership was smaller every day.

A humble start

In the beginning, more progress would be made with building than politicking. The board of control hired a Dayton architect named Grosskopp, who had served as a major in the Union Army and was a member of the GAR. Grosskopp's plans called for a two-story main building, 110 feet long and 46 feet wide. Residences would be two-story cottages—24 by 30 feet—with twelve on each side of the main building and connected to it by covered walkways. The buildings were to be constructed of brick at a total cost of more than $100,000.

On September 27, fifteen men began digging the basement of the main building. Shortly thereafter, bids were let to build three separate cottages identified simply as No. 1, No. 2, and No. 3. The board of control then turned its attention to opening a temporary home in downtown Xenia.

In November, the GAR rented a small building on East Main Street near the courthouse for $100 a month. (In 2010 it was still there, used as government offices.) The board of control hired the former hostess of a Put-in-Bay mansion as the first manager. When she left after a couple of months, Major M. S. Gunckel filled in as acting superintendent. Two teachers, two matrons, a seamstress, and a doctor also were added to the staff. First Lady Lucy Webb Hayes and several of her friends solicited donations of furniture, cookware, and clothing.

The first residents, James Doyle and John McNeely, arrived on December 16, cared for by Mrs. H. S. Edgerton, a matron from Cincinnati, and Mr. A. A. Hunt, a hospital steward from the Dayton Soldiers' Home. Two weeks later, at the first Christmas party, there were forty-four children who sat down to an elaborate dinner, presided over by Ohio's first lady. Afterwards, they opened presents under a tall Christmas tree. "I would give a thousand dollars for a picture of this occasion, painted on canvas," said Chaplain Collier in his remarks. Later, Governor Hayes would write, "Mrs. Hayes, with Mrs. Lovejoy of Columbus, ransacked the City of Columbus for money, books, gifts, etc., to make this occasion enjoyable for the orphans. The gathering on this occasion gave to the home great prestige."

The last children to arrive in 1869 were John and Rebecca Swift. Rebecca's stay would be brief. She was the only child to die in the Main Street Home and was buried in the Soldiers Plot in Woodland Cemetery.

By New Year's Day, fifty-three children occupied a space designed for forty-six. They attended the public schools in Xenia. William McCracken, who came to the Home in 1870 and was discharged nine years later, would go on to a distinguished career at The Ohio State University, where the college power plant still bears his name. His reminiscences were placed in the cornerstone of a school building in 1941: "The older children went to the old high school building on East Market Street in Xenia, the younger children went to the old grade school on West Market, just east of the railroad tracks. The old high school is gone and the West Market Street building has been replaced with a new one. We studied physical geography, algebra, Ray's higher arithmetic, elocution and grammar—no languages . . ."

In January of 1870, the GAR rented additional space on nearby Greene Street, and the children were permitted to play in the courthouse yard with kids from town. "One day when some of the children were playing with town children in the courthouse yard," recalled Albert "Abbie" Hudson, who lived in the Home at the time, "one of the Home children said or did something that caused one of the town boys to become angry and he called the Home boys 'poor charity kids.' William Kemp, ever present when a fight was on, overheard the remark and at once resented it and shortly the orphans home boys demonstrated fully that the blood of their fathers coursed through their veins. The one battle was sufficient; ever after the town boys and the Home boys got along fine."

After the three cottages on Poverty Knoll were completed, the board of control realized the new residences would be of little use without a kitchen and school classrooms. Construction of the main building was expected to take several years, so the board decided to put up a temporary two-story frame building and another smaller structure for use as a kitchen and laundry. The children would spend most of 1870 in their downtown quarters while the site was made habitable and the state legislature finally agreed to sponsor their new home in a melodrama referred to in the OSSO Home annals as "The Midnight Ride of Senator Gatch."

The Ohio General Assembly convened on January 3, 1870, in Columbus and organized itself in the wake of the '69 election. Governor Hayes had been elected to a second term and the balance of power in the both House and Senate had shifted a bit toward his party, the Republicans. But only a bit. The Senate consisted of nineteen Republicans and eighteen Democrats, neither party held a majority in the House, and a number of independent candidates had been voted into office.

Some Republicans opposed the idea of a Home. Some Democrats favored it. The votes of the Independents shifted as issues evolved and coalitions were formed. One observer described the muddled state of affairs as a "chaotic political condition." Into this maelstrom, Hayes delivered his annual message of recommended legislation—a forerunner of today's "State of the State" address. The governor cited the need for a state-sponsored orphans home.

"During the War for the Union, the people of the state acknowledged their obligations to support families of their absent soldiers and undertook to meet it, not as charity, but as a partial compensation justly due for services rendered. The nation is saved, and the obligation to care for the orphans of men who died to save it remains to be fulfilled. It is officially estimated that three hundred soldiers' orphans during the past year have been inmates of county infirmaries of the state. Left by the death of their patriotic fathers in this deplorable condition, it is the duty of the state to assume their guardianship, and to provide support, education, and homes to all who may need them. The people of Ohio regret that this duty has been so long neglected. I do not doubt that it will afford a great gratification to give this subject early and favorable consideration."

Indeed, early consideration was crucial. The Ohio Department of the Grand Army was running out of money. Delegates to the annual encampment that January were told that the state organization had only $1,116.23 in its treasury. Without more funds, it would have to close the temporary home in Xenia and re-locate the children. The GAR made an urgent appeal to Hayes for state assistance—an appeal the orphan governor forwarded to the lawmakers.

The friends of the GAR in the General Assembly tried to speed up the glacial pace of the legislature. Senator Potts, the veterans group's first commander, introduced a bill on January 7 to "establish an Ohio Soldiers' Orphans Home." It called for the creation of a board of managers and an appropriation of $125 for each child served by the Home. Over the next month, Senator Potts's bill moved through committee hearings, was modified extensively, and finally referred to a select committee in early February for further study, where it died.

A separate bill was introduced in the House by Representative Nelson Van Voorhees. It, too, called for a board of managers and setting aside $200 per year for each of the first one hundred children and $150 per year for each child in excess of one hundred. The Voorhees bill, like its doomed counterpart in the Senate, underwent a number of changes and was referred to a select committee. House members approved the measure and forwarded it to the Senate, which sent it back with amendments that were accepted by the House.

The final bill became law on April 14, 1870, the fifth anniversary of Abraham Lincoln's death. It established a board of managers, reserved a sum not to exceed $13,000 per year for the operation of the home, and established a formula of limiting reimbursement to $150 per year for each of the first one hundred children admitted to the institution and $125 for each child thereafter.

However, in a victory for opponents of the Grand Army, the new law specified that part of the property of the Reform and Industrial School for Girls, located at White Sulphur Springs in Delaware County—not the GAR's home already under construction in Xenia—would be transferred to the Board of Managers and used and occupied as the "Ohio Soldiers' and Sailors' Orphans' Home." The White Sulphur Springs institution was new, having been established in 1869, and it occupied a site previously used as a health resort.

While the struggle over the location of the OSSO Home would continue for some time, Governor Hayes wasted no time appointing a board of managers. On April 15, 1870—the day after the law was enacted—he sent his list of appointees to the Senate for confirmation:

J. Warren Keifer, of Clark County, for the term of five years;
James Barnett, of Cuyahoga County, for the term of five years;
Ralph Buckland, of Sandusky County, for the term of four years;
Benjamin. F. Coates, of Scioto County, for the term of four years;
Barnabus Burns, of Richland County, for the term of two years;
Judge Manning Force, of Hamilton County, for the term of two years;
John S. Jones, of Delaware County, for the term of one year.

One last opportunity remained for opponents of the Home to frustrate its sponsors. With the General Assembly set to adjourn for the season on Monday, April 18, opponents wanted to postpone confirmation of the governor's appointees and put off the opening of the home for at least a year. Supporters wanted the Senate to vote on the appointees before the lawmakers went home.

At 9 p.m. on Saturday, April 16, the board of manager nominations came before the Senate. By this time, two Republicans and one Democrat had left for home and the number of Republican and Democratic votes was equal. The vote for Commander Keifer resulted in a tie, as did several subsequent motions, including one for adjournment. Senator Potts, leading the fight for approval, saw that he had a deadlock and sent a message to Governor Hayes, who was staying in his office until the session ended. The note said, "Goepper is making a Dutch speech. We have them in a deadlock and they can't get out until Gatch comes. Will you send a committee to the depot and bring him forthwith?"

Senator M. D. Gatch was a Xenia resident. He had not been feeling well earlier in the day and had taken the train home, confident the Senate would approve the governor's appointees. Now his vote was needed to break the tie. Hayes asked the Little Miami Railroad to prepare a special engine and coach at the Xenia depot to bring Senator Gatch back to Columbus. The governor was also aware that calls for the other absent members had been sent out as well. After the railroad complied with his request, Hayes sent a message to the Xenia senator, asking him to return to the Senate chamber. A carriage provided by a local supporter of the Home brought Gatch to the station, where a locomotive with one car waited to make the eighty-mile trip back to the state capital.

To keep the Senate in session, Senator Goepper of Hamilton County launched into a multi-lingual filibuster. Speaking fluently in French, German, and English, Goepper whiled away the hours as the Senate waited to see who would arrive at the Statehouse first. In the course of the evening, each side made a number of efforts either to end the proceedings or keep them going. But in the end, Senator Gatch arrived and took his seat. The votes on the members of the board of managers were taken, and at 5 o'clock the next morning the governor was notified that his appointees had been confirmed.

Hayes summed up the evening in a letter to a friend.

"The hour of adjournment was fixed (for Monday) and if they could prevent confirmation for a few hours, the orphans' home was defeated for this year . . . Accordingly, the arrival of Senator Gatch gave the friends of the Home a majority.

"[Opponents] resolved to prevent its organization by a lawless, revolutionary and unprecedented resort to absquatulation. They fled from the chamber, Campbell and Hunt over to the [water] closet, others bolted out of the capitol and into the street. Hubbel of Delaware, did not remain out of sight, and Gusweiler, a Democrat assistant sergeant-at-arms, saw him, gave chase, and captured and brought him back, this made a quorum in the hall. The nominations were confirmed and the conspiracy defeated."

Over the next few months, the state would assume operation of the Home. At its first meeting on April 21, the board of managers noted that there were 125 children at Xenia receiving private support and that unless the state came to their aid at once, they would have to be dispersed. The board resolved that the children be accepted and furnished support and education.

The major issue facing the board of managers was whether or not the Home would be located at White Sulphur Springs, as specified in the newly-enacted law. Traveling to Delaware County on April 29, they found that the White Sulphur Springs site would require extensive modifications to be used as an orphans home. On May 29, the board adopted a resolution stating that the Delaware location would not serve, "comfortably and well, all of the children of deceased soldiers and sailors of the state of the class contemplated by the law . . ." The managers decided to accept, "as a donation or bequest, a suitable tract of land, of the number of acres provided by law, at a convenient and accessible point, with the necessary buildings and equipment thereon for the accommodation of not less than 250 orphans . . . ."

The only tract readily meeting that specification was the site in Xenia, Ohio, at the Pelham Farm.

With the academic year coming to an end in the Xenia City Schools, it was decided that any of the children living in the OSSO Home who wished to visit friends or relatives could do so as long as they returned at the beginning of the next school year. Transportation, both ways, would be provided by the Home. It was the beginning of a tradition that would last well into the twentieth century.

By August 1, 1870, the temporary administration and school building was completed by the Board of Control of the Grand Army. The orphans' new home was now ready for them.

On August 16, the GAR's board of control met and resolved "to convey to the state of Ohio, by deed in fee simple, the land held by said committee as trustees of the Grand Army of the Republic, together with all of the buildings and equipment thereon contained, placed there by this Board or any committee thereof."

And it was done.

The Grand Army would continue to play an important role in the life of the OSSO Home for many years. But on August 16, 1870, in Xenia, Ohio, something new and special was beginning.

At this time in America, orphaned children were decidedly not special. If they were in facilities at all, these facilities were usually infirmaries and asylums where the children shared space with adults: the aged, infirm, or the mentally ill.

The new institution in Xenia would give children their own population, their own facility. Unbelievably—in less than three years—this new institution blossomed from four original buildings into a *campus*. There was an administration building, a chapel, a hospital, a domestic building consisting of kitchen, bake shop, and dining hall, and twenty cottages. A barn and farmhouse was also part of the campus.

Almost immediately, it was at the forefront of the handful of such institutions in America. Not only was it caring for its children physically, it was educating them, and finding them a place in a world that had previously ignored them.

And so this place on a ridge in Ohio was no longer Poverty Knoll or Pelham Farm.

For Ohio's children of Civil War veterans, it was a Home of their own.

Building the Home *(1870-1900)*

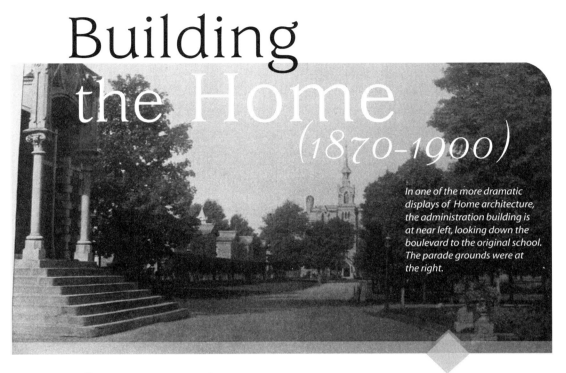

In one of the more dramatic displays of Home architecture, the administration building is at near left, looking down the boulevard to the original school. The parade grounds were at the right.

Ohio, the center of the universe

When it came time to draw up plans for permanent facilities, the Grand Army of the Republic turned to another Civil War veteran and one of the most renowned architects in America: Levi Tucker Scofield. The Cleveland native was a man of prominence in his day, known not just as the architect of grand Victorian buildings and monuments but also as the husband of a Cleveland socialite, and a friend and golfing partner of John D. Rockefeller. Scofield's commissions included the Ohio Penitentiary in Mansfield, the North Carolina Penitentiary, the Cleveland House of Corrections, the Asylum for the Insane in Athens, Ohio, and the Columbus State Hospital—the largest building under one roof in America until the Pentagon was built. But the architect always regarded the OSSO Home as one of his best projects.

Scofield recognized that the children needed air, light and space—especially

space—and thus designed a "home" that was not a grim, Gothic orphanage from the pages of Charles Dickens, but a complex of multiple buildings (including resident cottages) that had the look and feel of a traditional college campus with space for future expansion. Along with the administration of the Home and the board of trustees, the Cleveland architect urged the Ohio General Assembly to fund the construction of the various buildings. The legislators, though, had other priorities and were slow to get behind the Xenia project. So Scofield set off on a two-year excursion to Europe to improve his skills and broaden his perspective, which he put to good use with major artistic successes such as the Soldiers' and Sailors' Monument in Cleveland's public square and the "These Are My Jewels" monument in Columbus, honoring Ohio's prominent nineteenth century sons— Grant, Sheridan, Stanton, Garfield, Hayes, Chase, and Sherman. Busy with these and other projects, Scofield never again would spend time in design for the OSSO Home as he had done in 1870.

Most of the actual construction of the new buildings and grounds was undertaken by a local craftsman, Tobias Drees. A German immigrant, Drees traveled with his family to America in 1832. His parents acquired land near the town of Minster in Auglaize County, where they began to farm. To support the family, Tobias and his father went to work on the newly completed Miami and Erie Canal. At the age of 16, Tobias set off on his own, apprenticing himself as a carpenter to

An early panoramic photograph shows the Home administration building flanked by the cottages, imparting the message that ministration was not too far away.

the construction company of Crandall & Brown of Troy, Ohio. Crandall & Brown won the contract to build the Greene County Courthouse, a project that brought Drees to Xenia, where he got married, raised six children, and lived for the rest of his life.

After the courthouse was completed, Drees became an independent carpenter and contractor. Over the years he built many of the finer homes and larger business buildings in Xenia and other parts of southwest Ohio—among them the major buildings at the OSSO Home—and became a principal investor in the Xenia Twine and Cordage Company. He died in 1889.

Men like Tobias Drees and Levi Scofield had earned strong reputations for their creative design and sound craftsmanship. But as contractors they were at the mercy of Ohio's governor, state legislators, and trustees who held the Home's purse strings. The need for new buildings was only one of many priorities for the OSSO Home.

Ohio in the Gilded Age

Ohio in the late nineteenth century literally became the center of things.

Five of the seven U.S. presidents who were born in Ohio rose to power in the years between the end of the Civil War and the turn of the twentieth century.

From the very first days at the Home, Memorial Day was never an ordinary holiday. It was, after all, the day that explained why they were there. The familiar song from the Home band, played every year, was 'Flee as a Bird,' an old processional dirge.

The state produced some of the greatest innovators in American history—Edison, Kettering, and Hall.

Some of the most influential social and cultural movements in the history of the country—women's rights, temperance and prohibition, institutional care of the needy—began percolating in Ohio.

Ohio emerged from the Civil War with unprecedented economic, political and social power. Many groups sought influence with the state legislators and other officeholders. One of the most successful of these groups was the Grand Army of the Republic, which would become a powerful lobbying force in the 1880s and 1890s on behalf of the OSSO Home and its other supporters.

So-called "ripper" laws, which allowed legislators to reorganize the leadership of major state institutions, became one way in which the majority party could reward its friends and punish its enemies. The party in power, in other words, could remove the current leaders of the opposing political party and replace them with their own people. That is precisely what happened—not only in Ohio but in most states as well—for much of the nineteenth century. Most of the superintendents at the OSSO Home who were replaced during the thirty-five years following the Civil War to the turn of the century were quite competent. Each change in leadership at the top resulted in more staff turnover, with knowledge, experience, and skills often lost in the transition.

The Home faced many operational challenges in its early years, but none as potentially disruptive as the constant carousel of leaders.

> There is an orphans home not far away
> Where they feed you dog hash three times a day
> And O how those orphans crow
> When they hear that whistle blow
> O how those orphans crow three times a day.
> —student ode to the dining hall

The 1870s—The Home Defined

In 1871, as construction proceeded on the major buildings—first under the supervision of Levi Scofield and then Tobias Drees—the board of trustees and

Across the field from the old hospital, the power plant smokestack and (to its right) the administration building tower stand as sentinels over the Home.

Superintendent Griswold asked the Ohio General Assembly for $182,700, with $70,000 to be allocated for current expenses and the rest for construction. The legislators earmarked only $40,000 for expenses but provided the construction funds as requested, so the Home's trustees began letting contracts. Eleven additional cottages and a domestic building were to be completed by late 1871, a new administration building by early 1872, and a hospital by later that same year. The timetable also included construction of a barn, a farmhouse, a boiler house, and a chimney and heating system for the cottages and the domestic building. None of the projects, however, would be completed on schedule. The trustees blamed the contractors. "The board has not been remiss in urging, imploring, begging, warning, scolding and threatening contractors but all to no purpose. They have proved impervious to all attacks with a few honorable exceptions to discharge delinquent contractors and employ other parties to complete their contracts." It was a wish that was not to be granted.

Nonetheless, the new buildings that had been completed were soon put to good use by the Home as the institution continued to take in more orphans.

Dr. Griswold—who also was serving as the Home's physician—told the board that he was generally pleased with the health of the children. "I think we are particularly fortunate in our location," explained the superintendent. "The institution is situated on high ground, surrounded by pure air, and there are no swamps or other sources of malaria in the neighborhood." It was also fortunate that

The Home Battalion presents itself mightily, circa 1900, on the Home's parade grounds. The good townsfolk of Xenia, having their own army, slept well.

the Home was located south of the main rail lines entering Xenia and away from the nearby factories and the thick black cloud of dirty air that hung over the town throughout the year.

The Home had been open in its new location for more than a year before a death was recorded. On October 15, 1871, Charles Smith, of Guernsey County, died of "inflammation of the stomach and bowels in the fifteenth year of his age," it was reported. "He was one of our very best boys and his death cast a gloom over the Home." Generally, the death rate at the Home was quite low in its early years. But with a large number of young children living in close proximity one to another, colds, influenza, and other contagious diseases spread quickly through the cottages, classrooms and other facilities.

In 1872, two children died and several more were hospitalized after an outbreak of spinal meningitis. The following year, more than 200 children contracted conjunctivitis or "pink-eye." But by that time, a forty-bed hospital had been completed and Dr. Griswold had been joined by Dr. Leigh McClung, giving the Home two staff physicians. The work of the two doctors and much of the rest of the staff kept a measles outbreak under control, although one child died and more than 100 had to be hospitalized.

In September of 1872, the Home opened its new domestic building, which included a kitchen, dining room, and bake shop, as well as rooms for the officers and teachers. Much of the space in the temporary administration building was converted to classrooms. The domestic building and six new cottages—for a total of twenty—were served by a new boiler building. The barn and farmhouse were completed as well.

After the long-awaited new administration building was opened in May of 1873 and gravel roads and paths were laid around the Home, Dr. Griswold returned to his horticultural roots, planting 200 apple trees, 200 peach trees, 600 grape vines, and a large number of blackberry and raspberry bushes. It would be one of his best and longest lasting gifts to the Home.

The superintendent also decided that the clothing worn by the boys at the Home should be more military in style.

"One evening," remembered E. Howard Gilkey, "I was called into the little office of the superintendent and there was fitted on me a queer-looking gray uniform, which they told me was made from a pattern shipped from the military academy at West Point. The cloth was cadet gray. The buttons were brass and the absence of pockets as a receptacle for embarrassed hands was noticeable. We were rapidly outfitted with the new uniforms, blue navy caps being selected for our head gear. The uniforms were modified to meet the requirements of a peaceful student life." The gray uniforms would be standard attire "for boys of a certain age" until 1886, when the color of the uniform was changed to blue.

Joseph Morris wrote to his fellow ex-pupils, asking them to share their memories of the Home in the 1870s. Here are a few of the responses:

I was in Cottage 4 and 12. . . . We had the old wooden school house, no wings to cottages. Baseball grounds in front of the chapel, swimming pool at the bottom of hill near the gas house.

Remember the old frame school house? Early reunions were held in this building, dances and sleeping quarters for boys.

The first print shop with Orin Baker as boss? . . . The show, "Little Boy Blue," put on by teachers and matrons in the chapel in 1874? Joe Morris as "L.B.B."

Keifer's peach orchard south of the woods? Half a dozen boys will surely recall the time they played hooky from school and enjoyed the fruit and thought they had gotten away with it 'til just before supper, Mrs. Burroughs called us into her sitting room and changed our minds with the hickory sticks and sent us to bed supperless. . . .

It took most of a century before the old military traditions of the Home began to loosen. Here, the kids are marching to school.

Sewing carpet rags for the floor? No girls south of the main building and no boys north?

E. Manson, who donated complete baseball uniforms (but no shoes). Sent them to Jennie Nesbitt and she refused to allow us a peek 'til the first game? How Dan McCurdy was run off the field? He had borrowed a parasol and stood behind the pitcher 'til some fellow lined a hard drive through the pitcher's box and caught the parasol and away it sailed. Some girl yelled, someone started after Dan and did he run. Ah, those good old days!

In less than three years from the August day in 1870 when 124 children picked up their belongings at the Home's temporary quarters in downtown Xenia and made the walk to Poverty Knoll, the number of orphans in residence had grown to almost 600. "We have some bad and unruly children, but fully ninety out of every hundred are kind, obedient, and loving as any in the state," Dr. Griswold said in his 1873 year-end report to the board. The superintendent also informed the trustees that he had built a greenhouse—"without any appropriation from the state"—and gave them some numbers to chew on. "We consume daily about 300 loaves of bread, 300 pounds of meat, six bushels of potatoes, forty pounds of butter, the milk of sixteen cows, besides turnips, cabbages, and other garden vegetables. . . We have just placed in store two hundred barrels of excellent winter apples. We give the children apples two to three times a week."

It would be Dr. Griswold's last report. In 1873, the Ohio Democrats took advantage of voter dissatisfaction with the failing economy and with the scandals haunting the Grant Administration in Washington to get their candidate for governor, William Allen, elected over Republican incumbent Edward Noyes by a slim 817-vote margin. The 70-year-old Allen promptly demonstrated his party loyalty by presiding over the removal of most Republican appointees at state institutions under his control or encouraging the Democratic-controlled General Assembly to do the same with special legislation. After a newly-appointed board asked for Dr. Griswold's resignation, he and his wife left the Home on May 15, 1874, and returned to Elyria, where the superintendent spent his remaining years in retirement until his death in 1897. For many years his oil portrait would hang in the main hallway of the Grant Hall administration building.

Dr. Griswold's successor, Alexander Jenner, was also a trained physician from a family of doctors. Dr. Jenner's father and grandfather were physicians, so it was not surprising that Alexander chose to study medicine after growing up near Mansfield,

Ohio, where the Jenners had relocated from Philadelphia in the 1840s. Dr. Jenner opened a practice in the town of Crestline in Crawford County, where he was also active in the local Democratic Party, and served in the Civil War as a surgeon with the 28th Ohio Volunteer Infantry and 5th Ohio Volunteer Infantry. After the war, he served two terms in the Ohio Senate. He and his wife, Anna, were the parents of five children.

Dr. Jenner had a short—and controversial—term in office at the OSSO Home. He had been on the job only a few months when stories began to circulate about his morals, prompting an investigation by the board. After lengthy testimony from a number of witnesses, Dr. Jenner submitted his resignation. The Annual Report of the Board of Trustees for 1874 summarized the proceedings, stating, "The board at once accepted [Dr. Jenner's resignation] and dismissed the charges and specifications against him. The board has not thought that any more minute report of the charges or the evidence is required to be made public, or would promote the ends of justice or the good of the Home." Dr. Jenner took up residence in Dayton and remained active in local Democratic politics. For a time, he was connected with the Dayton *Leader* newspaper and opened a pharmaceutical drug business with his son, who was also a physician. He died in 1903.

Chief Matron Adelia Nelson presided over the Home for a brief two-month period while the trustees searched for a new superintendent. Their choice, William P. Kerr, was a prominent central Ohio educator—he had been head of the Granville Female College since 1845, and under his leadership the institution had become one of the most highly regarded schools in the state. One of Dr. Kerr's students at the Granville Female College, Ellen Hayes, remembered morning exercises at the seminary. "It is the hour for morning exercises. The day pupils have come and are gathered with the boarding pupils in the assembly hall of the brick building. Mr. Kerr enters and holds the door wide ajar while his teachers file in to their appointed places on the platform. A hymn is announced. . . . Mr. Kerr reads a short scripture lesson and follows with a brief simple prayer. Announcements are made and the students rise and go to their various classrooms. This chapel service, utterly free from perfunctory formalism, was quite in keeping with Mr. Kerr's sincere piety; his religion was suited alike to the realm of faith and to the concrete fields of good citizenship and brotherly kindness." William Kerr and his wife, who became chief matron at the Home, would bring the same piety and dedication to their new jobs.

Dr. Kerr arrived at the Home as efforts were underway to establish a vocational training program for the children. In their annual report in 1874, the board of trustees asked the governor and the Ohio General Assembly for the means "to train

There weren't many facilities like the Home, which offered a regular prep education, along with extensive trade courses. It was difficult to go through the place and come out unscathed by one kind of knowledge or another.

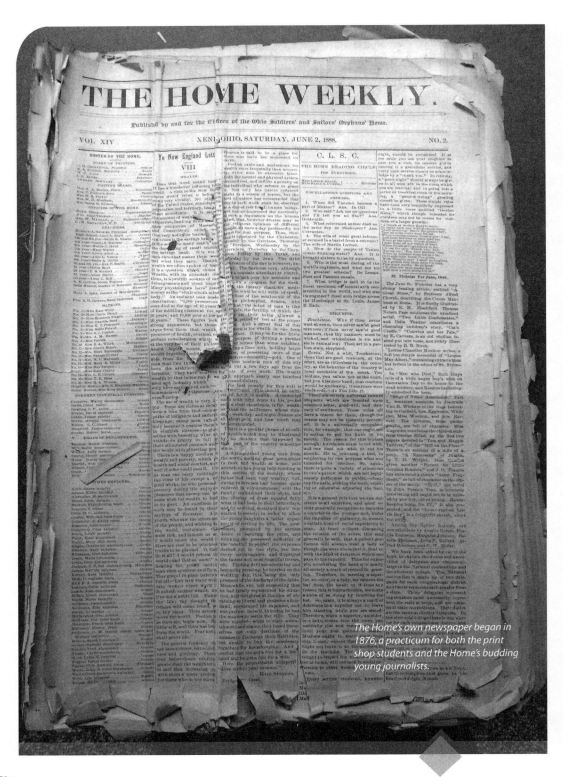

The Home's own newspaper began in 1876, a practicum for both the print shop students and the Home's budding young journalists.

[the children] and fit them for useful and profitable industrial vocations when they quit the Home and go out into the world." The "means" turned out to be $5,000 in the state budget. With the meager funds, Superintendent Kerr set out in 1875—in the middle of the worst economic depression in forty years—to train hundreds of children at the Home for the world of work. A second story was added to the Home's laundry building, providing space for a tin shop, shoe shop, and print shop. (On April 3, 1876, the first edition of *The Home Weekly* rolled off the presses in the print shop. The newspaper, produced largely by the children of the Home, would continue to be published, in different formats and under different names, for more than a century.) One of the classrooms in the old administration building was set up to teach telegraphy and another room was equipped with knitting machines. A blacksmith shop was opened in the boiler works and an engineer's shop at the base of the large water tower. The existing tailor, carpentry, and sewing shops were improved with new equipment, and space was set aside to teach as well as work in these areas.

Dr. Kerr's annual report for 1875 reflects his satisfaction with the Home's new Industrial School. Each child, he said, was attending traditional school classes for half a day and spending the other half learning a trade or performing various tasks around the Home and its farm. The superintendent also pointed out that "since the introduction of some industrial pursuits, there is very little truancy. . . . Under the new arrangement, we have and propose to have, better schools than ever before."

Ex-Pupil F.E. Bolton was among the first children to receive vocational training at the Home:

I was admitted to the Home in September, 1873, and discharged in August, 1875, at the age of sixteen. . . . When I was admitted to the Home, it consisted of the main building with the old dining hall, the twenty single cottages, a small hospital, chapel and the old frame school building and small frame barn. . . . There were about six hundred pupils in my time and we thought we were pretty fairly taken care of by the devoted teachers and employees who had charge of us. . . . The first industrial shops were instituted and some of us got a smattering of knowledge of what was going on in the world of business but not much, just enough to hunt for a job which it took most of us years to get.

After the success of the Democrats in the 1873 election, the Republicans turned to a proven vote-getter (and one of the Home's best friends)—Rutherford B. Hayes—to re-capture the governorship for the Grand Old Party. Hayes, who had served two terms as governor from 1868 to 1872, came out of retirement to win the 1875 election. With Dr. Kerr's party, the Democrats, now in the minority and his board of trustees now under Republican control, the Home's superintendent and his wife left the Home and returned to Granville, where he worked a few more years at the Granville Female College. Dr. Kerr resigned from the school in 1882, suffering from exhaustion and poor health, and died shortly thereafter at the age of 60.

In one sense, the OSSO Home returned to it origins in 1876. While, as expected, Governor Hayes appointed new trustees to the board, he also reinstated several members who had helped bring the Home into being, including J. Warren Keifer. With the past commander of the Ohio GAR serving as board president, the trustees chose one of Keifer's former officers in the 110th Ohio Volunteer Infantry—Major William L. Shaw—to be the Home's next superintendent. Major Shaw and his wife Rachel came to the Home from Eaton, Ohio, and were to be part of the story of the Xenia institution—off and on—for a number of years.

One might say that the new superintendent quickly "warmed to the task" by hiring an engineer to fix the Home's heating system. Many of the buildings were heated with steam, provided by boilers in a central boiler house. But the steam system had never functioned properly, either providing too much heat, too little heat, or sometimes no heat at all. Engineer David Evans would virtually rebuild the entire facility, and by 1877 the steam heat flowed evenly throughout the Home, presumably much to the satisfaction of the 600 children now living in the institution, as well as the staff. In addition to the capital improvements, Major Shaw also could take pride in having held expenses to just over $100 per pupil during his first year on the job. However, with Democrats back in power in 1877, Major Shaw filed his last monthly report with the board on July 19, 1878, suggesting it might be a good idea to one day invite former pupils back to the Home for a reunion. He left the Home the following day and nothing came of his suggestion at the time.

As the Home approached its tenth anniversary, the leadership of the institution was passing through some trying times. Major Shaw and his wife had been quite popular, as had Edward Merrick, the principal of the Home's school, but the three had been removed and the board had difficulty finding their replacements. Dr. George Keifer, a former trustee, temporarily filled in as superintendent and then reluctantly agreed to continue in the job on a permanent basis. Twice married with seven children, the 72-year-old Keifer had been practicing medicine for most of his adult life. He served in the Civil War as a surgeon with the 50th Ohio Volunteer Infantry at an age when most men were considering retirement. But by 1878, his

The Home's first real school building, which went up in 1878 and lasted for over sixty years.

health was failing, so he hired his son Asa to manage the Home's farm and assist with the rest of the superintendent's duties.

The Keifers presided over the opening of a long-needed and often-delayed brick school building on December 30, 1878. Then two months later—at approximately 7:15 in the morning on Sunday, February 16, 1879—with most of the children and the staff seated for breakfast in the dining room of the domestic building, someone shouted "Fire!" The basement of the administration building was burning.

The Home had its own fire wagon with a pump that also served as the sewage pump for the institution. In short order, a number of boys had retrieved the wagon and were pumping water on the blaze, using water from a pond at the base of the water tower. The Home's whistle was blown to signal the Xenia Fire Department for help. The town's firefighters arrived quickly and soon were pumping water from the pond as well on the burning building. With insufficient water in the pond to support two fire pumps, the Home's pumper switched over to the sewage collection tank and pumped several hundred barrels of raw sewage on the spreading fire. It was not enough.

Despite the best efforts of both fire teams, the administration building was totally burned out and almost two-thirds of the domestic building was destroyed. The combined fire-fighting effort went on for six hours until the fire was finally brought under control. Although several people suffered severe burns, no lives were lost. Despite a lengthy investigation, the cause of the blaze was never determined.

None of the cottages were damaged. Broken gas mains and water lines were repaired quickly. To help the Home cope with the loss of the dining halls, kitchens, and bakery, the people of Xenia contributed cooked food. Because the original walls of the domestic building and administration building were left standing, workers almost immediately began reconstructing (and fireproofing) both buildings.

Within three months, the domestic building had been rebuilt and was back in use. The administration building was finished the following year. Dr. Keifer and his family were not around, however, to see the completed structures. In April of 1879, the board asked for the superintendent's resignation and he complied without objection. Dr. Keifer returned to his home near Troy, Ohio, where his invalid wife died in May, 1880, at the age of 76. He followed her in death in November of the same year.

Dr. Keifer's successor was Nathan R. Wyman, a former member of the Board of Managers of the Dayton State Hospital, from Shelby County. As a young man, Wyman had rushed to California to seek his fortune in the gold fields. Not finding it, he returned home, taught school, and read law. By 1860, he was a probate judge.

Like many of his predecessors, Wyman fought in the Civil War, serving with the 99th Ohio Volunteer Infantry. After the war, he had returned home and practiced law.

Superintendent Wyman appears to have been an enthusiastic and energetic leader. He helped combat an outbreak of typhoid fever that sent more than thirty children to the hospital and killed one of them. He restored sound business management at the Home, and his staff successfully supervised the rebuilding of the domestic building after the fire.

Wyman also felt very strongly that the Home in general, and its boys in particular, needed a bit more discipline. "In May last," he reported, "a military organization was effected amongst the boys of the Home who were of a suitable age. The organization, designated the Home Cadets, has been found valuable in inculcating ideas of discipline and in affording the means of rewarding of merit by military appointment and promotion. . . . Flags, drums and fifes have been purchased for the organization, which consists of a battalion of four companies, under the command of Thomas M. Proctor. . . . The military band was instructed by W.D. Carpenter, who has charge of the Home's tin shops, without charge or neglect of his duties."

Superintendent Wyman was pleased with developments at the Home. "Yet the work is not finished," he added. "We are almost daily receiving new [children] and discharging those who have reached the age of sixteen. These help to swell the number that are an honor to our Home and the state." Wyman did not know it at the time, but his work, indeed, was close to completion. A Republican, Charles Foster, was elected governor in 1879 and by July, 1880, Nathan Wyman and his wife Mary went back to Shelby County, where he resided until his death in 1913.

Major William Shaw returned for his second stint as superintendent after being ousted just two years earlier by a Democrat-dominated board. He was the seventh superintendent in the Home's ten-year existence—and the sixth in six years.

The 1880s—The Home Defended

Despite the turnover at the top, the OSSO Home had a solid base of support in both political parties as well as the continuing and growing support of the Grand Army of the Republic. After a decade of growth, however, the institution had become a victim of its own success. It had run out of space.

Levi Scofield had designed a campus to handle a maximum of 600 children. But by the early 1880s, the Home's facilities and capabilities were being stretched

Here's a view of the Home's dining hall right around 1900, as the institution was reaching its full complement of buildings and cottages. The following prayer was used at each meal until 1930: "Unto Him who has said, Suffer little children to come unto me, to Him we give most hearty thanks for his goodness and loving kindness. He is our shepherd, we shall not want. God keep us, bless us, and save us, for Jesus' sake. Amen."

Before the 1900s rolled around, the Home had a first-rate farm, producing, among other things, a fine field of sixteen foot high corn.

to the limit as more and more eligible children were presented for admission to the institution. With the Civil War almost two decades in the past, it would have been reasonable to ask, "Where are all these children coming from?" The answer was, "All across the state." The OSSO Home enjoyed name recognition among families desiring a better life for their orphaned sons and daughters, while many smaller and less affluent rural areas had been unable to maintain facilities of their own at the county level during the economically depressed 1870s. Thus, expansion became a major issue for Superintendent Shaw and his wife Rachel when they returned to the Home in June of 1880. The Ohio General Assembly had decided not to fund any growth for the time being. Instead, legislators presented the Home with a fountain that had been located on the grounds of the Statehouse for several years. Their gesture, while appreciated, did not solve the Home's capacity problem, which Major Shaw brought to the board's attention in his annual report.

A total of 1,612 children had been admitted to the Home since it was established in 1869. Of that number, some 228 of them were full orphans, 191 had fathers only living, 1,072 had mothers only living, and 117 had both parents living.

In its first decade of operation, the Home had discharged 594 children, of which 175 had been released at the request of a parent, guardian or other interested party, and the rest having reached the age of sixteen.

Thirty-one children had died. Another 399 had been recorded as "absent," "transferred," having "run away" or "not returned from vacation."

That left 593 currently in residence.

In the spring of 1881, the Home began referring some applicants to local children's homes after the General Assembly clarified and simplified the state's child placement law. But the applications kept coming, and in September of 1882 the board finally passed a resolution increasing the capacity of the institution from 600 to 680. To accommodate more children, the trustees also authorized the staff to lengthen the tables in the dining room, shorten the beds to create space for more beds, and purchase additional furniture.

Major Shaw began looking beyond the boundaries of the Home itself. During his first stint as superintendent in 1878, he had reminded the board of its duty, under state law, to remain in touch with the children discharged by the Home so as "to report to the governor and the General Assembly in regard to these wards of the state." But when Shaw returned in 1880, he found nothing had been done to inquire after the condition of the discharged children, nor had any effort been made to bring them together. The superintendent vowed to follow the spirit of law—and he did.

The first reunion of discharged children was held at the Home over three days in September of 1881. One hundred and twenty of them came back for the event, a number which represented about one quarter of those who had been released from the Home since it opened in 1869. E. Howard Gilkey, one of the first children admitted to the institution, proposed that the returnees form a group called the Association of Graduates of the Ohio Soldiers and Sailors Orphans Home. After John Molloy, another early resident, objected to that name—he said if he had waited until he "graduated" he would still be at the Home—Gilkey suggested the group call themselves the Association of Ex-Pupils. The name was adopted and Molloy was elected president and Gilkey corresponding secretary. "It was the Major [Shaw's] idea to bring the ex-pupils back for their own good. Also, the sight of them might be a substantial help to the children still in the Home and show what Home training could produce in the way of good and respected citizens of the State of Ohio. So we met and completed our first organization. . . . Our friends of four and five years ago were gathered all around us, and we were carefree and happy in a good old way."

Major Shaw also shared his thoughts about that first reunion.

"While the number returning was not so great as was desired, the occasion was most gratifying and encouraging to the friends of the institution in establishing, beyond a doubt, the fact that the training received in the Home was productive of good results. The evidences were abundant that we are sending out children from here who, in almost every instance, will make good citizens."

One of Shaw's last proposals as superintendent would be a new industrial building in which the Home could consolidate its shops, classrooms, and training centers. After a Democrat, George Hoadley, was elected governor in the fall of 1883, Shaw undoubtedly knew it would only be a matter of time before a re-constituted board asked him to resign.

A series of windstorms of unprecedented force swept across several regions of the country in 1884, beginning with something called the "Enigma Outbreak." Over two days in February, more than sixty tornados touched down in ten states from Mississippi to Indiana and from Tennessee to the Carolinas and Virginia, destroying 10,000 structures and causing millions of dollars in flood and wind damage. Ohio had been spared, but two months later, a funnel cloud came swirling in from the southwest and dropped out of the sky, touching down near Miamisburg, Ohio, late in the afternoon on April 27. Instead of continuing on toward Dayton, the roaring, rotating column of air veered sharply east, heading directly for Xenia. As the tornado approached, however, it took another turn to the south and east, just missing the town—but not the Home.

The wind uprooted trees. It ripped the roofs off the hospital, the laundry, and several other buildings. The hospital roof was carried a distance of more than 500 feet before it came crashing to the ground. Pieces of roofing slate were driven into trees with such force that they could not be removed by hand. It was all over in a few minutes. Fortunately, no one was hurt. Residents and business owners in nearby Jamestown would not be so lucky, however. Its downtown suffered a direct hit. More than 300 buildings were destroyed, 600 people were left homeless, and several people killed in the storm.

James Bostwick was in the Home's chapel with the other children when the wind began whipping the trees outside. "I crawled under the long wooden benches," recalled Bostwick. "Dr. Moorehead, president of the Xenia Theological Seminary, delivered the sermon and I can still [hear him] saying in his loud bass voice, 'I, the Lord thy God, am with thee; fear not.'"

It took a couple of months to repair the buildings damaged by the wind, after which Major Shaw and his wife left the Home. Unlike many of the previous superintendents, Shaw's successor was not a military veteran, a physician, or a teacher. William J. Alexander was an attorney, a resident of nearby Spring Valley, a large landowner, and most important, a Democrat. But in April of 1885, after less than a year as superintendent, he and his wife, who had served as chief matron, resigned and returned to their nearby home and previous pursuits.

Dr. Cummins B. Jones, the Home's long-time physician in residence, became the new superintendent. Dr. Jones would accomplish several important tasks during his brief term as superintendent, not the least of which was accommodating the Board of Lady Visitors; the new panel was created by the Ohio General Assembly to inspect the Home on an annual basis and make any recommendations the ladies felt were needed to improve the institution. Dr. Jones also hired homegrown talent, noting in his 1885 annual report that the staff now included eleven former pupils, among them S.A. Dickson as superintendent of schools and E. Howard Gilkey as financial officer. It was on Dr. Jones's watch, as well, that the Home began a two-year project to replace every wooden bedstead and straw tick with an iron bed and spiral mattress—much to the delight of the children and staff, of course. "My experience during several years of service here has shown me that children who are properly governed in the cottages give but little trouble and make good progress in the schools and the various industrial departments," he concluded his report to the board.

Dr. Jones's days as superintendent would be numbered after Republicans returned to power in 1886 with the election of Joseph B. Foraker as Ohio's 37th governor. As governors before him had done, Foraker wasted no time realigning the Home's board of trustees by suspending some members and inducing resignations from others. As spring arrived, Dr. Jones's departure appeared imminent when Mother Nature intervened yet again. This time it was rain. Four inches in less than two hours. The May 12 downpour caused both branches of Shawnee Creek to overflow their banks, devastating the lowlands of town. Two hundred homes were destroyed and twenty-six people had been killed. It was, at the time, the worst disaster in Xenia's history.

High and (mostly) dry on the ridge above Shawnee Creek, the children and staff of the Home did their best to be helpful to their host city, providing food, shelter, and emergency assistance to residents affected by the flood. Here's ex-pupil James Bostwick, describing the death and destruction: "[It] washed out all of the bridges in Xenia, and hit Bar's Bottom below the Union Depot. A large number of residents were drowned. On Sunday afternoon, our matron took us to the old courthouse in Xenia where a number of bodies were lying covered with sheets, a gruesome sight

From top, the cottages, and an early photograph of the dining hall. At bottom is the hospital, the original building being finished in 1872 after a $7,500 appropriation. Its first doctors drove out from town, on the watch for a red flag the matrons hung on the cottage verandas if anyone needed a doctor.

but long to be remembered." (Shortly thereafter, Bostwick experienced a family tragedy when his sister Elsie, on vacation in Dayton, was thrown from a buggy and suffered a broken arm. She was admitted to the Home's hospital. "In her weakened condition, [Elsie] was easy prey for the Black Diphtheria rampant at the time and lived but two days. The Home officials contacted my father and he got to see her shortly before she died. They buried her at midnight. I didn't know about it until the next afternoon. My father had to be fumigated before he could see us.")

Dr. Jones left in October after hiring a contractor to move the old frame administration building so a new industrial building could be built on the site.

Ex-pupil Fred Barr left a lengthy description of life at the Home in the late 1880s:

Arrived February 24, 1886, in [the] charge of an uncle, as both of my parents had died. Spent two weeks in quarantine at the hospital. Then entered portals of No. 14 (called by some the "Angel Cottage"). Thirty-two wildcats, full of mischief but not mean or destructive, and the matron, Mrs. M.C. Maynard, strict but just, and having the respect of all.

There were just twenty cottages then, housing 644, making thirty-two to a cottage. When we went to bed we had to climb over the ends as they filled the room nearly solid; single beds with mattresses were later furnished, but then we had straw ticks. One event each year was carrying all the ticks to the barn, emptying the old and filling with new straw. We were not satisfied until they looked like big footballs, so for a few nights, we went to sleep in one bed and awakened in another. . . .

Everyone had some duty to perform. We arose at 5:30, washed and dressed, and helped to dress the little ones. Yes, we had all ages up to sixteen in each cottage. No. 14 had one, Gardner Gearhart, who was only eighteen months old when he came. And they were treated as well as if they had been in their home families. We then marched in line of twos to the dining room, later marched back to the cottage, made up beds, tidied up the cottage, picked up some leaves and scraps on the lawn, shined our shoes and at the whistle marched to school to drum and fife.

Each morning, detail slips were given to each matron, with lists of boys under 14 who had been detailed for half a day to various jobs—such as gardening, florist, herding cows, helping janitors, picking fruit. Boys and girls 14 and older worked half a day at their trade and went to school half a day, with also a study hour at eight.

For recreation in those days we had first and second hardball teams who played each other and sometimes won over crack outsiders. Each cottage had a scrub team, also a football team. Every boy wanted to play. In football, we had no rules,

·the FALLS, O.S.·S.O. HOME ·XENIA, OHIO · '88 ·

no goal lines, just battled the ball from here to there, got bumped up some, gave the hospital a few jobs, but had fun.

There was a good-sized pond where the power house is now located, also a 'frog pond' east of that. When [the ponds were] frozen, we all skated. Most boys had skates and sleds, and ice hockey, or 'shinney' as we called it, was a favorite with many [and] gave the hospital some more patching jobs.

In winter, frequently on Friday nights when there was no study hour, the tables in the dining room would be stacked on each other along the walls, and there would be dancing, mostly square dances. . . . I remember when we first saw waltzing. This was mostly by employees, since girls were a kind of poison ivy. We did not get to hardly touch or speak to the little dears.

Four of the new 'circle' cottages, 21-28, were completed by December 1, 1888. Some time later, 29-30 were mostly filled, this leaving all of the west old cottages for girls. At the same time, the dining room was enlarged by a wing on each side of the basement. The chapel was enlarged in the same way, by wings on each side. The chapel services were held in the afternoon in those days, [with] different preachers from Xenia each

Sunday. Some we liked. The young student preachers held Sunday School. Some put us to sleep. There was a theological seminary in Xenia, to the joy of the girls especially. Two cottages doubled up as a class, sometimes one of girls and one of boys.

In the last years of my time in the Home, each morning at breakfast time, a black-eyed, smiling little girl, Ruth Given, came around to collect matron's reports and leave detail slips. Well, you could not expect a big boy of 15 to notice a pint-sized girl of 12, but when they met at the advanced ages of 22 and 19, three years meant little. She still has that sunny smile. How do I know? I have lived with her over fifty years. Thanks, old Home.

Dr. C.B. Jones's replacement was a man well in step with the politics of the time. Noah Thomas was born in Madison County in 1835 and was a student at Antioch College until he joined J. Warren Keifer's 110th Ohio Volunteer Infantry in the Civil War. Thomas fought in many of the major battles and was severely wounded at the Battle of Cold Harbor in 1864, resulting in the amputation of his left arm.

During his four years as superintendent (1886 to 1890), Major Thomas sought to take in more orphans, including the 400 on the waiting list and another 250 housed in county children's homes at the OSSO Home's expense. In his annual report to the board of trustees in 1887, the superintendent wrote, "The saving of the Union could not be postponed for an examination of the treasury. This was not a matter for even secondary consideration. The time to care for these children is now. Delay is dangerous, as it would have been in the matter of saving the Union. Now is the accepted time. If you hear their voices, harden not your hearts. . . . To delay this matter is a shameful discrimination against the best interest of a class of children who are soon to form largely the citizenship of the state."

Thomas had little trouble convincing the board that these children should have the advantages the Home provided. The trustees recommended an appropriation of $40,000 to expand the Xenia institution, but the General Assembly was a tougher sell. So the Civil War major brought in some reinforcements—the Grand Army of the Republic—to present a united front in Columbus. The Ohio GAR had become one of the largest departments of one of the most successful advocacy organizations in American history, and the OSSO Home was important to it. In April of 1888, as the GAR prepared to bring 90,000 Union veterans to the capital city, the state legislature approved the expenditure of $25,000 to build four new double cottages at the Home and expand its children's dining room. When Thomas and most of the Home's residents came to Columbus to participate in the largest gathering of Union veterans since the end of the Civil War, they had a lot of people to thank.

In the fall of 1889, with Ohioans electing a Democrat, James E. Campbell, to be their next governor, Noah Thomas saw his superintendency coming to an end. Fortunately, he had accomplished most of his major goals. The Home now had more than 900 children in residence. Sixteen additional acres had been acquired for further expansion. A lake had been built on two-and-a-half acres at the extreme western end of the Home grounds with $800 from an anonymous donor; the identity of the donor was kept secret until after his death, at which time it was named McDowell Lake. But before Major Thomas took leave of the institution, he would help manage the worst crisis in the history of the OSSO Home. The following description of the crisis is found in the 1890 year-end report of staff physician Dr. C.M. Galloway:

During these six months ending on April 15, when the general quarantine was removed and the schools and industries were again opened, 234 cases of diphtheria—many of them complicated with scarlet fever—were treated, of which number thirty-five children died. We also lost one of our nurses from diphtheria after an illness of only four days—Miss Olive M. Smith of Xenia.

Scarlet fever in a mild form prevailed during this time also, and 240 cases came under treatment, of this number two died. Another death occurring from an overdose of medicine taken [by the patient] while in delirium from la grippe, was the only fatality resulting from about 400 cases of this strange malady, that also became epidemic among our children and employees during the months of February and March, 1890; later a child twenty months old died of tubercular meningitis. Lack of hospital accommodations prevented the proper handling of such a great number of sick children and the trustees abolished a part of the industries and gave us three wards in the industrial building. The schools were also dismissed and the rooms used as convalescing wards.

Cottages 27 and 28 were used as scarlet fever wards while the children with la grippe and a few with pneumonia were kept in their respective cottages while convalescent.

The general health of the Home since the 15th of April has been excellent.

In the wake of the epidemic, the Home hired its first full-time resident physician, Dr. T. Van Duprey. (Most of the early physicians made calls at regular times each day, while maintaining practices in Xenia or other nearby places.) The state board of health also recommended construction of a new hospital with 150 beds. Two rooms in the old frame administration building had served as the Home's original hospital. The current free-standing hospital, built in 1872, had only 34 beds.

On Saturday afternoons, in good weather, the boys took their weekly bath in a small pond there. The story was that two boys had once drowned in it, their deaths the origin of the graveyard behind the chapel.

The diphtheria epidemic of the winter of 1889-1890 added many more.

Jake Cupples in Cottage 18 was first, and sudden. Another boy in the same cottage died the next day, and the next day, a girl, Elsie Bostwick of Cottage 15.

School was closed, but the epidemic went on through the autumn and into the spring.

Thirty-five children died, and even the young nurse, Olive Smith, not much older than the students, fatally stricken and also buried behind the chapel.

Here's how former pupil Fred Barr remembered the tragedy: "In the fall of 1889, school had just got going when an epidemic of diphtheria and scarlet fever started. Soon the schools were closed, the hospital was full, seats were removed from school rooms and cots placed instead. There was no resident doctor then. Each cottage had a red flag to hang out front. A Xenia doctor came out each morning. On seeing a red flag, he would stop, examine a child and treat them or send them to the hospital. . . .

"All who died were buried at night and I will never forget the sound of the rumble and crunch of the farm wagon with one or sometimes more coffins, and several men with lanterns walking beside the wagon. We would look toward the little cemetery, and often someone would start the song we last learned at school, *The Future*.

Charlie Gearheart, age 4, died, and Miss Maynard was grief-stricken. When Eddie and Bob Chenoweth were stricken, the other boys in Cottage 14 were taken to the old industrial building and placed in solitary quarantine.

Miss Maynard, it was said, never again punished another boy.

Trustees requested $60,000 for a new building and received $5,000 to remodel the old hospital and add two cottages for hospital purposes.

Among the expenses of the Home for the year 1890 was one lonely line: *Head stones…39……$390.00.* A monument marked the grave of Nurse Olive M. Smith, who was buried with the children she died trying to help.

Noah Thomas and his wife Alice submitted their resignations, as requested by the board, on April 1, 1890, and went home to London, Ohio. Thomas would serve as a member of the local board of education, four terms as a city councilman and five terms as a justice of the peace.

Major Thomas was succeeded by General Charles Young who, at the time, was the highest ranking military figure to serve as superintendent of the Home. Born in Albany, New York, in 1838, to a family of "substantial financial circumstances," Young enlisted in the Union Army at the age of 22. He fought in many of the Civil War battles and served on the staffs of generals Daniel Sickles and Joseph Hooker. In the Battle of Chancellorsville, he was struck in the neck by a piece of shrapnel and was feared to be fatally wounded. But he recovered and served through the rest of the war. General Young was one of the few Democrats in Ohio who also had the trust and confidence of several of the state's leading Republican officeholders, which would serve both him and the Home well during his term as superintendent.

The 1890s—The Home Determined

The long, terrible winter of 1889-90 would cast a long shadow over the Ohio Soldiers and Sailors Orphans Home. The cycle of recurring and overlapping epidemics showed just how ill-prepared the Home was for the onset of contagious disease. A number of steps were taken to improve and maintain hygiene. In addition to having a physician in residence, the Home was cleaned and refurbished. Anything considered to be a possible source of infection—furniture, bed clothes, even books and toys—was either cleansed or discarded. New arrivals were put under temporary quarantine to reduce the chance of infectious disease spreading quickly through the institution. The quarantine system would be kept in place for the rest of the Home's history. In the two years following the diphtheria outbreak, similar outbreaks occurred in a number of schools, institutions and villages, but never again would the Home see an epidemic like the one in the winter of 1890. A lesson had been learned.

An 1891 list of "Rules To Be Observed By Those Occupying Rooms In

Administration and Domestic Buildings" addressed health and hygiene by staff:

Scraps of paper or cloth, fruit parings or remnants of any kind will be deposited in buckets provided for such purpose. The slop pails will be used for water only.

Slop pails, water cans, brooms, towels and clothing must be kept within rooms and not left in halls.

No dirt shall be swept into the halls from rooms. While sweeping the rooms, the doors leading into the halls must be closed.

The rooms must be kept neat and in order, and ready for inspection at all times, and pupils must not under any circumstances be detailed or asked to assist in keeping said rooms in order.

No bathing shall be allowed after 10 o'clock PM and the bathroom must be kept in order at all times.

All persons residing at the institution are expected to be in their rooms by 10 o'clock PM (at which hour the building will ordinarily be locked) and lights to be out at 10:30.

General Young and the board were pleased that the health of the Home was so much improved, particularly at a time when more children were being admitted to the institution. The trustees, dissatisfied with the amount of money provided by the state for the maintenance of soldiers' orphans in county homes, accepted the transfer of 113 of these orphans to the Home in 1892. By law, the Home could keep children until they were 18, but because so many had applied for admission, it would be several years before all children entering the Home stayed until the age of 18.

In his annual report, General Young described the reunion of the Association of Ex-Pupils as "one of the most interesting events of the year," and well it should have been. It was the group's tenth anniversary. Olga Brumagem of the Class of 1901 had many fond memories of her first reunion and her days at the Home:

I well remember the first time I ever saw the Home. The first relay of Phillips children had been to the Home and had been discharged. Dess and I listened to their stories of the Home for years. . . . We wanted to go, we begged to go . . . and so finally she [their mother] made application and we were accepted and passes sent for us to come. We had to change trains twice, at Kenton and at Springfield, and finally arrived at Xenia about four o'clock in the afternoon. . . . Someone told us to go in at the big gate and walk until we came to some big stone steps. And so we did. I still have the picture in my mind, two little girls in white dresses, with ribbon bows on their shoulders, with long white ribbon streamers. The latest style for children in those days, I'll have you know. Each of us had hold of one handle of the lunch basket, two cute little twins, believe it or not. What a strange world for us to enter.

I have many memories of the time I was still a pupil there. One funny one. That year they were letting boys and girls have parties. First, the boys would invite the girls and then the girls would invite the boys. One time Paul Ramsay invited me, and then found out I was in the hospital, so he invited another girl. But I didn't know that. The girls in my cottage got word to me that I had an invitation, and Miss Elmore said I could go. So on the great evening I got ready and started out and Paul saw me go by his cottage. Was he in a panic? He rushed around trying to find someone to take me on. But when I got to my cottage, I found out he had invited someone else, and I went back to the hospital, a disillusioned female.

Then I remember my first reunion. Brother Hal and [I] went together. I was just eighteen and had taught my first term of school. . . . They had a masquerade dance and Hal and I went as John Alden and Priscilla. I thought we made a swell couple and I thought we should have won first prize, but the judges didn't. . . .

Memories! All of my dearest memories are of the Home. A child in school there, graduated there, courted there and married there. An ex-pupil here in Cleveland was married to a man ten years and he never knew she had been in the Home. Can you imagine me keeping still about the Home ten years?

I don't want to miss "remembering" those exciting ball games we used to have at [the] reunion. Cleveland vs. Cincinnati and the way those Brenneis boys played ball. Hal played ball the year we were there together and did himself proud pitching. If we weren't so old, wouldn't it be great to have one more game with the same boys playing? You will understand how, when the president called for slogans for reunion, I would write, "Where Friends and Memories Meet."

In 1893, General Young updated state legislators on the Home's industrial programs, proudly referring to the institution on Poverty Knoll as a "university of manual and technical training." Its science department was "attracting attention from other schools and universities," boasted the superintendent. Steam power and other labor-saving devices had been introduced in most of the shops and training classrooms. General Young also had requested $10,000 for a new engine and power house. Of the 900 residents of the Home in 1894, a total of 272 were enrolled in classes teaching industrial trades, which accounted for a good proportion of the children over the age of fourteen—the minimum age to enter the job training programs. The *Home Review* published the following letter from Nevin Jordan,

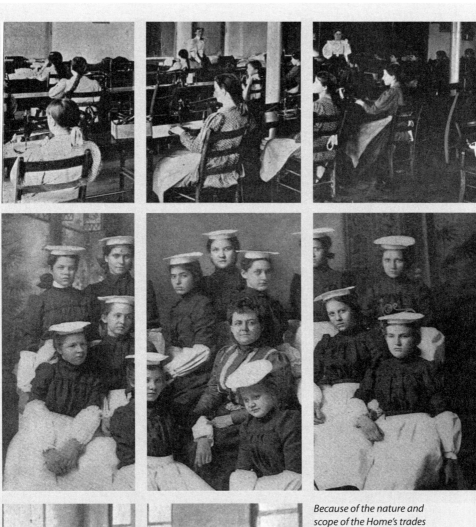

Because of the nature and scope of the Home's trades program, its students left the campus with the equivalent of two degrees: a high school one and another in the practical arts. Pictured here are, at top, the Home's sewing class shortly before the turn of the nineteenth century, the cooking class, and the Home's cobbler shop.

Leaving Home
Perry Sawyer's trip

Perry Sawyer, leaving the Home in December of 1891, bound for Fostoria with no money and small prospects, returning to his family, who were too poor to keep him for long. At 2 p.m. in the afternoon, the train stopped at Upper Sandusky and everybody got off to get something to eat.

Except Perry.

"A man was occupying the same seat with me and when he came back he brought me a ham sandwich with mustard." Perry recalled. "It was a fine sandwich. I have never tasted anything so fine, and I have eaten at least a thousand ham sandwiches to see if I could find one as good.

"I have even stopped several times at the same restaurant, seeking the same sandwich, but to no avail. As vividly as I sought the sandwich, I recall that day. I was on my own. My folks were too poor to keep me. It was a gloomy kid who arrived in Fostoria that December. Then at table, a girl who once lived next door burst into the house jubilant because she had found a job. I asked her if I might have one, too. She said she heard that, indeed, they were hiring boys. The Home had taught me to strike while the iron was hot, so I asked her to take me with her, and the man put me to work that very night.

"I have been going ever since…"

These croquet-playing orphans had this stereo photograph of them and their cottage sent to Lucy Hayes.

who learned his life-long trade at the Home:

I was taken to the Home in 1890 from Troy. I was put in the hospital for two weeks, then I was put in Cottage 16. I left the Home on June 26, 1896. . . . When I was fourteen years old I was placed with David Evans, who was the plumber on the Home grounds, and he put me in the old boiler room where the new dining room stands now, then down to the gas house as we had no electric lights in the Home. The gas house was down by the pond. I stayed there awhile and then went to the plumbing shop. I have followed plumbing and tin work all of my life and still work at it. . . . One of the grandest monuments The Grand Army of the Republic ever laid in the State of Ohio was when they laid the cornerstone for the O.S. and S.O. Home so that you brother and sister exes and I could get our start in life.

General Young and his wife left the Home in 1895—of their own volition—to manage the Soldiers' Industrial School in Scottsdale, Pennsylvania. They were replaced by David Lanning and his wife Letitia as superintendent and chief matron. Lanning had served in a number of capacities in state government, including as a captain in the state adjutant general's office. He saw the leadership of the OSSO Home as the opportunity of a lifetime, even if the experience of his predecessors had proven otherwise.

Superintendent Lanning took over the administration of the Xenia institution during difficult economic times, but with the ongoing and vigorous lobbying by the GAR, and affiliate groups like the Woman's Relief Corp and the Sons of Union Veterans, the Home continued to receive the funds it requested from the state. The Sons of Union Veterans held their 1895 state encampment in Xenia in June, followed by the annual reunion of ex-pupils. "They visited the Home in a body, spending the afternoon and evening," Lanning stated, referring to the veterans group in his report to the board. "In the evening the Home gave them a banquet, [attended] by about 200 persons. The following week came the reunion of the ex-pupils, when about 250 returned to their adopted home, with as much pride and enjoyment as do the soldiers of the late war gathered at their regimental reunions. It was as intelligent and refined a gathering of men and women as I have ever met."

(In the same report, the superintendent informed trustees that he had permitted the boys at the Home to go swimming in McDowell Lake in the evenings and allowed the girls to try the "modern method of bathing" in the afternoon, for which no further explanation was offered.)

In 1896, Superintendent Lanning reported on a significant change in the

McDowell Lake was a year-round source of recreation at the Home and the envy of outsiders who had no pool and ice-skating rink in their own backyards.

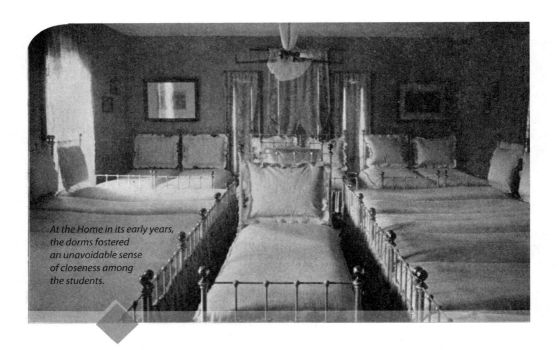

At the Home in its early years, the dorms fostered an unavoidable sense of closeness among the students.

children's living quarters at the Home. The cottages originally had been equipped with three-quarter beds, made of wood and lined with straw-filled mattresses, each to accommodate two children. The beds had been replaced with iron beds and mattresses in 1885. Now, "these old landmarks," as Lanning referred to them, were removed and replaced by single beds to be occupied by one child. "The placing of single beds in the cottages crowded the dormitories," acknowledged the superintendent, "but now each child has his own bed and it is much more pleasant for the children."

In 1897, Governor Asa Bushnell, from nearby Springfield, made several visits to the OSSO Home. Unfortunately, the children were also visited by another infectious disease as well. After having been largely epidemic-free for most the decade, the Home experienced an outbreak of measles. A total of 369 children came down with the highly contagious infection, but only one child died in this latest outbreak of illness, which says something, perhaps, about the Home's vastly improved medical care and hospital facilities.

The anxieties associated with the measles epidemic, combined with the normal stresses of work, took its toll on Superintendent Lanning. While delivering a political speech at City Hall in Xenia in the fall of 1897, he was stricken with a paralytic stroke. With Lanning no longer able to perform his duties, the board appointed the Home's financial officer and ex-pupil, Orin Baker, as acting superintendent. David

Lanning and his wife resigned on January 17, 1898. In February, Nelson Fulton, a former board member and area resident, was named the new superintendent. His wife Hallie became chief matron.

Over the course of the year, steady progress was made in wiring most of the Home's buildings for electricity. A seventy-five-kilowatt generator was installed and soon was providing power to the campus. The generator provided power not only for electric lights but also for a new telephone switchboard and for the equipment used by a newly appointed full-time dentist.

Meanwhile, the U.S. became involved in its first major conflict since the Civil War. The destruction of the Battleship *Maine* in the harbor of Havana, Cuba, in early 1898 quickly led to the Spanish-American War. More than 300,000 troops were mobilized to fight in the war and 15,000 of them came from Ohio. Of the more than 3,000 deaths of American servicemen in the war and the 260 fatalities of men from Ohio, the great majority were caused by disease.

The Ohio Soldiers and Sailors Orphans Home was founded as a refuge for orphans of the Civil War era. Now it would soon become a home for orphans from America's most recent war as well.

Nelson Fulton and his wife did a creditable job as superintendent and chief matron. But in April of 1900, they were asked to step aside after General Charles Young and his wife Cora, who had left the Home several years earlier to work with soldiers' orphans in Pennsylvania, expressed a desire to return to the OSSO Home. The board, "in the best interests of the institution," welcomed the couple back to Xenia.

The 1900 reunion of the Association of Ex-Pupils drew the governor of Ohio, George Nash, as well as members of the Ohio Sons of Union Veterans and its Ladies Auxiliary, who were holding their annual encampment at nearby Springfield. John Jones, president of the Home's board of trustees, spoke at the reunion banquet, noting that "54 vocations were represented among those present, [including] clergymen, lawyers, physicians, teachers, electricians, and every known profession and occupation."

That same year, Ohio GAR commander Elias Montfort, sent a letter to a fellow member of the veterans organization—President William McKinley. "I recently made an inspection of the Ohio Soldiers and Sailors Orphans Home," wrote Montfort, "and found about 900 children of the war veterans and was very much gratified with the splendid showing in character, education and culture of the children of our deceased comrades. A battalion of four companies has been organized, equipped, and drilled by an officer, late of the regular army. The military bearing and martial spirit of the boys was very commendable. I was astonished at the accuracy of their movements and the enthusiasm which they manifested."

In thirty years, the Home had come a long way since a procession of children trudged up the slope to Poverty Knoll. Much had been accomplished and much remained to be done. But at the dawn of a new century, the future looked bright.

Circa 1894——The boys poured the contents of the medicine cabinet——cod liver oil, Scotts emulsion, arnica, and worse——into a gallon can with a screw top, hung it over a gas jet in the store room, and while Mrs. Tong was reading the Bible, it exploded, giving great emphasis to the scriptures . . .

SKATING WAS FUN ON OLD SHAWNEE CREEK AND MᶜDOWELL LAKE.

These orphans *are a select class (1900-1930)*

CHAPTER

3

In 1912, students dressed for picnics. Here, some of the graduating seniors appear dressed for success.

Finding one's way to the farm

By the turn of the century, the Ohio Soldiers and Sailors Orphans Home had become one of the most successful institutions of its kind. Poverty Knoll, the forested ridge with one barn-like building and three brick cottages of thirty years earlier, now had manicured lawns, a three-story administration building, more than two dozen cottages, and hundreds of children at work and play.

Visitors making their way up the winding lane to the crest of the ridge discovered a model campus. In addition to the children's cottages and the majestic edifice housing the Home's administrative staff, there were two schoolhouses, a chapel, a main hospital and four cottage hospitals, a laundry, several industrial buildings, a mechanical building, boiler and engine houses,

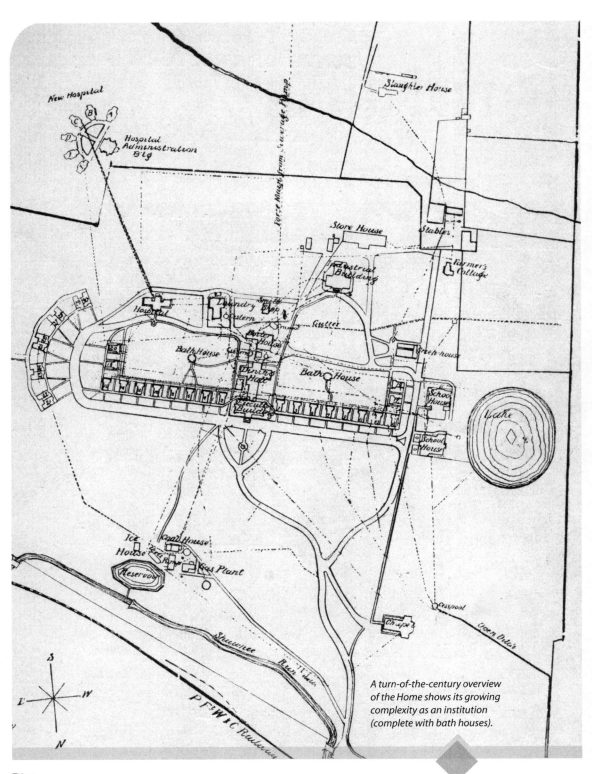

New Hospital

Hospital Administration B'l'g

Slaughter House

Fort Wayne from Sewerage Pump

Store House

Stables

Farmer's Cottage

Industrial Building

Hospital

Laundry

Smithy Shop

Cistern

Gutter

Porter House

Green house

Bath House

Dining Hall

Bath House

School House

Electric Burial

School House

Lake

Ice House

Coal House

Feed Pump

Reservoir

Gas Plant

Chapel

Cesspool

Crown Point

Shawnee Run

P Ft W + C Railway

S

E   W

N

A turn-of-the-century overview of the Home shows its growing complexity as an institution (complete with bath houses).

an electrical powerhouse, a water pumping station, a gas house, greenhouses, and farm buildings. A guest arriving on the grounds after dark might have thought he or she was dreaming. America still had a predominantly rural population in 1900. Most people lived in the country or in crossroad villages that were dependent on nearby farms. Theirs was a world lit by fire and pulled by horses—a world that rose with the dawn and paused at dusk. Here on the "Home farm," as it was called, a long column of uniformed boys and well-dressed girls marched back to their cottages every day after work—cottages with electric lights, steam heat and indoor plumbing. The sewerage system, noted one resident with pride, utilized manure "made on the premises" to improve the land.

The Home had survived various calamities—fire, flood, epidemic disease, windstorms—in its first three decades. No less challenging than the whims of Mother Nature had been the changing political winds. The veterans of the Grand Army of the Republic had fought hard to get the Home established and then supported as a state agency. But every time a new majority party took office in Columbus, heads rolled. More than once, the Home's leadership had been replaced at precisely the point in time it was most needed. Yet the institution grew and prospered, despite the setbacks.

The OSSO Home offered a quality of life and the promise of a better future not always found in a county Children's Home or a domestic arrangement. Superintendent Charles Young in his annual report to the General Assembly in 1902 drew attention to the residents' well-rounded education. "This is the first institution in the land, a third of a century ago, to teach *at public expense*, trades and literary branches," Young pointed out. (In an earlier report, the superintendent declared that "a child . . . employed a half a day at industrial training will keep up in study with one who goes to school all day.") He also shared the favorable comments of two of the Home's notable visitors in 1902—U.S. Senator Mark Hanna of Ohio and General Roeliff Brinkerhoff, chairman of the state board of charities. Senator Hanna, who was preparing to run against President Theodore Roosevelt in 1904, described the reception he received from pupils and employees assembled in the chapel as "inspiring." Brinkerhoff, on the other hand, was a man not easily impressed. He had witnessed the good and bad of more than thirty years of reform in prisons and asylums. But he liked what he saw in Xenia, and spoke at length about "the extended and excellent reputation of this institution, especially its industrial features," reported Young, "which he said have no equal anywhere . . . in the number of trades taught." It was welcome praise, coming from the man who had founded the Ohio Historical Society in his living room and been present at the birth of more than one university.

Clearly, the people at the Home—at least in their own view—had been doing more than a few things right. And it was not simply WHAT they did. It was HOW they did it.

The whistle and the work

The OSSO Home had been established by a veterans organization calling itself the Grand Army of the Republic for the sons and daughters of Union soldiers and sailors, so from the outset there was an expectation that it would be run, at least in some respects, like a military installation. The boys wore uniforms. The girls, too, dressed alike as age and tasks dictated. And there were rules. Lots of rules. By 1900, the list had grown to forty-eight, many of which addressed the conduct of the Home's employees with respect to the children:

Rule No. 5. *Friendly relations should be cultivated among all connected with the Home and altercations are forbidden.*

Rule No. 7. *No officer or employee will make any distinction in the treatment of the children of the Home on account of the cottage, room, office or shop to which they may belong, but will act towards them as though they all belong to the same cottage or family. . . .*

Rule No. 9. *Under no circumstances will any officer or employee having charge or coming in contact with the children, apply to them any language or epithet calculated to humiliate or degrade them.*

Rule No. 13. *The children shall not be addressed by their last names alone or by any nicknames or false names. Correct use of words and language shall always be encouraged.*

Rule No. 14. *Corporal punishment should be resorted to only when all other remedies have failed and, when necessary, no artificial instrument or cruel means shall be employed. . . .*

Rule No. 47. *No child of the Home shall be detailed, or otherwise required to do personal service for any officer or employee of the institution.*

For much of the Home's history, the lives of its children were governed from dawn to dusk by one "commander," as a full-page tribute in the 1940 *Home Review* characterized the steam whistle that—beginning in 1873—called the boys and girls to their daily activities and entertainments. "All who have ever lived at the Home have one common memory. We may have lived there under different

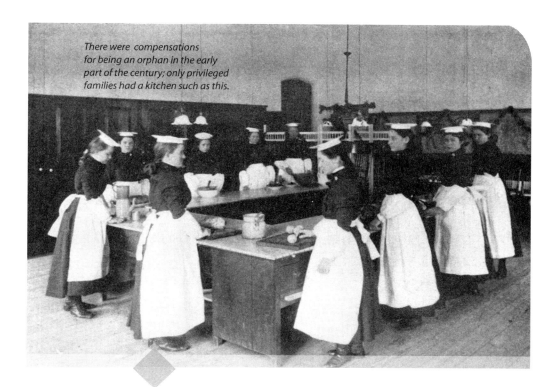

There were compensations for being an orphan in the early part of the century; only privileged families had a kitchen such as this.

superintendents, different officers, supervisors, teachers, and even under different conditions during the changing years. But every one of us had one common commander; a commander that gave us an order the first morning we awoke there, and the last morning we spent there; a commander that controlled our going and coming, that called us to our work, and sent us to our play; in fact a commander that controlled with precision and punctuality every step of our daily program from the first day to the last day of our stay there."

The tribute concluded with a poem written by former pupil Olga Brumagem (1901):

THE HOME WHISTLE

It wakened us at early morn,
When on our beds we slept;
And sent us to our rest again
When darkness o'er us crept.

It called us to the dining room.
And to our work at school.

It sent us to our daily task,
Our every step did rule.
Of yore it sounded loud and shrill,
But now its tones are sweet,
When once again we hear its call,
Where Friends and Memories Meet

There were various signals throughout the day. One long blast from the Home whistle woke Olga and the other children in the morning. Another long blast, followed by a short blast, summoned them to school during the day. Two short blasts just before dark meant they were to return to their cottages. After one long blast and the playing of "Taps," it was lights out, heads on pillows. The Home's daily schedule stayed pretty much the same for many years.

Under the supervision of longtime Superintendent of Instruction Thomas Edwards, the OSSO Home became a model educational facility. In the primary grades, each pupil began with full days of classes, which later became half days of school and half days of training in "The Trades." Some occupations—like telegraphy, stenography, and bookkeeping—were taught as extensions of the regular school curriculum, as were cooking, sewing, drawing, musical instruction, "physical culture," and military training. Others were extensions of the "Industries and Trades" curriculum, which, in their own way, kept the Home in operation as a small world unto itself.

By 1900, the number of trades taught in the Home had been expanded considerably from earlier years: printing, electrical and mechanical engineering, blacksmithing, woodworking and carpentry, tin shop, shoemaking, farming, butchering, baking, clothing, painting, and barbering.

Here's the *Home Weekly*, giving the more than 100 members of the 1906 "Discharge Class" a heartfelt sendoff as they prepared to leave the Home and make their way in the world:

"As the hour draws near for departure to each of them naturally comes a feeling of uncertainty and suspense as to what the future may have in store for them. And their matrons, teachers and friends here will watch anxiously for news of their future success. They have now finished their preliminary training, and while some may continue studies for a short time, even that will be amid different surroundings; so that all will be called upon to act on the education and habits acquired during the time spent at the Home.

"The training has been practically the same for all, but will the results be the same? If each would act the very best he or she knows how, according to the

If the outside world was viewed by the caretakers of the Home as a practical place—and it was—then its signal operation might have been its vocational offerings. The Home had one of the earliest vocational programs anywhere, and soon it had the widest offerings.

The voc building opened around 1870 and before long there were classes in everything from baking, blacksmithing, and carpentry to horticulture, tailoring, and woodcarving. In effect, the shop boys, being able to perform most any task, were the Home's caretakers. By the 1930s, the Home's shop graduates—because of the variety of their experiences with machinery—were judged superior to the graduates from Ohio's largest high schools.

The fellows in the electric shop, for instance, learned to do everything from electrical theory to the repair of the electric fly catchers in the dairy barn, and the boys in woodworking built a packing crate for Dick, the Home's old cavalry horse. The boys in the metal shop put a new tin roof on Cottage 19, and two Home boys were running the downtown Xenia movie projectors.

"And last but not least," wrote the *Home Review* in December of 1934, "William Thomas has been sleeping on the woodpile."

Tom Ferguson was still running the tin shop in the 1930s, having arrived at the Home after apprenticing in the various tin shops of Cincinnati, Dayton, and Springfield. Perhaps because he, too, was an orphan, the boys were drawn to him, carrying away from the Home the picture of old Tom, his hat tilted back on his head, arms folded, chewing a wad of Beechnut, and meditating upon some problem a kid had brought him that soon would not be a problem.

He had a tin replica of the battleship *Maine* on a shop shelf, its craft all the endorsement Tom ever needed. He was forever doing something for the boys, making giblet stews, or pigeon fries, or cooking up his tomatoes-and-onions dish that held sway over anything that came from the Home dining hall, even if the boys were suspicious of where the pans that held Tom's treats had come from or what they had previously held.

Ham radio was the Home's new craze during the 1930s, presided over by Mr. Schleip's kids at the electric shop, who wired the cottages with buzzers and drove everyone batty with their Morse Code practice. The longer-range ambitions of the maintenance electrician, Court Wilkins, hurled his voice across the country where one of Mr. Wilkins' shortwave conversations with a fellow in backcountry Texas was interrupted by a loud blast. A large rattlesnake had crawled into the Texan's shack where it was summarily dispatched by the Texan's shotgun, to the chagrin of Mr. Wilkins, who was left deafened on the other end.

Not to be outdone with the new medium, the boys in Cottage 18 made a crystal set, using a window screen as their antenna. To warn them when the cottage matron was coming, the boys sprinkled toilet cleaner on the cottage stairs so that her crunching footsteps alerted them. It was difficult to tell which was more inventive, the crystal set or their early warning system.

Early on, the Home boys had fallen under the thrall of the old power plant.

There wasn't much the shop couldn't do. They made shoes, for instance, then they repaired them, as many some years as four pairs per student.

Shoe repairing class O.S.-S.O. Home. C.B.N.

"When we unloaded coal from the cars and wheeled it into the boilers," one of the students wrote, "how the flames leaped out with ferocity. How thrilled we were to actually shovel coal on Sunday, thereby missing church where the other fires of intensity were mentioned but without any particular effect on us.

"They gave us asbestos gloves when we held the steam rod while blowing out the boiler tubes, and ran back and forth on the planking inserting and withdrawing the rod. We watched the ever-lighted clock for the fireman to blow the whistle that regulated our day. How amazed I was upon first hearing the sound of the whistle at its source.

"Upstairs, the engineer peered at the complex gauges and charts, and it appeared he almost caressed the machinery as he oiled, greased, and regulated it. The bigness of it was breathtaking. The Home power plant instilled in me a fascination for all power plants that I have never lost, and I visit them at every opportunity…"

Before the Home's old electric generating plant went into retirement, the boys who studied electricity had graduated into some of Ohio's top places—Fred Barr was an engineer with Dayton Power and Light; Ed Grove the superintendent of maintenance for the Columbus, Ohio, schools; Bliss Haskell was an engineer at West Virginia Steel & Mfg.; Foraquer Thornton and Ed Noice worked for the Municipal Light Plant in Columbus.

And there was Will McCracken. He graduated from the Home in 1879, then went to Ohio State when the university consisted of four buildings, 336 students, and twelve faculty members. He became chief engineer in 1886, helped introduce electricity to the campus in 1893, spent six decades at OSU and served under five presidents. He was known for always keeping his hat on, ready to rush out and answer any university call, and in 1953 he received the university's Distinguished Service Award.

In 1940, the Barnett Vocational School in Texas wrote the Home to ask about the course of training used in the Home's shoe department. Texas's voc-ed department was preparing to introduce shoe repairing in thirty-one cities but could find no text on the subject. The Home had overcome the same problems earlier on, and could now supply Texas with a series of units to cover the subject.

The Home's shoe shop supplied shoes for the students, then repaired what it had supplied. About this time, each Home kid went through about three pairs of shoes each year, and repairs were made to nearly four pairs per student. The budding shoemakers had other talents, too: "The shoemaker's kids sewed covers back on baseballs after the game was ended because some kid connected and batted the covers off," said Lloyd Brewster.

Their work wasn't just shoes and baseballs, either; it was also the foot itself. They learned "Practipedics," the study of the human foot, its functions and ailments, and they were astonished to find out that the fifty-two bones in one's feet made up about twenty-five percent of all the bones in the body. Most of them would never again look at the foot in quite the same manner.

In late 1950, the shoe shop repaired 1,835 pairs of shoes; the print shop had a profitable year selling its own Christmas cards; the auto shop was doing a booming business starting cars (due to the extremely cold weather); the metal shop made new dust pans for all the cottages, then ran out of material for the new towel racks; and the general shop was busy repairing everyone's sleds. At one point in the 1950s, Albert Fisher was very energetically building a boat.

Clarence Burke was still the custodian in the trades building. He worked as a mechanic where he had been friends with the Wright Brothers when they were struggling inventors. Among Mr. Burke's prized possessions was a photograph he took, with his box camera, of the first airplane flight in Dayton, out at Barr's Station (now the site of Wright Field). He found the Wright boys unprepossessing. "Hard to believe that they were working on something so great," he said, a kind of object lesson for kids who were trying to find their own applications.

The kids were, in effect, keeping the Home running. There wasn't much they couldn't do. In 1963, for instance, the boys in the woodshop built new racks for the library, made forty T squares for the art room, a kitchen cabinet for Mr. Joslin's house, a room divider (with trellis and planter) for the beauty shop, a Ping Pong table for Taft A, repaired ten sleds, and constructed a Santa and reindeers for the Christmas band concert.

Mr. Hansford Jackson, the Home's horticultural supervisor, grew from a tiny seedling an eight foot tall banana tree, when in maturity produced from thirty to fifty bananas, which were short, extremely sweet, with brown peelings.

The kids even learned how to give haircuts. They did it so well, in fact, that even the governor liked to get his hair cut at the Home. Governor James Rhodes loved the place, and whenever he was anywhere close by, he showed up for a haircut.

That's what the lore always said, anyway. One thing for sure about the place. Its ability to teach and train youngsters how to make, build, repair, and maintain most anything was unparalleled. That much wasn't lore; it was all on the record.

teachings received at the Home, there is no doubt that success, though perhaps not riches or fame in every case, would follow. Circumstances will change but the same Christian principles of right and honor prevail in all places, and the one who heeds these principles will have the character founded upon the rock that will not be upset by the first wind that blows past him."

Their pupils, of course, would come and go, but some of the Home's instructors remained at the institution for many years. One such beloved figure was Tom Ferguson.

Born February 9, 1869, Thomas Ruel Ferguson was raised by a Batavia, Ohio, family after his parents died within a few years of each other. At a young age, he went to work as an apprentice in a tin shop in Maysville, Kentucky, and was employed over the next several years in tin shops in Dayton, Wilmington, Cincinnati, and Springfield. In 1899, Ferguson came to the Home to manage the tin shop and serve as an instructor. Perhaps because he, himself, was an orphan, or because he liked teaching as much as tin work, Ferguson stayed for the rest of his life. By the time he died in 1933, he had become a legend.

Some of Tom Ferguson's best students, like George Strain, became prominent in their fields. Arriving at the Home in 1904, Strain graduated in September, 1910, at the age of 16. A profile in the *Home Review* in 1939 revealed that "George learned the sheet metal trade under the able leadership of Tom Ferguson and as has now proved, it was to his good advantage. . . . Upon leaving the home he worked in Akron and Springfield and for the last sixteen years he has been an officer in the Sheet Metal Workers International Union." In 1939, Strain was appointed state director of industrial relations by Governor John Bricker.

Another of Ferguson's students remembered what it was like to work with him. "His boys and friends were first and utmost in his thoughts and he was continually doing something for them. The picnics, the annual suppers were always high spots in the lives of the kids, as well as for Tom himself, and many a boy has stood around a shop stool with a can of white cherries on it and speared one when his turn came. It was in the sharing equally, as well as in the mutual joy for the gift, that great lessons were taught us, lessons we can never forget."

Life at the Home was not all work. One of the earliest surviving photographs shows a group of girls and their matron standing in front of their cottage, each girl holding her favorite plaything or possession: a doll, a wagon, a hoop, a parasol. A visitor to the Home on a spring afternoon undoubtedly would find a baseball game underway. By the 1880s, the Home was fielding its own team.

William "Mike" Thrasher remembered his playing days in a letter to the *Home Weekly* in 1921. "I can look back on my time in 1887-1888 and see how the boys

The Cadets of 1920 had a distinctly martial bearing; the area teams all knew about the Home teams; they were as good as they looked.

were always looking for Saturday to roll around. We had in those days a team that went on the field to win, and I wish to state we were very seldom defeated. We played clubs from Charlestown, Cedarville, Columbus, Springfield, Dayton, Yellow Springs, Sabina, Wilmington, and Xenia . . . Gee, those were good old days." The Home's "Cadets" began their 1908 season by thrashing Xenia Theological Seminary, 13-1, and went on to play high schools, as well as the colleges of Cedarville and Antioch.

The chapel

It was a foregone conclusion that the Home's children would receive a regular dose of religion, given that the "father" of the institution was a local pastor and that its founding organization, the Grand Army of the Republic, strongly advocated religious values. George Collier, who had been chaplain for the Grand Army of the Republic, was a major force in energizing the GAR to keep the home on its priority list. The Home chapel was named after him. The OSSO Home was a state-sponsored institution in a country founded upon specific guarantees of religious freedom and the careful separation of church and state, but these guarantees in no way diminished the importance of religion in citizens' lives.

The chapel was the second-oldest building on the campus. It was a never-changing constant in the Home's long history.

The children from the Main Street Home gathered at City Hall to receive their first sermon, delivered by Reverend P. C. Prugh, pastor of the Reformed Church and leader of the local campaign to establish the orphans home in Xenia. Reverend Prugh taught the first Sunday school in the nearby YMCA. After the Home moved to the Pelham Farm on Poverty Knoll in 1870, regular church services were held in the dining hall of the temporary administration building and then in the dining hall of the domestic service building. When the weather was warm and pleasant, Sunday services were sometimes held outside on the lawn near the cottages. Local ministers and students from nearby Xenia Theological Seminary conducted the services on a rotating basis—and did so without compensation of any kind for more than a decade. As many as forty volunteers from local churches and the seminary taught the weekly Sunday school classes.

In 1872, the General Assembly approved funds for the construction of a chapel near the point where a road entering the grounds reached the top of the ridge. With a seating capacity of 1200, the chapel was not just a place of worship. It was the Home's concert hall, theater, and assembly center. Holidays were celebrated there. Former residents would have fond memories of Christmas and Memorial Day, long after they left the Home. The Grand Army and other veterans groups, as well as the Association of Ex-Pupils, made sure that every child had a memorable Christmas, continuing the tradition started by Ohio First Lady Lucy Webb Hayes when the Home was founded in downtown Xenia. The same could be said for Memorial Day, when long lines of children—the boys in uniform carrying flags and the girls in white carrying flowers—marched from the school to the cemetery behind the chapel, where the Home buried its dead. There, the marchers put flags and flowers on the graves and sang hymns. One child was given the solemn responsibility of reciting the Gettysburg Address. Ohio Governor Andrew L. Harris delivered the Memorial Day address at the cemetery in 1907.

Dorothy Cox Skelly remembered the Memorial Day celebrations of her youth in the 1920s: "We would march, boys and girls. We were paired off into sizes and grades. . . . I led a good deal of the times, up in my teens. I remember being about 12. I had to walk with my brother and this was insulting to me, at that age. So I went behind what is now the museum. We played back there and there was poison ivy. I put poison ivy all over my face and arms hoping I would get poison ivy and not have to march in that parade. I didn't break out until the day afterwards.

"We had a Memorial Day song. . . . We had this basket of flowers the girls carried and the boys carried a flag. And when we sang 'We deck these halls today' we'd lean over and stick them in the ground. It was a very beautiful sight and we were very proud of it."

The Memorial Day parades were a magnificent occasion at the Home, connecting the children by its splendid ritual to their country's past and it was made knowable by the palpable emotion of the day.

With the terrible economic depression of the 1890s behind it, the Ohio Soldiers and Sailors Orphans Home seemed poised to face the challenges of the new century. Despite the declining number of Civil War orphans that had forced similar institutions in other states to close, the OSSO Home had the continued support of the local community and the Grand Army of the Republic. It also drew strength the Association of Ex-Pupils, whose numbers had grown because the Home's system of care and culture, education and work, discipline and dedication had earned it the loyalty of both the children and the people who served them.

The Progressive Movement

Many of the larger social movements of the so-called Progressive Era at the time were not as disruptive in the Home as they were in the world around it.

Alcohol had been a problem in Xenia and most of southwest Ohio in the early days of frontier settlement. But the efforts of churches and other religious groups had minimized the problem by the turn of the century, and the OSSO Home prohibited the use and possession of alcohol on its property. Violators faced swift and severe consequences.

Xenia, like most communities in the Midwest, was racially segregated. While black people and white people worked together, shopped in the same stores, and attended many of the same events, they lived in separate neighborhoods and attended separate schools. Yet because blacks had served in the Union Army, there was never any serious question that eligible children of African-American veterans would be admitted to the Home. They attended the same classes, learned the same trades, did the same chores and attended the same events as the other residents.

In the beginning, though, there were not many black children in residence. Black men wanted to enlist immediately in the Union Army but were not permitted to do so. Of the approximately 350,000 Ohioans who fought in the Civil War, only one African-American regiment—the 5th United States Colored Troops—was formed in Ohio. Ultimately, several hundred thousand African-Americans would serve in the Union Army.

With the Home admitting greater numbers of children, both white and black, in the early 1900s, segregation in housing became the accepted practice. But African-American children continued to participate in all other activities of the Home.

In general, the roles of women were considered subordinate to those of men, but with a few notable exceptions. In the years after the Civil War, Ohioans Elizabeth Blackwell and Victoria Woodhull shattered traditional stereotypes, working in

In the separated society of its time, it was unusual for any institution to be as color-blind as the Home. (At rear, left, is Hat Noland, one of the Home's great benefactors.)

jobs—Blackwell in medicine, Woodhull in politics and finance—normally reserved for men. Reformers Lucy Stone and Harriet Tyler Upton were leaders in the women's rights movement, which set the stage for the suffrage amendment to the United States Constitution in 1920.

By 1900, women had twice served as acting superintendents of the OSSO Home. Much about the treatment of gender in the Home was egalitarian. Girls and boys attended most of the same classes. It was only in the trades curriculum that differentiation by sex became obvious, apparently due to a recognition of where jobs would be found and who was likely to find them. Military training was a masculine enterprise, but units of girls practiced close-order marching and "wand drill" as a complement to the "manual of arms" practiced by the boys. When the armory opened in 1904, it was used equally by boys and girls.

Because of the strong support of Ohio's veterans organizations and the

Association of Ex-Pupils, the OSSO Home enjoyed funding and state support at levels not available to Children's Homes funded by local government. It seems there could be little objection to an institution that did so much so well. But of course there was.

The state and the child

One of the differences between the Progressive Movement and earlier reform movements was journalism's enormous influence on politics. There had always been passionate advocates. The American Revolution had Tom Paine and the abolitionists had William Lloyd Garrison. Lucy Stone argued the case for women's rights. Henry George preached the merits of the Single Tax. But a new breed of reporters came of age in the years before WWI, writing in depth on every aspect of society, politics, and culture, opening windows to an America many of its citizens had never seen. With advances in printing, newspapers and periodicals became cheaper to publish. Competition led to in-depth reporting as well as lurid headlines—and a lot more people reading a lot more news a lot more often.

Critics, among them President Theodore Roosevelt, suggested that reporters were only interested in turning over rocks to see what might be living in the darkness beneath them. Roosevelt described them as "muckrakers," which reporters took as a compliment. There were a lot of muckrakers turning over a lot of rocks. Lincoln Steffens examined the politics of selected towns and wrote, *The Shame of the Cities*. Upton Sinclair looked at the meatpacking business in his novel *The Jungle*. Ida Tarbell politely called her series of articles *A History of the Standard Oil Company*, which led to the breakup of one of America's largest companies.

Few subjects in American life, though, captured the heart and attention of its citizens than stories about its children. Muckrakers looked at the schools and found students not learning. They found youth living in slums. They also looked at child laborers. By 1910, more than two million American children between the ages of 10 and 15 were on the job—many working six days a week, ten hours a day, for wages significantly lower than their adult counterparts. Many more children even younger than 10 years of age were working in America's mines, mills, and factories.

Progressive reformers, with the backing of organized labor, called for the abolition of child labor. Most labor unions saw working children taking jobs away from adults by working for less money for longer hours. Reformers also called for improvements in education, settlement houses, and social services for people in need. But change was slow in coming.

Viola King
graduate of 1930

"I went to the Home in 1914 at the age of 2. They thought I was a smart little girl because we kept our shoes lined up in the storeroom, and I knew which were mine. Of course, I knew them. They weren't like anyone else's. They were black patent leather bottoms with red leather tops.

"The teachers came early in the morning to help dress all the little kids. Many mornings I woke up to find myself sleeping between the matron and her husband. I suppose they carried me in during the night. They were so kind.

"There was another matron, Mrs. Eisenhower. I loved her, too. Even after I left the Home, I sent her roses. Cleveland, where I was, had two Sunday papers with all the funny papers and I would say, 'Let's send them to Cottage 13 for a rainy Saturday afternoon. Sometimes I'd send her money to order ice cream for a kid's birthday. When she got sick, I paid her hospitalization. The night before she died, she wrote me a letter and said, 'Thanks to you, darling, I can be in a hospital and I have your picture right by my bed, your smiling face,' and she died during an operation.

"I loved my 4th grade teacher because she understood children. It was embarrassing for a child to have to go to the bathroom, so in the middle of class she'd excuse everyone. It was so kind. She knew how restless the children were, so she let us go to the fire escape and watch a robin build its nest. When she walked up and down the aisles, she always stopped and put her hand on my shoulder.

"My 5th grade teacher drew a big map and told us what certain cities did. Xenia had a hemp factory so she found a piece of hemp and glued it onto Xenia. She read to us every noon for fifteen minutes, and again at the end of the day, and over the course of a year she read us three or four books.

"My brother bugled under the flag pole for every meal and we kids sang *Coffee, coffee, coffee without any cream. Porky, porky, porky without any lean. Soupy soupy soupy without any beans…*

"Once, three girls did something, I don't remember what, and had to have their hair cut like a boy and wear the boys' uniform and march around the flagpole. And Millie Adams liked this boy and wrote him a note and the Chief Matron who was horrible made Millie walk through the dining room, and the boy stand up, and the matron read the note, which said, *Your hair is like a bale of hay, your eyes are very queer, your mouth is like my cellar door, but still I love you dear*.

"We had the most beautiful dress parades, and the band boys traveled a lot. One time, they went to Washington and a group of women put on a fancy dinner, crystal and sterling, all this beautiful stuff on the table for the orphan boys. The waitresses hadn't poured water in their glasses yet, but there was water in the finger bowls, and the boys drank all the water in the bowls.

"Later, my grandson-in-law asked me what war impressed me the most and I said, 'Of course, the first World War.' The Germans had those awful helmets with the point on top, which scared the kids. Sometimes at night, I couldn't sleep, thinking 'Those big German soldiers can get off the train and walk right up the chapel hill and get us.' Then I'd say to myself, 'No, the big girls locked the door.' And it was okay…."

Since the end of the Civil War, the growth of cities and industries drew ever larger numbers of children of both native and immigrant newcomers to urban America. Many were on their own or were surviving in desperate poverty with single or disabled parents. Inevitably there were more children than there were jobs and something needed to be done to help the children who could not help themselves. Orphanages established prior to the American Civil War could not handle all of the children in need.

A number of new initiatives were tried. Under the leadership of Charles Loring Brace in 1854, large numbers of children were removed from the poor neighborhoods of eastern cities and put on "orphan trains" for re-settlement with families in the rural Midwest. The system was popular for a time and lasted for a number of years. But it was increasingly criticized as well. Some of the children had been tricked into heading west, where they had to work long hours with their new families in rural and small town America. And in the worst cases, they were abandoned by their new families. The "orphan train" programs tried hard to meet lofty ideals, but simply failed far too many times.

Another new alternative to help children in need were institutions like the Ohio Soldiers and Sailors Orphans Home. Established in the wake of the Civil War after intensive appeals from veterans' organizations, these homes for veterans children were established in ten northern states. Some lasted only a few years. Others in Iowa, Indiana, Illinois, Pennsylvania, and Ohio had strong and continuing support. But there were still many children needing assistance.

Least attractive of all the options were the poorhouses or infirmaries that operated under guidelines drawn from the English Poor Law of 1611. The Poor Law stipulated that all who needed assistance—the young and old, the sick and healthy, the physically or mentally disabled—were to be gathered together in single facilities to receive "indoor relief" or given a small sum of money as "outdoor relief."

A few states, including Ohio, responded to the public distaste over children living in the poorhouses and infirmaries by attempting to disperse these minors and others with special needs. Ohio established independent state treatment facilities for the blind, the deaf and the mentally ill, and in 1866 followed up with a law permitting counties to establish—if they so desired—independent Children's Homes at county expense. The law looked good on paper, but most counties either could not or chose not to open these facilities. By 1870—four years after the law's enactment—more than 1,000 children were living in fifty-seven poorhouses or infirmaries around the state.

In 1874, a new state law allowed counties to place children in local orphanages as long as the cost was the same as "similar institutions," but the measure did not prohibit the continued placement of children in poorhouses. And so, the poorhouse is where orphaned children often found themselves.

An 1884 law stated that any child eligible for a county Children's Home or other charitable institution could not be kept in an infirmary or poorhouse. If a place could not be found in the county of residence, the infirmary director was required to place the child in the nearest acceptable Children's Home or in "some other proper charitable institution" approved by the state board of charities. This particular law was amended to permit counties to continue to place children in the county infirmary, provided they were kept separate from adult paupers. Until well into the 20th century it was still permissible for county infirmaries to keep the aged and children who were insane, epileptic or mentally defective, under the same roof, even though state treatment facilities for the insane had existed since 1821. In what was considered to be a positive development at the time, infirmaries were prohibited in 1914 from accepting any person with pulmonary tuberculosis unless a separate building was provided for them.

A search for answers

Most of the recommendations made by the White House Conference of 1909 concerning minimal standards of care for dependent children had been in place at the OSSO Home from the outset.

Cottages were recommended; the Home had them.

Education was recommended; the Home had a system of formal and trade education equal to any in the state.

In terms of medical care, the Home had survived horrific outbreaks of disease far better than many of its neighbors and had kept complete records on its residents.

In short, much of what the White House Conference found lacking in American institutional care already was present in the Ohio Soldiers and Sailors Orphans Home. Strictly speaking, the only desirable form of assistance the Home could not provide was a family, although many of its former residents might disagree even with that assertion.

Across three decades

General Charles Young returned as superintendent on May 1, 1900. He and his wife Cora had been away for five years managing an experimental industrial school

An elegiac scene at the front entrance, probably around 1913, showing the magnificent approach to the Home.

in Scottsdale, Pennsylvania. With their managerial experience, the Youngs were the right people, in the right place, at the right time. The OSSO Home was becoming a big business. It cared for more than 850 children in residence—a number well above the institution's capacity. It processed 139 new boarders, while discharging 162 residents. Annual expenditures approached $200,000.

A total of 406 children were enrolled in the Home's trade schools. The trades that provided better pay and more opportunity were changing, so Superintendent Young saw to it that chemistry and physics were added to the high school curriculum. "We now have twenty-six trades in operation and our children are learning each of them," he reported with pride. In 1901, the Home's electrical engineer organized a school of electrical engineering and mechanical drawing.

One pupil who took advantage of the new offerings was Charles S. Hart, who came to the Home in 1895 and left in 1901.

"I believe it to be the finest institution of its kind in America, and I have always been very grateful for the fact that my father was a soldier which in turn permitted me to have the advantage of the Home as a child, the advantage of wholesome food and regular hours, which built up my physical reserve, the educational and moral influences of the people who were in charge of the Home at the time. . . . Leaving the Home at the age of 16, I was given a drafting job during the years 1902 and 1903 due to the kindly interest of Fred W. Ballard, who was editor of *The Engineer* magazine in Cleveland, and had been chief engineer of the Home."

After attending Ohio State University and graduating from Yale, Charles Hart worked for the Hearst news organization, served in World War I, and eventually became the publisher of *World Adventure* magazine.

"We can remember how we were bored when ex-pupils told us to be grateful for our advantages but as a matter of fact I think there were many of us, just as there are many now in the Home, who appreciated what it was all about and knew that we were having advantages that come to few youngsters of our age," he concluded.

Some of the major problems facing General Young and the Home's staff were related to the physical plant. It was simply too small. Soon, even more children would be eligible to come to the Home as a result of the Spanish-American War of 1898 and a new law passed by the Ohio General Assembly in 1901.

"The trustees are authorized and required to receive into the Home, under such rules and regulations as they may adopt, the children and orphans residing in Ohio of such soldiers and sailors who have died or who will hereafter die by reason of wounds or diseases contracted while serving in the military or naval forces of the United States, and are found to be destitute of the means of support and education; and the children also of permanently disabled or indigent soldiers and sailors found destitute as aforesaid; and all children admitted shall be supported until they are 16 years of age. The board of trustees may however, retain such children until they arrive at the age of 18 years and retain all children of the graduating class."

Under the new law, the OSSO Home would admit children from any of the Ohio's future soldiers and sailors as well.

The first children of a Spanish-American War veteran to be taken into the Home were Grace and Enid Campbell on November 4, 1901. There soon would be others. Fortunately, the war had lasted only four months and casualties were low. More died from disease than combat. Nevertheless, the Home would need to upgrade its facilities to accommodate the anticipated growth of its population. And these were not the first children to be taken in as a result of the war. The Ohio 4th Regiment soldiers brought back a Puerto Rican boy, Cornelio Vargas, who had served as their interpreter, but they were unable to care for him. Warren Harding, then state senator, introduced a resolution allowing the 13-year-old to be cared for by the Home until he was 18 years old. Showing his gratitude over forty years later in one of his many letters to the *Home Review*, he wrote that he would be at the next reunion and "the Home has a warm spot in my heart."

Superintendent Young, a Democrat, stayed on good terms with Republican Governor George Nash and most of the legislature. He needed their support to make the physical changes at the Home during what would become a period of transition for the institution. Longtime Trustee David Jones died in 1903 and was replaced for yet another term by one of the Home's original trustees, General Warren Keifer.

In 1904, after Keifer retired and Governor Nash appointed ex-pupil Dr. James Bemis to the board, General Young and his wife Cora felt it was time for them to go as well. The superintendent was 66 years old and had accomplished much of what he felt was needed to put the OSSO Home on firm footing. While some new construction was still needed, the major improvements to heat, light and water supplies had been completed. In 1903, most of the major buildings had received a coat of paint. And in 1904, the armory was opened.

General Young's replacement was yet another veteran of the Civil War. Captain James L. Smith of Cleveland arrived in September, accompanied by his wife Alice. Following longstanding tradition, Mrs. Smith became chief matron of the Home.

In 1904, a new fire service was put in place with the purchase of a new hose cart.

In 1905, a vegetable green house 100 feet long by 20 feet wide was built for $900.

In 1906, the Home produced 365 gallons of maple syrup and harvested 1200 tons of ice from a frozen McDowell Lake.

In 1907, the board authorized the purchase of a linotype machine to improve the appearance and size of *The Home Weekly*.

In 1908, the Home suffered through a lengthy bout of epidemic scarlet fever and another outbreak of diphtheria. Fortunately, not a single child died from these diseases. Meanwhile, the Ohio General Assembly allocated $65,000 for construction of a new power plant.

Captain Smith and his wife returned to Cleveland in 1909. They returned because they were Republicans and incoming Governor Judson Harmon was a Democrat. They were replaced by another Clevelander with Civil War credentials but the correct political affiliation. E. D. Sawyer had served in a number of government capacities, including Cuyahoga County sheriff. A political opponent of Progressive Mayor Tom Johnson, Sawyer thereby had the support of some local Republicans as well. There was one major problem with Sawyer's appointment as the Home's new superintendent: he did not have a wife who could act as chief matron. Acting Chief Matron, Anna Dunbar, was appointed to the position permanently. "Mother" Dunbar had been a matron at the Home since 1876 and was well-acquainted with its day-to-day operation—probably a good thing since E. D. Sawyer's previous experience as a soldier, sheriff, and state oil field inspector did not provide much experience in running a children's home.

Undaunted, Colonel Sawyer spent his time trying to turn the Home into a place where a good time could be had by all. His remarks to the Association of Ex-Pupils Reunion in 1909 summed up his point of view. "No one could be prouder than I to be called 'daddy' by all these children. I love them and I believe in my heart that they love me. I know of no nobler work than this and I can never tire of it." The superintendent demonstrated his affection for the children by purchasing a motion picture projector so silent films could be shown in the chapel. A report in *The Home Weekly* of his recent activities in July, 1909, ended by noting, "Every move the Colonel has made since coming to the institution has been one to give pleasure to the children of the Home. He is one of the biggest hearted men in the state."

Colonel Sawyer made his most lasting impression on the Home by naming its various streets and drives after Ohio Civil War generals—Sheridan, Custer, McPherson, and so on. On July 15, 1910, he resigned and returned to Cleveland. Taking his place as acting superintendent was Financial Officer Joseph P. Elton. Elton's permanent appointment as superintendent and of his wife Margaret as chief matron was made on April 15, 1911. Joseph Elton had been a former sheriff of Highland County and influential in county Democratic politics before coming to the Home in 1909. The Eltons' stay at the Home, while interrupted a bit, would be quite lengthy.

A new round of construction began at the Home in 1911. A steel flagpole was erected in front of the administration building, placed on the exact spot where the dedication ceremony of the original Home site on July 19, 1869, had been held. Then, in 1911, with funds from a bequest by John Ross and Mary Hissen, a granite memorial gateway was built at the Home's entrance.

The Home faced a new challenge as a result of the Progressive politics of the period. A law passed by the General Assembly had mandated that all state institutions be placed under the supervision of one central controlling agency. Friends of the Home exercised their extraordinary lobbying power, however, and an amendment to the bill excluded the Home from agency control.

In his first biennial report, Superintendent Elton stated, "The Home is classed as one of the benevolent institutions of the state, yet our pupils have never been considered the recipients of charity, for it has always been conceded that in their education the State of Ohio is merely liquidating a debt she owes to the defenders of the nation and for his widow and orphan, and I cannot believe the taxpayers of the state would consent to have one comfort or one pleasure taken from these active growing boys and girls, not one of whom is here by reason of any fault of his own."

In 1912, a Spanish-American War veteran was appointed to the board of trustees for the first time and a silk American flag was presented to the OSSO Home by the United Spanish War Veterans. Meanwhile, its resident population had declined from 702 in 1910 to 630 in 1912 due to fewer children being admitted while further improvements were made to the grounds and buildings. More than fifty years later, Laura Mae Vining recalled what the Home had been like in her childhood in 1912.

"It has been many years since I was a pupil at the Home but nothing dims my memories. The picture of the old white cottages tore at my heart, especially as dear old Cottage 15 showed up so plainly. How many times I marched up the old veranda to take my place in the big dining room where the long white tables were set with the big white bowls which we younger girls carried filled with food from the kitchen below. Does anyone remember those wonderful 'pound cakes' we had every Sunday night? My! My! How we girls in Cottage 15 used to gripe when dear old Miss Smith would take the remainder of the cake over to the boys in Cottage 30! These are my brightest memories as are those of beautiful Lake McDowell where we skated in winter and walked around in summer. . . .

"One thing I remember clearly is the iron steps in the administration building where I visited with my brothers . . . on Sunday afternoon. Miss Grapes would also invite me to Cottage 30 to visit them. The back lawn had a maypole swing where we played so often after school. We had many a fine time sliding down the walk leading

There was a formality to the rituals of the Home, which, after all, was based on military models. This is a photograph taken early in the 1900s and shows the students marching off to their classes.

to the bath house when it was icy. I still have a picture of the dog 'Beans' who was a friend to all.

"I am very grateful that I could have such a happy childhood as I know the sacrifices each and every parent makes for his children in this world."

By 1914, the grounds encompassed 360 acres, including the addition of sixty-seven acres of the nearby Sullivan farm acquired by the board of trustees for $15,000 in 1913. One hundred acres constituted the grounds of the Home, another 100 acres was in pasture or timber, and 160 acres was in cultivation. Board members believed more land was needed for farming and gardening.

The year 1914 also marked the arrival of a memorable teacher: Miss Gertrude Straley. An article in the *Home Review* in 1936 highlighted her contributions to the institution: "Miss Straley, for 22 years teacher of the second grade at the O.S. & S.O. Home has resigned her post as teacher to retire from the profession. . . . Miss Straley has kept a record of different children since coming to the Home. Her record of teaching aggregates 957 pupils. . . . She has kept the same room for all of these 22 years, never a change. She also taught Sunday school nearly all the time.

"Miss Straley is noted especially for her Rhythm Band in which many of us had the honor of being a part while in the second grade. . . . Miss Straley had a bird parade for May Day which stretched across the front lawn to the school building occupied by the grade children. Miss Straley says that one of the things ex-pupils always notice that is missing in the room is the large picture of the American flag in the sky on the front blackboard. This picture was put up by Miss Straley in 1918."

Sadly, the Home in 1914 reported its first death in six years. It was noted, however, that the child who died had only been in residence for eight days. Meanwhile, the hospital facilities were expanded, with a new veranda surrounding the main building. And a new detention ward to stop the spread of contagious disease had become quite effective in its work.

The war years and after

The Home saw a number of changes in 1915 with World War I underway in Europe. The U.S. maintained a policy of strict neutrality, but the conflict abroad led to greater interest in military preparedness at the Home. For the first time in a generation, the uniforms worn by the boys were changed. They wore khakis during the summer because the material was less expensive, cooler and easier to keep clean than the previously worn blue-jean uniforms, which were kept for dress purposes and cold weather. In addition, the boys battalion and its color guard went on the

Lloyd Brewster
Class of 1925

"Do you remember when ginger snaps were plentiful and could be used as flying saucers, and when you could mix your butter in your syrup only if you did not owe the next six months' allotment of syrup to some kid, that along with your pie? Of course, if you had been a bad little kid, the matron might divert your pie to some model boy of those years—who is now probably laid up in some garage or used car lot.

"When if you were lucky you had yourself a carrier, like an enlarged money belt, in which you carried some turkey to your cottage, of course not exactly with the matron's concurrence? Why was it that food taken from the dining room always seemed to taste better? Do you remember how lucky you felt if some buddy had not gotten into your locker in the washroom and swiped your food bank?

"I would certainly love to have the recipe for that Sunday night pound cake. I know it took plenty of butter to make it. Daisy yellow with a rivulet of chocolate running through it and old Daddy Horn sculpting it into the cake pans made in the tin shop.

"Do you remember the haywagons in which we were taxied to the train station? What a thrill when the horses started hauling their cargo of light-hearted kids with their canvas suitcases and tickets pinned to their clothing for safekeeping. Miss Bauerle always had lunchboxes for the kids—two, if you were going far…"

The view of the old school from McDowell Lake—the students' preferred campus view: from their swimming hole.

road to demonstrate their preparedness. In June, 1915, the battalion attended the Annual Encampment of the Department of Ohio of the United Spanish War Veterans in Chillicothe. The boys participated in a street parade and later performed the Manual Drill in their dress uniforms. The Home's band attended the National Encampment of the United Spanish War Veterans in Louisville in the same year. The expenses of both trips were covered by the veterans groups.

Annabelle Flower Heller's memories of 1915 were of her teachers and the cottage where she lived: "How well I recall Viola Sypherd, my first and last teacher; Mrs. Carrie Reymour Preston; Miss Woodrow; then our 'special' teachers, Miss Sara Collins, music; Miss Alice Perry, writing; Miss Lottie Hunt, drawing; Miss Eloise Clough, stenography. Then we would not forget our matrons, Mrs. Smiley and Mrs. Elder of No. 15. My eyes were cast on other matrons than my own, for instance, Miss Hess, then our beloved Rose Bauerle. I feel we should say, 'Ladies, take a bow.' (Sara Collins wrote the home Christmas carol in 1887 and it was sung each Christmas after.)

"It is proper to give honor to those whom honor is due, but all of these I have mentioned and many others deserve a special recognition. Our dear Professor Edwards, who had the interest of so many at heart, and who worked so tirelessly toward an education for those who really sought more.

"All in all I feel we owe so much to many who were so faithful and long suffering with many of us. The dear Home was a real savior for many who had never known a real home. I bow with the greatest of reverence. When I know of the success of a boy or girl from the Home, I feel it as keenly as though it were my own . . . . "

In 1916, the Home remodeled the Sullivan family farmhouse for use as a nursery, which was occupied by twenty-four children and a matron. Meanwhile, the political wheels of Ohio politics turned once again in the Republicans' favor when Frank B. Willis defeated James M. Cox in a race for the governorship. Like his predecessors, Willis decided that the leadership of the Home should be from his political party. Joseph Elton and his wife left and Judge J. S. Kimbrough was installed as the new superintendent.

By all accounts, Judge Kimbrough was a kind, competent man. But he soon found himself dealing with a variety of misfortunes. During the winter of 1916, the Home's hot water heating system proved inadequate. It was the following spring before repairs and improvements were made. Thus, a lot of people were very cold for a very long time. Some were sick as well as a new diphtheria epidemic struck the Home, forcing officials to quarantine the sick children for several months. One died from the serious bacterial infection. Another died over the winter of pneumonia unrelated to the epidemic.

With the U.S. entering World War I in April of 1917, newly re-elected Democratic Governor James M. Cox permitted Republican Judge J. S. Kimbrough to remain as the Home's superintendent. But by July, the judge had resigned and Governor Cox had replaced him with former Superintendent Joseph Elton.

The war years of 1917 and 1918 were difficult ones, of course, for all of America. The U.S. had not been involved in a major war for more than fifty years and many people had never experienced the sacrifices involved in such a major struggle. To obtain the manpower needed to fight the war, a draft was imposed for the first time since the Civil War. The federal government took over operation of the railroads. National, state and local Councils of National Defense set priorities for wartime production and enforced quotas. Many goods and fuel products like coal became unavailable or were in extremely short supply. A number of young men who were ex-pupils of the Home went off to war, and nine of them died in combat.

Life at the Home, however, was not substantially changed by the war. Viola Pebcroft King was 5 years old at the time.

"It was in the newspapers and matrons or teachers would sit and talk to the big girls," King said, recalling the war years. "Big girls were knitting scarves and socks . . . real ugly color . . . khaki is what they had then. I sat up and watched them knit, and once in a while a big girl gave me needles and let me do two rows. . . .

"Such beautiful songs came out. . . . I still remember all of them. I was born harmonizing. A little kid can harmonize. And the big girls would stand in a group and cuddle me up and let me harmonize with them."

The most memorable event at the Home during World War I did not take place until the great conflict was almost over. In the summer of 1918, a particularly virulent form of influenza became a worldwide pandemic. In crowded army camps and heavily populated areas, the flu's toll was devastating, with thousands and then millions of people succumbing to its complications. It was not the flu itself, but the pneumonia it induced that killed people, especially those in their late teens and 20's. Influenza arrived at the Home in October, and more than 600 children and several employees would be stricken.

With the hospital full, five cottages and three school rooms became temporary hospital wards. People from nearby towns and many of the mothers of children came to the Home to help when so many were ill. Because of the prompt action of so many, and because the disease hit older children hardest, only sixty-five of the 600 cases of flu turned into full-blown pneumonia. Of the sixty-five children contracting pneumonia, three died. It was the worst epidemic since diphtheria struck the Home in 1890.

The Association of Ex-Pupils held their annual reunion in the summer of 1919,

The girls, as well as the boys, wore uniforms into the 1930s. It took the difficulty out of one's early morning decision-making.

celebrating the Home's 50th anniversary. It was one of the largest reunions in the Home's history and one of the most poignant, for a memorial service was held to remember the nine ex-pupils who lost their lives in World War I.

Recognizing that many more children would be coming to the Home as a result of the war, the board of trustees made a study of what it would take to increase the capacity of the Home by fifty percent. It was determined that the construction of ten new cottages, one new school building, one new laundry building, an expanded hospital, an expanded dining hall and the purchase of 250 additional acres would cost more than $400,000—the equivalent of two years of the Home's operating budget. With an economic downturn resulting from the peacetime conversion of war industries, and with many other problems facing the state, the board chose not to act immediately on the proposals.

The Twenties

America changed during the war years. The bright hopes and the belief in the inevitability of progress that characterized the country's Progressive Era were shattered by the horrors of World War I. In Ohio, Republican Harry L. Davis won the governorship and took office in January, 1921. The service of Joseph Elton and his wife at the Home came to an end. Elton would follow his wife to Delaware, where she became head of the Girls Industrial School for seven years. Eventually, the Eltons returned to their home in Hillsboro, where Joseph Elton died in 1936.

Elton's successor, Sylvis Garver, served previously on the board of trustees and therefore knew how the Home operated. Born in 1869 in Defiance, Ohio, Garver fought in the Spanish-American War with the Sixth Ohio Volunteer Infantry and left the service with the rank of first sergeant. His wife, Anna Noble Garver, was intimately acquainted with the Home as well. The new chief matron was an ex-pupil. She met and married Sylvis Garver after leaving the Home.

The Garvers were sympathetic to the changing values of the times. As one account from that period states, "Special attention was given to granting the children all the freedom consistent with good government, and the holding of social parties at the armory was received with great delight, and afforded a pleasant relief from daily routine." In their annual report to the governor in 1921, the board of trustees reported that "(the Garvers) have succeeded in making the children happy, and at the same time preserved the rules of discipline which always must exist in this or any institution of like nature."

In June, the Home band made a trip to the United Spanish War Veterans of Ohio encampment at Lorain and entertained the veterans. It was a happy band that returned to the Home, for the veterans had presented the children with new instruments valued at $1200.

In the early 1920s, the Association of Ex-Pupils raised the money needed to build a library. The new Memorial Library was formally dedicated in July, 1925. By then, the long-planned new high school building was well under construction. The impetus for this project had come from the Ohio Department of Public Instruction and its recognition of the OSSO Home's schools as "public schools." Classes taken in the Home's four-year high school program were now more easily transferable to other Ohio schools. The Home also was eligible to compete with other public schools in scholastic, athletic and other competitions.

In 1923, Democrat A. Victor Donahey was elected governor of Ohio. Unlike many of his predecessors, Donahey, a relatively conservative Democrat, did not use the occasion of his election to remove every Republican holding office at state institutions. In fact, he even appointed some Republicans to government positions.

The open approach pursued by Superintendent Garver apparently did not meet with everyone's favor at the Home. Ultimately charges of mismanagement and lack of competent controls were investigated by legislative committees. No charges were ever brought formally, but Sylvis Garver and his wife resigned on June 30, 1925.

Here's a familiar scene at the Home, probably a reunion, with lots of speeches, which could make a young lad (lower right) positively comatose.

The Home band in 1919, performing in Akron, was a handsome outfit—small in number, mighty in sound.

Garver returned to his home in Defiance, where he died in 1936. His replacement was Thomas E. Andrews. Andrews, a Republican, was appointed by Donahey, the Democratic governor, which may speak well of both men. Andrews had been born in Union County, Ohio, in 1875. Moving to Marion, Ohio, as a young man, he served in the Spanish-American War and as a first lieutenant in World War I.

Superintendent Andrews brought a variety of administrative and management experience to the Home, and over the next two years the results of his expertise of Thomas Andrews began to be seen. The laundry building was completely remodeled and stocked with new equipment at a cost of more than $14,000. Architects also were retained to remodel the cottages and the administration building. By late 1927, the remodeling of the cottages was well underway. The job included an addition to the rear of each cottage with a bathroom with shower, new linen and clothes closets, a realignment of the stairway giving more room for the matron, and a rear exit for the children.

On April 10, 1928, Thomas Andrews and his wife resigned from board. He had accepted a position with the Ohio National Guard as an inspector in the mining areas of southeastern Ohio, where violent confrontations between labor and management had become quite common. Andrews remained on the National Guard's administrative staff until his retirement in 1938. He died in Marion in 1960.

The board appointed the Reverend Norman King of Bluffton, Ohio, to be the new superintendent on May 30, 1928. He came to the Home with his wife as chief matron, but their stay would be short-lived. According to one account, "Superintendent King inherited many troubles and quarrels of the employees and to smooth them out properly he reckoned it would take a regiment of the National Guard."

Not having the Guard at his disposal, King lasted nine weeks before resigning. He later served as a chaplain at the Soldiers' Home in Dayton for three years prior to World War II. After serving one year as a frontline chaplain, he returned to the Soldiers' Home, where he died in 1942.

Reverend King was followed by Major and Mrs. Charles Burton as the superintendent and the chief matron of the Home. Major Burton had served in the Spanish-American War and World War I, and had strong support from the incoming Republican administration of Governor Myers Y. Cooper.

During the late 1920s, Ohio veterans organizations lobbied the governor and the General Assembly to commit funds and support to the building program proposed by the Board of Trustees of the OSSO Home and the various study committees and planning commissions that had looked at the institution in some detail in recent years. The veterans' push would pay off. By late 1928, the cottage remodeling, which had been proceeding slowly, received a new infusion of state money. Two separate residential halls for senior boys and girls were completed. The boys' building was named for Theodore Roosevelt and the girls' residence for Lucy Webb Hayes, wife of former governor and President Hayes. A new hospital building was named for General J. Warren Keifer, another leader in forming the GAR in Ohio and an original Home board member in 1870.

Superintendent Burton made a number of changes in the operation of the Home. He rearranged the occupancy of the cottages so that children of the same age would be living together. He established the rule of marching to chapel in company formation. Under his direction, a radio loudspeaker was placed in every cottage. Burton also worked with the teaching staff to improve the quality of the education offered to all of the pupils. The board of trustees noted in their annual report, "The schools have taken on new life." With a little more time, Burton might have accomplished more of what he had set out to do. He had won the confidence of the pupils, the staff and his board. But his health began to fail and he was forced

Some of these guys were there at the very beginning—this is the 1927 Home football squad, the second year of football on the hill.

to resign in December, 1929, after only two years as head of the Home.

Charles Burton had health problems, yet he and his wife managed to have a good time with their friends at the Home in the days before they left. In the early weeks of January, 1930, the Burtons attended a dinner given by the pupils in Hayes Hall. "As the pupils are just taking training in cooking, the meal was one worthy of mention," noted *The Home Weekly*. It was reported that the couple also enjoyed themselves at a farewell party in the Hayes Cottage. "Almost every means of entertainment was provided except dancing. Major Burton joined us in playing cards, the game at this time being Old Maid. After becoming Old Maid three times he had to serve the penalty by standing on his head. This of course was a very striking picture. After the game ended lovely refreshments were served which consisted of candy, popcorn and lemonade."

On the day the Burtons left, they attended an assembly in the high school auditorium, where both bid the children farewell with a parting admonition to "play the game square."

On January 19, 1930, Charles Burton— definitely a hard act to follow— would be succeeded as superintendent by a man who had not sought the job but who, over many years, would change the Home more than most of the men who had previously held the position. His name was Harold Hays and he came to the Ohio Soldiers and Sailors Orphans Home as both the institution and America were about to be tested by some of the most trying times in their history—the Great Depression of the 1930s. How Hays and the Home met those challenges are the stories of which legends are made.

Circa 1905—When girls were discharged from the Home, they were given $15, a new blue worsted dress, a change of clothes that had been worn, and a trunk to put them in.

A good American home (1930–1940)

Here's good student form off the board in the summer of 1938 as the kids use their lake to thwart the heat.

CHAPTER 4

A drive around the Home, c. 1930

The Ohio Soldiers and Sailors Orphans Home survived a a disastrous flood, a deadly diphtheria epidemic, and a merry-go-round of superintendents in its first three decades. Now, after another three decades in which advocates of foster care and adoption argued against its very existence and Civil War veterans faded away, the OSSO Home not only survived, it flourished.

An ex-pupil re-visiting his childhood home for the first time in a number of years would have been both reassured and surprised by the layout of the Home in 1930. Its campus was still green and pristine. Many of the original buildings remained in service. But the institution was much bigger. The Home, which began on a 100-acre site carved from the forest in 1870, now occupied a 400-acre spread, with over half of the land used to grow the crops and raise

109

the livestock that sustained the 700 children and several dozen staff members living there. Here's a "Description of the Home," written in 1930:

The main entrance to the Home Grounds is on Route 68 and has a fine granite memorial gateway. . . . The original entrance to the farm was a lane from what is now Detroit Street. In later years it was used very little except by the street car company which served the City of Xenia until the street car line was abandoned. The street car service was replaced by a bus service each half hour up to ten o'clock at night (The William Pickel Bus Line).

Passing through the Memorial Gateway, one's first impression is that they are entering a fine military reservation. If driving, you will proceed up the winding driveway to the top of the hill. . . .Arriving at the top of the hill in your car, the heart of the Home and its beautiful campus come into full view; to your right is an object of interest—the Home chapel set in the midst of a small grove. Directly in the rear of the chapel is the Home's most sacred spot, the little cemetery, "God's Acre," where are

The Home's replacement hospital, built in 1930, went up at the same time as the new vocational trades school and Hayes Hall.

buried less than 100 children, that have been taken by death during the sixty years of the life of the Home.

At the top of the hill, the driveway forks to the right and the left. Turning right the first building is the senior high school, which contains the gymnasium, swimming pool and large assembly hall seating 1,000 persons. The second building is the grade school. At the grade school building, one may continue straight ahead to the farm buildings or turn to the left to the main east and west drive to the Administration Building, passing the west row of cottages.

However, returning to the fork of the road at the top of the hill one may turn to the left and follow the driveway passing on the left the ex-pupils' fine Memorial Library Building (erected by former Home students) in memory of the Grand Army of the Republic; a short distance to the east and on the right is the Home flagpole where Old Glory floats every day in the year; to the left below the brow of the hill is located the Home Power House.

Continuing to the main drive in front of the Administration Building is a fountain

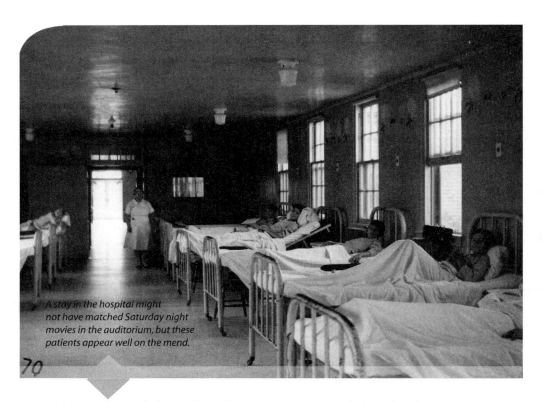

70

which was formerly located on the State House Grounds in Columbus.

From the Central Administration building, the original sixteen cottages stretch out to the east and west with a frontage of 1500 feet—all facing north. At the east end of the eight cottages (No. 16), the line turns directly south and two cottages (18-20) are built facing east. The old cottages on the east of the Administration Building are given even numbers, two to twenty. Opposite No. 16, 18 and 20 are on the left, five double cottages built in a semicircle facing west. The double cottages are given mixed numbers 21-30 inclusive. A short distance southwest of No. 20 cottage is the sixth double cottage (31 and 32) formerly the Home's first hospital. Also to the south and west of No. 20 is located Col. Roosevelt Hall for discharge boys (boys preparing to leave the Home).

A little farther to the southeast on the left is the second hospital group erected on the Home grounds, being known as the cottage plan of hospital. The central brick building is used as the residence of the Home physician. To the west on the left is the beautiful new Hospital building, recently erected and modernly equipped; and appropriately named for one of the most earnest and active members of the Grand Army in founding the Home—Major General J. Warren Keifer. The hospital represents the state's third effort to furnish the Home with adequate hospital and dental facilities.

Driving on west, to the right is the Mannington Armory, and nearby to the right is the old laundry building. In the rear of the Administration Building and attached thereto, is the Domestic Building, containing the kitchen, bake shop, children's dining room and employees' rooms on the second floor. The whole plan with the cottages forms an Egyptian Cross.

South of the Domestic Building are located the Store buildings with ice plant, electrical and machine shops and the blacksmith's shop.

To the west of the Armory on the right, is first, the Industrial Building, second, the new Laundry building, and on the left the old frame shops building and the dairy barn.

Continuing west to the junction of the farm road to the left of the junction is the horse barn, the carriage barn and almost straight ahead the farm house. Turning to the right on the east side is the greenhouse, the discharge girls' residence—Hayes Hall, cottage 19 and 17 and on the left the Junior High School building; at the junction of the main east drive, turning to the right eight cottages are passed, which completes the drive back to the Administration Building. Cottages on the west side of the Administration Building are odd numbers, one to nineteen.

In the rear of the central school building is McDowell Lake, covering two and a quarter acres of ground. The lake is named in honor of Captain McDowell of Xenia who donated the funds for its construction.

On the old Reid farm on the Burlington Pike is a fine residence, which has been converted into a duplex, now occupied as a residence of the Schools and the supervisor of Trades.

There are fifty four buildings on the grounds.

The original administration building from 1870 had been moved and now served primarily as a storage facility. (It would be torn down in September of 1931.) There was a new school building and several new cottages and dormitories. An article in the *Home Review* described the new General J. Warren Keifer Hospital, which had opened in 1928:

Inside . . . are four bright, cheery wards decorated with gay paintings on the walls and bright colored curtains at their many windows. There are four private rooms for more serious cases. The other rooms include: a modern kitchen, dining room, lobby, office, two clinic rooms, the doctor's office, a sewing and linen room, x-ray room, laboratory, operating room and a dentist's office.

Statistics for April, 1936, to April, 1937 . . . the daily average of children in the hospital was 21; the daily average of children treated in the clinic was 27; 61 new children were admitted to the Home; 592 physical examinations; 178 x-ray examinations; and 817 light treatments were given.

In the dental department there were 1600 appointments with students and five appliances made for orthodontia cases. There was no epidemic throughout the year and only one case of contagious disease. It is also interesting to note that in the last three or four years there has not been a single case of pneumonia.

Most of the students in the Home recall the German measles epidemic in November and December of 1934. . . . In that epidemic there were 305 cases of Rubella (another name for German Measles). This shows that 48 percent or almost half of all Home children contracted the disease. Then in 32 of the 305, some complication or second illness or infection set in.

A 1940 article praised the skill and dedication of the hospital's staff:

The Consulting Medical Staff, of which every member is a volunteer, represents the best in both the medical and dental fields. These men give their services without charge and respond to all calls from the Home promptly. They give both their talents and their time freely and without reserve, being paid only with the knowledge that their services have made the Home and some student better. To them we owe our undying gratitude.

Another busy place was the greenhouse. The *Home Review* of April, 1937, described preparations for the spring season:

As spring comes along, everyone becomes intensely interested in flowers. During the winter the cottages, school rooms, dining rooms and the hospital have been kept well supplied with lovely potted plants from the greenhouse.

Do not be surprised to see spring flowers popping up in various places as there are about two thousand bulbs planted around. Along the creek approximately four thousand additional perennial plants are being grown.

There are two thousand hyacinths, narcissus, and tulips in the greenhouse. Unusual plants are limited to a small number because of lack of space to give them. . . . If you fancy cut flowers better than potted ones, there are lovely flowers to cut too. They are larkspur, Calendula and a few others.

Mr. Peterson has planted 27,000 annuals, which will bloom during the summer time. In this huge amount of flowers, there are forty-five different varieties.

Vegetables such as peppers, cabbage, cauliflower, tomatoes and eggplant, which are raised in the vegetable gardens are started in the greenhouse, then transplanted to the outside garden.

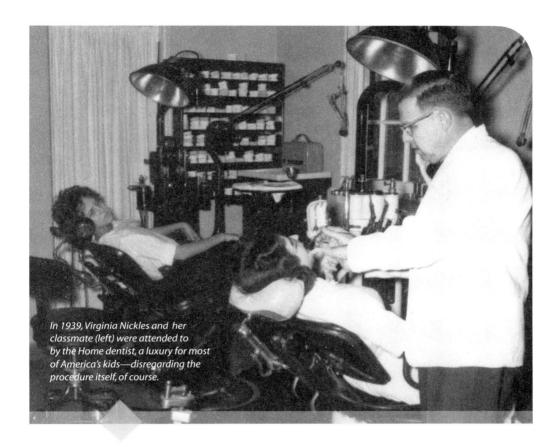

In 1939, Virginia Nickles and her classmate (left) were attended to by the Home dentist, a luxury for most of America's kids—disregarding the procedure itself, of course.

The laundry employed ten women and two men:

Monday morning, the girls send their clothes to the laundry, and they are washed and dried. Tuesday the boys' soiled clothes are sent to the laundry. While the boys' clothes are being washed and dried, the girls' laundry is ironed.

Wednesday the girls' laundry is sent back to the cottages, and the boys' laundry is ironed and sent back Thursday. And as you might know, the boys' clothes are twice as dirty as the girls'.

Besides washing and ironing the clothes of the children of the Home the laundry also washes the bedding, towels and curtains of each cottage. The laundry also washes the aprons, table cloths, napkins and other linen used in the kitchen and dining hall and the clothes, aprons, bedding and other items used in the hospital.

The Reid farmhouse, which had been acquired with several acres when the Home expanded, had become a staff dormitory. Originally, it was to be converted

The Home laundry, by 1939, used 48,000 gallons of water each week—and a barrel of soap.

into a nursery, but after establishing a poultry farm next door that was mandated by the state legislature, Home officials apparently decided that employees could live alongside the chickens even if the young children could not.

Not as visible to the ex-pupil's naked eye—at least not from behind the wheel of, say, his Model "A" Ford Roadster—would have been the problems of an aging infrastructure. Several of the Home's fifty-four buildings needed to be torn down and replaced. The armory, built in 1904, needed improvements. The board of trustees had asked the Ohio General Assembly for funds, but Ohio, like most Midwestern states, was governed by people who were relatively conservative, both politically and fiscally, regardless of party affiliation. Republicans and Democrats listened to the board, as well as the Grand Army and other veterans groups strongly supporting the Home, because it was prudent to do so. But when action was called for, partisan politics often got in the way. So did Governor A. Victor Donahey. During the late 1920s, Donahey, the popular, fiscally conservative, three-term Democratic governor, had regularly trimmed budget requests during one of the greatest economic booms in American history. By 1930, every state institution, including the Ohio Soldiers and Sailors Orphans Home, had a backlog of unmet needs.

Social service organizations felt that the Home should modify, or even abandon, some of its traditions due to the shrinking number of Civil War orphans in residence. While veterans groups saw the uniformed children marching to mandatory school, church and recreational activities as a reminder of the institution's military origins and as a remembrance of the men whose sacrifice led to its creation, there were only sixteen Civil War orphans at the Home in 1929, and within a few years there would be none at all.

While several new cottages and dormitories for girls and boys about to be discharged were built and substantial renovations of the older cottages were made, the fact remained that most housing at the Home had been built more than fifty years before. The inability to get funding for a library finally led the Association of Ex-pupils to raise funds for the construction of one. The building is now the Home museum.

The Association had celebrated its 50th reunion in 1930 and during the decade attendence at reunions rose to over 500 each year. The larger membership allowed the Association to take on projects such as the library.

The Captain Comes to Xenia

Although the OSSO Home continued to do what it did best—educate and nurture young children—it came under considerable pressure from state officials in 1929 to do an even better job with even fewer resources. And the pressure came right from the top.

Newly-elected Governor Myers Cooper sought to make good on his campaign promise to restrain spending and demand stricter accountability of all state agencies. The Home felt the heat, in particular, from two government offices: the Ohio State Board of Health, whose director inspected the facilities and recommended that sanitary and health conditions be brought up to standard; and the Ohio State Board of Education, whose superintendent of public instruction prepared a "comprehensive program of instruction" that resulted in a streamlining of the Home's vocational education curriculum.

J.E. Balmer, hired as director of vocational instruction, persuaded the Home's board of trustees to "abolish trades no longer profitable" and use the trade

The winding drive into the Home presented an idyllic approach, qs well as a sense of expectation.

Captain Hays: making the Home even more modern.

schools for "education and maintenance only"—not for "production." The state subsequently approved $75,000—a large sum for the time—for construction of a new vocational education building. Under Balmer, the Home's vocational program would become one of the best in the country and one of the institution's greatest strengths.

After Superintendent Charles Burton stepped down for health and personal reasons, the board of trustees met in special session in Columbus on January 11, 1930, to discuss the vacancy. Governor Cooper advised the board to use "great care" in the selection of a new superintendent, reminding trustees that their choice must be able to work with the veterans organizations, the education and social service communities, and, of course, the governor himself. Eight days later, the board had its man.

Harold Hays was born near Washington Court House, Ohio, in 1897. He graduated from the Washington Court House High School in 1915 and attended Ohio State University for a year and a half before returning to his hometown to serve as executive director of the local YMCA. Hays re-enrolled at Ohio State in 1918 and immediately was sent to Officers Training School. After receiving a business administration degree in 1923, he enlisted in the Ohio National Guard and two years later joined the staff of the Ohio Civil Service Commission. By 1930, he was the Commission's chief clerk and examiner.

Timing is everything, as the saying goes, and it certainly was true of Captain Hays's arrival in Xenia. With the Great Depression coming to Ohio, the OSSO Home needed a young, articulate, energetic leader with business and government experience as well as a military background, someone open to new ideas and new ways of doing things if the orphanage was to survive the greatest economic catastrophe in American history.

The Great Depression Comes to Ohio

Times were bad. Very bad. Many institutions like the OSSO Home would be forced to close during "The Lean Years," as one historian would describe the Depression. In Ohio, steel mills, tire producers and glass factories that were part of the industrial corridor stretching from Pittsburgh to Chicago began laying off workers at an alarming rate. By 1932, unemployment had reached 37.3 percent across the state and was as high as 50 percent among industrial workers in many of the major cities.

America's newly-elected president, Franklin Delano Roosevelt, was not all that different from his predecessor, Herbert Hoover, in many of his basic assumptions. FDR believed budgets should be balanced, the private sector should be given freedom to act, and government should not be all that big. Roosevelt, though, also was a pragmatist who would pursue almost any strategy and try almost any tactic, conservative or liberal, to jump-start the economy and restore the country's badly shaken confidence. As a result, budgets became unbalanced, the private sector became more heavily regulated, and government grew bigger. The federal government became involved in social welfare, education and direct care of the needy during the Depression as it never had before, making funds available for institutions like the OSSO Home, which had put new initiatives on hold, including repairing or replacing buildings and improving the education and social service programs.

For the children who came to the Home in the late 1920s, the Depression would define their entire experience there. This wasn't a camp where rich folks dropped off their spoiled kids for the summer. It wasn't a prep school for the privileged. The Home's boarders came from broken families—families torn apart by death, disease or disability affecting at least one parent because of their service to their country. They needed a safe haven, a place to learn and grow and prepare for the future. The Home and its friends were determined to give them that future.

Action on Many Fronts

Captain Hays soon became quickly involved in the Home's day-to-day operations. The superintendent helped confirm locations for a summer camp. A strong believer in the Scouting movement, he increased the pay of the Home's

Another familiar scene at the Home: A dozen of Miss Hilty's Peter Pan girls in their best dresses in front of their cottage. Miss Hilty is wearing the hat, otherwise just one of the girls.

teacher who also served as scoutmaster. He authorized payment of $1,000 for new fire equipment and fire bells for each of the main buildings on the campus, and supervised the removal of several very dead trees from the grounds.

Captain Hays had no trouble adapting to the semi-military approach followed by the Home with its rigid schedules, uniform appearance and discipline. It was, after all, a mirror image of the military world of which he was very much a part.

But he soon came to realize that the Home was just that—a Home—and it was not a military base. With its heavy emphasis on military training and social discipline, the Home was in some ways like a military boarding school. But since much of its population was feminine and not part of the military units, the Home was something of a traditional boarding school as well. It also was a very sophisticated vocational training school. Such vocational training— if it was to be found at all—was usually to be had only in a large urban high school.

In June of 1930, Governor Cooper attended the Home's commencement ceremony and delivered a sobering assessment on the health of the economy, warning that budget cuts might be in the offing. Hays took what today would be called a pro-active approach, accompanying the president of the Home's board of trustees to Columbus to discuss funding needs with the Child Welfare Committee of the Ohio American Legion. The alliance between the Home and the veterans lobby had been in place for some time, but Hays would strengthen their already close association.

Effie Wisely of Fayette, Missouri, was hired as chief matron after Hays informed the board that his wife had no interest in the position. (Instead, Mrs. Hays became her husband's unpaid assistant on all Home matters.) Mrs. Wisely, on the other hand, was a tough, no-nonsense veteran of life in children's homes, and apparently her reputation preceded her. Here's how she remembered her arrival at the Home:

One supervisor made the remark, "What is this place coming to anyway? A chief matron! How is she to know what the superintendent wants done?" . . . The children openly challenged our right to be here. We have a vivid remembrance of one evening in the children's dining room when we were stopping by to make an announcement about some general rules and regulations we hoped to put into effect. We were greeted with catcalls, raspberries and hideous groans. We may have appeared calm enough outwardly, but our inner feeling was anything but calm. By this time we had a pretty good understanding as to how they felt. However, we stood our ground. . . . A great deal of our time was spent gaining the respect and confidence of those with who we had to work.

This was the teaching staff for the Home's school year 1935-1936. Given their generally happy appearance, the picture may have been taken early in the year.

Mrs. Wisely went on to describe the Home's admission process:

Our department has the first contact with the new children after they have been accepted by the board of trustees. When a child enters the Home he is received in our office, taken to the hospital where he is received by the receiving physician or one of the nurses, assigned to a cottage where he is to live after his period of observation at the hospital is over. . . .

Next in importance to the receiving cottage would be an understanding supervisor who could help these newly admitted children over the most difficult part of their lives, the separation from their own family and friends and the adjustment to new surroundings and strange people. . . .

We advocate above all else, kindness accompanied by a certain amount of firmness. We do not believe a supervisor would ever get far without kindness, and yet if she lacked the second qualification she would not get anywhere, as children are prone to take advantage of kindness alone.

Betty and Gladys, co-eds at the Home in 1936, roll into spring.

Betty and Gladys Mar. 1936

While Mrs. Wisely and Mrs. Hays agreed that the boys' blue and gray dress uniforms and khaki daily wear were sufficient, both women thought something had to be done about the girls' clothes. "Their everyday school dresses were made of blue gingham, middy blouse style, with sailor collar trimmed in white braid and long sleeves and pleated skirt," explained Mrs. Wisely. "Their blue serge for winter and their white Indianhead dresses for Sunday summer were all made over the same pattern as the blue gingham, except that the blue serge was trimmed in red braid. A big red tie was worn with each of these dresses and it was an unpardonable sin to be caught without it on. . . . These dresses were all being made at the tailor shop."

New dress designs were proposed by Mrs. Wisely and Mrs. Hays and accepted by the board. But when the dresses came from the tailor shop, the ladies were surprised. "How that particular garment could have been produced from the pattern used, we have not been able to figure out," remarked Mrs. Wisely. At the urging of Mrs. Wisely and Mrs. Hays, as well as Captain Hays and a considerable number of young ladies, the board closed the Home's dressmaking department and bought the girls' dresses ready-made in shades of green, tan and blue. The white dresses continued to be worn but without the sailor collars and with slightly shorter sleeves. Other changes in the styles and varieties of girls clothing would follow. Boys in the senior discharge class were permitted to wear casual clothing when they went to town for social events.

These may not seem like big changes today, but at the time they had a striking impact on the children. As ex-pupil Catherine Dussell Pritchard recalled, "We were all so excited as we thought [the dresses] were beautiful." The girls were beginning to dress like girls everywhere else.

While times were changing, and so was the Home, Superintendent Hays insisted that the institution maintain the high quality of its food service—not an easy task, as staff dietician Bessie Handy explained in the *Home Review*. "If even in the small home, so much of the housewife's time and energy is devoted to the food service, how important it is that this phase of institutional activity be properly administered. Increase the number in the family to that represented by the children and staff here, add to it the number requiring special dietary consideration, also parties, picnics and gatherings of various types requiring meals, recognize that each individual has special food fancies and desires and you may possibly be able to appreciate the task of providing satisfactory food service." The job surely got tougher for Miss Handy and her culinary staff with the departure of Pastry Chef Minnie Jenkins in 1938. The *Home Review* estimated that Minnie Jenkins had made 124,000 pies, or 150 a week, since 1922, and noted that her 24,960 cakes "vanished as rapidly as the pies!"

Catherine Dussell Pritchard loved the food.

"We had candy every Thursday, ice cream on Wednesday and Sunday, and pie on Fridays. We had varied desserts at other meals. We had our own baker and such delicious rolls each Sunday. Also, on Sundays, we had beef tenderloin steak, steam-cooked in butter, that just melted in your mouth. I don't remember ever having anything I didn't like except sweet potatoes. If we didn't like something, we told our superior and she'd give us a small taste, which we had to eat or we didn't get dessert. We had milk three times a day."

Richard Moffat, a member of the 1934 discharge class, wrote about some of the changes during his time at the Home:

It was during the regime of [Superintendent] Hays that dress became more casual—beginning first with the girls. It was a big step and severely frowned upon by the diehard matrons when the girls were permitted to choose three dresses, of three colors. . . . Along with it girls were allowed to copy the hair styles worn elsewhere and the day of the shingle-bob for everyone disappeared. Girls for the first time took on the look of girls.

In the 1920s, everyone, boy or girl, went to bed wearing a nightgown. In the 1930s, normal nightwear-pajamas . . . were not only permitted. They were purchased and issued.

In the 1920s, the boys lined up in formation on the circle, with the bugle corps providing the martial music for the trek, by the cadence to school in the morning and after dinner. . . . The girls marched in twos—not by cadence however—from their cottages to school and back. . . . By 1930, the boys and girls were walking to school like boys and girls anywhere.

The parade ceased to be daily, but the noon drills continued, and in the warm seasons, the Sunday parade continued to be a mark of distinction at the Home. No one could argue that there was not a sound basis for it—the boys and girls were the sons and daughters of servicemen. Probably no corps of cadets anywhere could match the precision of Home boys, many of whom were later to serve in branches of service in World War II—some of them as drillmasters.

The Home had Boy Scout troops, but no Girl Scout troops. That would change during the 1930s, thanks to Captain Hays, who was a believer in the benefits of Scouting. Upon his recommendation, the board bought full uniforms for both the boy and girl scouts and handed out a "Trustees Medal" for meritorious service to the Home—not that everyone was always behaving with the decorum deserving of a medal. Ex-Pupil Ruth Beyer Long told of learning proper manners from the matron of her cottage:

On Sunday afternoons, we were allowed to promenade from 2 to 4. You promenaded around this parade ground and of course you were visible in front of God and everybody, and so that's what we did on Sunday afternoon. Or if it was a cold day, you might go in the cottage and read the paper or magazine or something like that and then on Sunday night from 7 to 9 you could have a date and the boys would come to our cottages and we might play checkers. We were never allowed to play cards in our cottage because Miss Bell did not want us crossing our legs. She said it was not lady-like for you to cross your legs. . . We sat with our feet on the ground and our hands in our laps in a lady-like manner.

While the girls learned to be lady-like, the boys slipped away to a special place,

Mike came from a small place called Centerfield where he grew up wearing his mother's galoshes to school because he had no proper shoes and going without lunch because there was no lunch. When the school authorities noticed, and because Mike's dad was a veteran, Mike was placed in the Home. It was 1928, and he was 9.

His earliest memories were of being a "newkie." A newkie, Mike said, was where "everybody wants to get up there and see what kind of shoes you got and if they'll fit them, and maybe they'd try to trade theirs for yours." But Mike barely had shoes.

He recalled blind Betty, the horse who pulled the garbage. Betty knew the cinder path from dining hall to hog lot so well she could traverse it without eyesight or guidance. Mike was astonished at the big rats that ran along beside the wagon, as he and the other kids threw rocks at them.

The boys were taught to darn their socks by stretching them over a light bulb, and he learned to go to the tailor shop and press his own shirt and pants for the Sunday parade.

Sometimes, his classmate John Rope would run off, but he always came back where he was punished by the matron, Mrs. Ubert, who made him wash her feet.

"I think he probably just wanted to run away because a fuss was made over him when he came back." Mike said. "I was afraid if I got out here, I'd never get back."

Mike played center on the famous Home team of 1937 that was never scored upon. He played center because, the coach said jokingly, Mike was one of the few who could actually remember the numbers.

Their coach was also their source of information about growing up, although he was a man of few words. In hygiene class, when the boys asked him about sex, the coach said that if they insisted on having sex with somebody get protected. "You won't get into any trouble," he said. "And that's all we knew about *that*," Mike said.

In the Home butcher shop, he learned to be a meat cutter. When he graduated from the Home, he was given $50 and a suit of clothes, off to Cleveland where he met an Englishman with his own meat market, and Mike worked for him.

"I thought that if I was lucky, I would be able to someday own a store. And that's what happened to me. I wound up with an IGA store in Hebron, Ohio. So my dreams came true."

In 1969, after Mike retired, he came back to visit the Home, learned that the place was having trouble running the swimming pool, and he and his wife returned from Florida to help the Home with maintenance.

"I told Mr. Stephans, Yeah, I'd help him. I used to work at the pool when I was a kid. That's the reason I knew how to get all the necessary ingredients in it and keep it safe for the kids. So I did that, I went to football games and ran around with the line, monitored the kids having their gymnasium things, chopped wood, all the little jobs that came up.

"The Home was good to me. I never saw many kids that weren't impressed with the way we were living, and it's a shame there aren't more places like it. I don't suppose the word 'orphanage' sounds so good to some people, for some reason. But we never minded it. We *liked* the word 'orphanage.'"

The decorous young ladies of Peter Pan use the small dining room—complete with tablecloths and, of course, manners.

remembered ex-pupil Robert Impson:

> When we were growing up at the Home, we had a place called Shantytown. It was down behind the superintendent's, just across the creek and near a field where they planted crops. That field separated Shantytown from an orchard—a Home orchard. Shantytown was a place for boys. . . . Probably you went there as early as you thought you could survive there. . . . We had to dig holes in the ground and out in the woods. Most of the [shanties] were underground. They would lay boards across the top. Maybe they had discarded and thrown a rug out of one of the cottages. . . . We'd haul that back and put it over the boards and then put dirt over the top. It was a beautiful place to hang out. We'd get down there . . . and talk about girls. It was a nice place to grow up. . . .

For more complex problems, Hays and the board of trustees sought outside help. In June of 1932, they consulted with former state director of public instruction,

J.L. Clifton, sharing their concerns about the quality of the children's education and a clash between the Home's vocational and traditional schools. Clifton urged the Home to hire the Bureau of Educational Research, part of the Ohio State University's College of Education. A team led by Dr. T. C. Holy met with the board and laid out a plan in which the bureau would study the "native abilities" of the Home's pupils, occupational opportunities for the children, and the curriculums of the academic and vocational schools. Holy's team also would review the personnel, physical plant, school organization, and extracurricular activities.

Over the next several months, dozens of Ohio State faculty and staff descended on the Xenia campus. They came from departments within the College of Education and from the School of Social Work. Representatives from the Ohio National Guard, the Ohio Department of Education, the Ohio Department of Welfare, and the Association of Ex-Pupils also participated in the project.

The final 173-page report included 107 specific recommendations regarding curriculum, staffing, facilities, and administration of the Home and its schools. The board adopted all but two of the suggestions—a dental hygienist was rejected for lack of funds, and loosening of dress restrictions already had been accomplished.

"The Survey," as it came to be called, set the direction for academic accomplishment at the Home for the next decade. Most of the proposals later adopted for expansion, construction, changes in personnel or policies—specifically with regard to education—can be found in the Bureau of Educational Research's comprehensive report.

"We ate our meals in a real big dining room. That was the only time I got to see my brothers... I can remember one time... they used to serve peanut butter in a big bowl and nobody at the table wanted any. I ate that whole bowl of peanut butter and I got sicker than a dog. They had to take me to the hospital to pump my stomach. I must have been in my 40s before I ate peanut butter again."
—— Helen Theil, Class of 1936

Building a Better Home

A number of the recommendations in the report linked programs to buildings not yet built, but raising money for construction projects in the shadow of the

Great Depression would not be an easy task. The battles over buildings began almost as soon as Captain Hays arrived at the Home in early 1930. During the previous administration of Charles Burton, funding had been obtained for a new hospital and separate dormitory for the girls' discharge class.

By 1930, Lucy Webb Hayes Hall for senior girls was ready for occupancy and joined Roosevelt Hall for senior boys. The long-awaited J. Warren Keifer Hospital opened and the power house was renovated.

With these major projects completed, the board brought vocational education under the supervision of the superintendent of schools (a newly-created position) and began construction on a new vocational trades building at a cost of more than $120,000. The new building was dedicated as the General James Barnett Vocational Trade School in May of 1931—named after a long-time board member and advocate of education at the Home.

Trustees also approved a plan to replace the 1887 industrial trades building and allocated funds to tear down an old grandstand and make needed improvements to the athletic field. The state initially rejected, then granted a request for emergency funds to replace the pasteurization plant so the Home could continue using milk from its farm. With the economy getting worse, the Ohio General Assembly funded two more construction projects: a new domestic building and the Peter Pan Cottages that would serve as a nursery for the Home's young children. The total cost of the two contracts was more than $742,000.

There had been a time when children like Viola Pebworth had been admitted at age 2 in 1914. But in recent years, for a variety of practical reasons, children under the age of 4 were not permitted to live at the Home. But Peter Pan was—and remained—a state-of-the-art nursery for many years. Like many other innovations at the Home that did not reach other institutions for a number of years, the methods and approach of Peter Pan were as close to family living as one was likely to find in an institution.

George White, a conservative Democrat, replaced Myers Cooper in the governor's office in early 1931. White was generally of the opinion that government ought to live within its means, and thus made life difficult for institutions like the OSSO Home that persistently needed increased funding.

A number of changes were made in living arrangements at the Home in 1932. In recent years, children had been assigned to cottages by age, each child moving from cottage to cottage as he or she grew older. They made many new acquaintances and lived with a number of different adults. Home officials, however, decided to return to an older system whereby children of several different ages were placed in

Here's a pair of young classmates, on the grounds in springtime of the mid-1930s.

the same unit, thus permitting children from the same family to live together in the same cottage.

Many of the newer buildings had been given the names of people notable in the history of America and the institution itself. But most of the older buildings had only a number or a generic name—administration building, domestic building, laundry building, and so on. In September of 1932, every building at the Home was given a name. Veterans organizations and the Association of Ex-Pupils had been asked to recommend names and many of them were adopted. The administration building became Grant Hall, in memory of President Ulysses S. Grant. The school buildings were named for U.S. presidents McKinley, Lincoln and Wilson. Each cottage received the name of a prominent figure from American history, the Civil War, the Spanish-American War, World War I, or a person associated with the Home, such as Olive Smith Hall. Smith, a nurse, died at the Home during the great

This aerial overview of the Home was taken in 1930. If the pilot was from out-of-town, he might would have wondered what college campus lay beneath him.

diphtheria epidemic of 1890. The Gettysburg Armory and the Argonne Athletic Field were named after the famous battles. On an inside wall near the front door of each building was a small framed statement explaining the significance of the person or battle remembered. Various veterans organizations adopted specific cottages named after servicemen, providing the residents with gifts on holidays and at other times of the year. The re-naming of the buildings was an inexpensive but effective way to strengthen the bond between the Home and its supporters.

The dining hall was named after board president William T. Amos, who died in early 1932 after a lengthy illness. One of his last acts as a board member had been to approve the letting of a contract for the new dining facility. Colonel Amos also had given the go-ahead for construction of the new nursery serving forty-three boys and thirty-four girls between the ages of 4 and 8. The matrons and staff named each of the cottages in the "Peter Pan" complex after nursery rhyme characters: Jolly Roger, Jack Horner, Boy Blue, The Gables, Miss Muffet, BoPeep, and Wendy. After Peter Pan opened in 1933, head supervisor Helen Lindsey wrote a lengthy description of the Home's state-of-the-art nursery that conveys something of its charm:

Each cottage is in the charge of a supervisor whose college course has included definite training in Child Care and Elementary Education. Although her main duty is to care for the children (their physical, mental and spiritual welfare), she has other important duties such as keeping the cottage clean, mending and planning constructive and educational activities.

Assisting in four of the six cottages are Antioch students who are here for a five to ten week period under the Antioch Co-Op Plan for the purpose of gaining experience in child care and training.

(At 6:30 a.m.) in Wendy, the fifteen girls of ages six, seven and eight are burrowing their noses in their pillows for the last time and then dashing for the bathroom, where they dress. By 6:45, they are through dressing and start making their beds which are ready by breakfast time. When the 7:00 whistle blows, the girls of Wendy and BoPeep and the boys of Jolly Roger and Jack Horner at the other end of the cottages follow the tunnel route to the dining room.

Those of you who are used to the hushed tones of the sound-proof Main Dining room may be shocked by the babble that greets you here. The children are seating themselves at small tables planned for four or six. At many of these tables there is a cottage supervisor or a co-op student in charge. The children best able to take care of themselves are placed at tables without supervisors. With the tap of a bell comes a

Catherine Dussell Pritchard

Class of 1940

"My supervisor, in Cottage 3, was Mrs. Simes. I was frightened of her because she wore thick green glasses and somehow she always seemed to know what we were going to do before we did it. One day, she grabbed the wrong girl and spanked her, and Mary Burns, the real culprit, was hollering and crying as if she was being spanked. She begged the other girl not to tell her and Mrs. Simes never knew she spanked the wrong girl. In time, I came to love Mrs. Simes…

"We had a large elementary school with a sandy bottom swimming pool behind it in which we swam in the summer months. In winter, when it froze over, we were allowed to ice skate on it— if the white flag was flying. If the red flag was up, skating was a danger and we couldn't go near it. When we couldn't skate on the pool, we could pour hot water on the walk and slide down that. We also had an indoor pool, something special in the 1930s. The black children swam with us and we all had to know how to swim to pass Physical Education.

In Beauty Culture, we learned how to give permanents, learned the repair of electric cords in Electric Shop, did blueprint drawings, made sandals, pulled up turnips, and milked a cow—

Home inventiveness was clearly evident at camp, when the Home kids were inspired by long summer days to improvise.

the Devil made me squirt one of the boys, and I hopped off and he didn't get me back.

"My first experience on the switchboard was traumatic because I disconnected the superintendent. I was cringing in my shoes when I saw him come out of his office. I thought, *Now I've done it*. But he was so understanding, and I quickly said, 'I'm so sorry, this is my first day.' I was hoping his compassion would take over. I'm sure he sensed how frightened I was. He said very gently, 'Don't worry about it, Catherine. We all make mistakes. When they call back, just reconnect me.' I was so relieved. That day, he taught me patience in a way I've never forgotten.

"During the summer, we were allowed to go to camp for two weeks. We learned crafts, slept in tents, and had such a wonderful time that when we found out if you got poison ivy you must stay in camp an extra week to get rid of it, some of us wiped poison ivy on ourselves to stay an extra week. I was the only one who didn't get it, and I had to return to my cottage.

"When I returned for my 55th reunion and I heard my name—*Catherine Dussel*—called by my favorite teacher, Jane Pavey, we ran to each other and embraced and shed tears of joy."

This was the barn built after the devastating fire of 1933. Its impressive architecture made it an icon of the Home.

silence and then the morning grace, "Father We Thank Thee."

Almost all the children have good appetites. . . . By 7:30 breakfast is over and we go back to the cottages. . . . With school beginning at 8:00, there is not much time. . . . There goes the whistle and all except the kindergarteners are out of their cottage doors and off to school. . . . They too are off now, and the supervisors sit down to catch their breath; but not for long, for these morning minutes are precious and the four year olds will be back at 10:30 for the rest of the day and the other children arrive at 11:00 to 11:15.

(Now) it's after 11:15 and the children are beginning to arrive. They will wash their faces and hands and have a few minutes to play before dinner. And now the familiar buzz as the children troop in for dinner. The grace we use at dinner and supper is a very simple one—"Thanks to our Father, we will bring; for He gives us everything." This change was necessitated by the fact that our children did not understand the "Gloria" and we were surprised and not a little amused to hear one of our six year olds singing, "And to the Son and chew the Holy Ghost," varying it the next week to "stew the Holy Ghost."

During the period after naps—2:30 to 3:30—the cottages are buzzing with activity for it is at this time that our educational activities are carried on. In the evening after supper, the older children have one half to three-quarters of an hour for active play outdoors or in the cottages. The four and five year olds take their showers and gather for story hour. . . . Not only the smallest children but the others are also now in bed. "Old Man Sunshine's" prayer has been sung: all the children have been kissed good-night. Silence reigns—at least for the present.

Ex-Pupil Mary Blake remembered a verse she learned after arriving at the Home in 1937:

A gum chewing gal and a gum chewing cow seem alike somehow, but oh, I see it now, the intelligent look on the face of the cow.

At the depth of the Depression in 1933, two large barns on the Home's farm were destroyed by fire. Workers saved the livestock and a large dairy barn. The construction of a new barn would become a federal Civil Works Administration and the Federal Emergency Relief Agency project. The barn was designed at Ohio State University and became one of the largest farm structures—175 feet by 146 feet—in the United States. Federal workers also helped develop playground space and assisted the Ohio Highway Department in laying down a 1,500-foot cinder driveway from the Home's hospital to the Peter Pan cottages and beyond.

In 1934, the Home's farm supervisor, Robert McWilliams, called attention to one of the findings in the "The Survey" of 1933, which stated that "the Home farm cannot be justified alone as a business enterprise." McWilliams was instrumental in correlating the activities of the farm and the Home's agricultural school. The *Home Review* gave the following accounting of the farm's operation in 1936:

"The Home milks an average of fifty cows daily, produces 5,270 gallons of milk per month and pasteurizes 5,000 gallons. . . . Mr. Wones reports that he now has under his command 249 spring pigs. He has established a new record for nursing young pigs through the severe cold winter of last year. His loss of pigs was very low while that of most farmers ran to the high mark of 50 percent loss. The farm received 166 bushels of certified seed potatoes. The farmers and farm boys made good use of the rainy days cutting the seed in preparation for planting. Twelve acres of potatoes have been planted."

The Home's cows also won prizes.

"The . . . dairy herd made a splendid showing during the summer County Fair season, and also took some prizes at the Ohio State Fair. Nine head were shown at the Greene, Champaign, Miami and Darke County Fairs. . . . The Home won 7 Grand Champions, 24 firsts, 13 seconds, 4 thirds."

A "Most Extravagantly Conducted Institution"

In January of 1935, Martin L. Davey took office as Ohio's fifty-third governor. Davey, a conservative Democrat, was born in 1884, the heir to his father's successful tree surgery business. He spent most of his time, however, in politics. After stints in Congress and as mayor of Kent, Ohio, he lost his gubernatorial bid in 1928 but came back to win the 1934 election.

Governor Davey immediately made a number of enemies in both Columbus and Washington. Home officials, who were dealing with an outbreak of measles that left over half of the 650 children ill, weren't happy either when Davey didn't seem overly concerned by major cuts in the institution's budget. In his defense, the governor claimed he had been guided by the results of a major review of all state agencies by Colonel C.O. Sherill. The Sherill Report, though, generally approved of the operation of the Home. The budget standoff continued through the fall of 1935 and into the new year, when Davey used his weekly evening radio address to single out the Ohio Soldiers and Sailors Orphans Home as "the most extravagantly conducted institution of its kind in Ohio." It was a curious accusation, given the fact that the Home was the ONLY institution of its kind in the state. Nevertheless, Davey went on to say, "Merely because the home at Xenia takes care of the orphans of Ohio soldiers and sailors, it is not a sacred cow, toward which we must take a worshipful attitude and never even raise a question about its cost or its business management."

Facing re-election in 1936, Governor Davey perhaps felt that it might not be helpful to have every veterans group in the state angry with him, so he re-appointed the American Legion president to the Home's board of trustees and finally compromised on the budget.

Harold Hays stayed at the Home for another three years before moving on to tackle the problems of another state institution—the Boys' Industrial School in Lancaster. He commuted between Xenia and Lancaster until Captain Francis R. Woodruff took over as superintendent of the OSSO Home on January 1, 1940. Captain Hays would see action in the South Pacific during World War II, earning a Silver Star, Bronze Star, Legion of Merit and the Purple Heart, and was also called to active duty during the Korean War. In 1955, he left the Boys' Industrial School and became director of the Ohio Selective Service. He died in Columbus in 1960 at the age of 62.

When Harold Hays left the Ohio Soldiers and Sailors Orphans Home, it was a better place than when he arrived and for a number of reasons. Not the least

This was the Home's first structure built specifically for a school. Worn out by the generations, it came down in 1940.

The Peter Pan cottages on Christmas morning, of 1939. It was a scene just like any other home that might have had a dozen boys in the house.

On a pleasant day in April of 1938, what better way to waste an afternoon than watching the cadets practice?

of these were the changes he made in the culture and social life of the Home. Also important were the organizations that found new life during his tenure. But perhaps his greatest legacy was the quality and number of people he employed and worked with during the 1930s. More than twenty people came to the Home during that period and stayed for their entire careers. They improved the Home with their work and their dedication to the children. They set the standard for the employees coming after them.

J. E. Balmer, supervisor of vocation education, made a good vocational program one of the best in the nation. Harley Waldren, the academic principal, increased the reputation of the school, and most important, both men always had time for the students.

There were academic teachers Madge McCoy (arts), Hannah McKenzie (grade school), Jane Pavey (English), Mary Elizabeth Rhodes (English), Professor Seall (band), and J.R. Rooney (English and drama), all of them not only excellent teachers but gave many extra hours to their students.

Glendon Lakes (carpentry), Harry Van Cleaf (metal shop), Johnnie Trunnel (shoe shop), Rocky May (print shop), and John Baldner (auto shop)—trade school instructors—were no different.

Houseparents and administrators also came and stayed: Herman Gill (military instructor), Austin Gill (laundry), Robert McWilliams (farm), Mary Neville (nurse), Helen Farrington (houseparent and dean of girls), and houseparents Florence "Melvie" Melvin, Mary Re Minnich, and Edith Neeld. All gave their time unstintingly to both the Home and the students.

A Good Life at the Home in Hard Times

The vigorous practice of Christian religion was an integral part of the life at the Home from the day it opened in Xenia in 1869 under the supervision of Superintendent Luther Griswold, a practicing minister. Roman Catholic children were regularly transported to Xenia for services, while chapel services were strongly influenced by the liturgy and doctrine of the Methodist, Presbyterian and Baptist churches.

Captain Hays implemented several initiatives designed to make religion more relevant, more often, to more people at the Home. Hays believed that if young people received a large dose of religion each Sunday, they might soon be more moved by fatigue and boredom than devotion, so he made Sunday school optional

Field Day, 1937, one of the Home's most anticipated events. It was here that William Dezarn, a football halfback, ran a 10.1 100-yard dash for a new Home record. Speed was obviously in the family, for D. Dezarn set the 220-yard dash record at 22.8 during Field Day of 1936.

instead of mandatory. If children had the option, they might come willingly to Sunday school and be more likely to continue their religious development after leaving the Home.

In 1932, Reverend Cecil C. Hankins became the Home's first full-time chaplain.

"Many ministers depend upon their sermons for the influence of their spiritual knowledge. Not so with our situation. We realize the value of the Sunday morning service in providing opportunity for worship, training and spiritual relaxation, but we doubt the contentions of some who believe that 80 percent of our total influence to be derived from the pulpit. On the other hand, we attempt to make religion a personal matter, and establish such procedures and practices as will help the child 'to stand firm under the pressure of life.' This is done through example, participation, counsel and advice."

Chaplain Hankins helped plan the Home's recreational program until a recreation director was hired later in the decade, and was responsible for the two Boy Scout troops and their eighty-plus members. He spent much of his time, though, reorganizing the Sunday school, forming a variety of new religious organizations, and preparing religious classes to be taught as part of the regular academic program of the Home.

"Voluntary church organizations have been formed and are contributing to the education of the children in a fine manner," he explained. "Training is secured in Christian leadership, in discussions of moral and spiritual subjects, and through supervised recreational activities of a Christian significance. The Intermediate Christian Endeavor takes care of about sixty children of the ages of 12 to 14 inclusive, while the Young People's Society appeals to the youth of 15 years and above."

The biggest single change in religious practice at the Home came two years later after Chaplain Hankins invited Dr. Richard E. Shields of Chicago to speak to the entire student body in the chapel. As the secretary of the Community Church Workers, U.S.A., Dr. Shields was helping to form congregations of the new non-denominational Christian church across the country. He saw the non-denominational Home as a logical place for such a congregation. Within a few days a committee of pupils and staff began working on a "new form of church organization," and by February of 1935 more than 100 pupils had registered to become members of the new Community Church for Christian Youth.

Dr. Shields returned to the Home on February 24, 1935, and installed the officers of the Community Church during a formal ceremony at the chapel. The balance of the morning's program was reported in the *Home Review*.

"The charter book, made by the Home departments of arts, printing, and shoe shop and written by a student from High School, was presented by Col. H.R. Mooney of the Board of Trustees of the Home to Superintendent Hays, who then presented it to Rev. C.C. Hankins. Rev. Hankins then turned the charter over to Carl Linsmayor, representative of the church officers.

Cornelius Malone and Henrietta Cloud took the card seriously. After graduation, they were married, joining that large host of ex-pupils who did the same, becoming known as "double-Ex's."

"Letters of congratulation were read by Rev. Hankins from the following persons and organizations: American Legion, Department of Ohio; Col. H.R. Mooney, President of the Board of Trustees; P.R. Hayward, director of the young people's work of the International Council of Religious Education; and R. Carl Stole, representative of the Community Church Workers, U.S.A.

"A beautifully bound pulpit bible, a gift from the Ohio Department of the American Legion auxiliary, was received at the service."

Captain Hays believed the children would be more interested in the operation of the Home if they were directly involved in its management. So, in addition to the largely student-managed Community Church, the superintendent created a Students Home Council complemented by individual Cottage Councils. There had been student councils earlier in the history of the Home, but they did not have the strong support from the staff and administration. These new groups proved to be popular as students liked being involved in the decisions affecting their lives at the Home.

In Music and Marching

An early historical account of the Home noted that its band and the military organization were "closely interwoven as to be almost inseparable." The Home also

These are the marksmen who brought home the 1933 championship. Before Kevlar vests, the Home boys bulletproofed themselves with a chest filled with their own medals.

had a chapel choir, various singing groups, and even an orchestra from time to time. But the major focus of musical interest was the band.

The largest single organization of young men at the Home was "The Battalion," and participation was mandatory. From the earliest history of the Home, the marching feet of Cadets were accompanied by music of one form or another. The first band in 1870 was a fife and drum corps whose major purpose was to keep the military company marching in step. By 1887, the fife and drum corps had become a band using instruments donated by the Sons of Veterans of Ohio. A full-time music instructor was employed. Later, a complete set of silver instruments worth more than $1,200 was donated by the United Spanish War Veterans of Ohio.

As the Home's band became more proficient, its military company became more professional. Military training had always been an important part of the life of the institution, but the Military Department also became, by default, the office that administered punishment for various transgressions. First Lieutenant

William J. Graham attempted to address what others might have perceived as the department's heavy-handed role in keeping order among the children.

"I believe that the common opinion in regard to the function of the Military Department is that its first duty is some sort of discipline more involved with a paddle, kept well-polished and well-oiled in a dark room, or some other more dreadful form of persuasion, and it is my desire to correct these opinions and enlarge a little on the first duty of the Military Department here. . . . This duty is to conduct the training of the unit as prescribed in detail by the War Department and the mission is to 'awaken' in the student an appreciation of the obligations of citizenship, to prepare him to discharge his duties as a citizen and to qualify him as a military leader.

"The object of the basic course is to qualify the Cadet to perform the duties of a non-commissioned officer of the lowest grade in the army for which he is being trained. It can easily be seen that the R.O.T.C. is a vitally important element in our national defense as it is expected to furnish the bulk of the officers required in the event of a war."

Ex-Pupil Clarence "Mike" Ford recalled his military training: "When you got to be 12 years old, they gave you what they called a wooden dummy, a Civil War gun that was cut off and made small . . . When you got just past 12, you're introduced to a big rifle . . . They weigh 8 ½ pounds . . . You have to throw them around and put them on your shoulder and walk around. They had some beautiful parades. Every Sunday we had a parade."

When the Cadets weren't marching with their rifles, they put their weapons to use on the rifle range. Beginning in the early 1930s, the Home's rifle team was regarded as one of the best in the local area and received national attention as well. The team's success could be attributed, in part, to good coaching by military advisor Perry Swindler, strong support from the administration, and the enthusiastic interest of pupils—both boys and girls.

"The rifle has had much to do with the exploring and building of this great nation of ours," reported the *Home Review*. "In the days of our hardy frontiersmen, the minutemen, the soldiers of the Civil War, and later the 'doughboys' went over there [as] cocksure 'Yanks' depending on their rifles quite a bit. . . . At first, boys went off in small groups, to try as best they could, to aim at anything which was a likely target. Shooting for girls was practically unheard of; all of this has been changed. Now girls and boys shoot under careful adult supervision, by following the direction of the coach, one can become a good shot, that is if he so desires."

The Home's rifle team won regional, state and national contests. In 1934, the squad shot a perfect score and captured first place in the bi-weekly national team match sponsored by the National Rifle Association. The Home produced some of the finest marksmen in the country during the 1930s. Of the fourteen marksmen in the United States certified as "Distinguished Riflemen" by the National Rifle Association in 1934, three were OSSO Home Cadets—David Baker, Ralph McKinley, and James Shriner. Shriner was named "National Interscholastic Gallery Rifle Champion of 1934." Over the remainder of the decade, the Home's rifle team would continue to be one of the best in the country. In 1939, Cadet Lieutenant Thane Robeson won the title of "Regimental Small-Bore Rifle Champion" as well as "Distinguished Rifleman" by the NRA.

The Home's band adopted the same precision and discipline as its military counterpart, playing at statewide and local veterans meetings and even performing occasionally at national gatherings. For a time in the early twentieth century, the band didn't take its music on the road as often because of the time needed to travel to and from events, but the purchase of two motor buses by the Home cut down on travel time and allowed the band to schedule more appearances.

After performances at veterans events around the state in the summer of 1934, the band returned home to play at the reunion of the Association of Ex-Pupils over the Fourth of July holiday, when, according to tradition, former residents gathered in front of the administration building and tossed flowers into the fountain to remember ex-pupils who had passed away. The boys in the band then were released for a month's vacation before returning in early August for another round of touring.

Under the direction of instructor Harold Seall, the Home's band performed in Sandusky at the state convention of the American Legion, then traveled to Pittsburgh for the national convention of the United Spanish War Veterans where they were judged to be the "snappiest" and best band to appear in the convention's annual parade. The band closed out the summer with an appearance on WLW radio in Cincinnati to benefit the American Legion Child Welfare program.

While the band enjoyed much success, the orchestra was still a work in progress for "Professor" Seall, as he was known. The orchestra had its ups and downs over the years, and by 1931 had been inactive for some time. When Captain Hays asked why the orchestra was in limbo, he was told that most of the stringed instruments had no strings. The board subsequently set aside funds, instruments were repaired, and the slow rebirth of the orchestra began. The Ohio Woman's Relief Corps, an auxiliary to Civil War veterans groups, had sought a major project to benefit the Home for a number of years and found one in the orchestra. With instruments,

Ruby Lee Garrison
Class of 1935

"On stormy nights we jumped into bed with one another and cuddled up and sat at the window and watched the lightning. I was afraid of the lightning until then. I said, 'Let's watch it,' and Jessie Hall said, 'No, I don't want to watch it,' and I said, 'Let's do.' So we sat and watched the rain and lightning, and from then on, I wasn't afraid anymore.

"One time my sister and I decided we were going to run away. It was about a half hour before suppertime. We got to the bottom of the hill and the whistle blew and she looked at me and I looked at her and she said, 'You hungry?' I said, 'Yeah. Are you?' She said, 'Yeah,' and I said, 'Okay, let's hurry up and get back before the kids all get in the dining room.' So we hurried back up the hill and got there just in time.

"If you ask me why we were going to run away, I'd say, 'Well, you know how it is. Kids sometime think it's better on the outside than on the inside. I'd know where we thought we were going, but we didn't get very far. We got to the bottom of the hill and it was supper time. Kids, just kids…

"One night we got kind of boisterous and we swung on the light pulls. Once in awhile the boys would sneak over to see us, when the matron was asleep. We went outside, and we'd sit on the swing with them, just sit there and talk until we got tired and they went home to their cottage. It was the best years of my life, that's what I always tell everybody."

At end of the cottages, looking east, are Cottages 20 and 21, part of the circle cottages (five buildings, ten cottages). The photograph was taken from in front of the administration building.

willing musicians and good instruction, the orchestra just needed a nice place to play. The Woman's Relief Corps provided them with one.

"In spite of a cloudy sky and a biting wind," reported the *Home Review* in 1936, "the new band shell was officially dedicated at the OS&SO Home on Wednesday, June 3. The Woman's Relief Corps, through whose long and untiring efforts the shell was made possible, was present in considerable number, as were several distinguished guests from all over Ohio. Miss E. Jane Bailey, former member of the Board of Trustees of the Home, then gave a short speech in which she introduced Mrs. Ruth E. Hanson, chairman of the band shell committee of the W.R.C. and an ex-pupil of the Home. After a few remarks in which Mrs. Hanson stated the Woman's Relief Corps is working just as much for the present boys and girls of the Home as it did for the boys and girls of the veterans of the Civil War, the Home girls chorus sang an original song about the band shell, which was written by the chairman. The song dedicated the band shell 'to the boys in blue.'"

At one point during the festivities, Rose Warner, president of the Woman's Relief Corps, simply said, "We hope that the children of the Home will enjoy the band shell as much as we have enjoyed raising the money for it."

For the next several decades, this was one of the Home's truly special places.

In Sport

By the early 1930s, the Home fielded a limited number of sports teams. A full-time supervisor of recreation was hired to develop a program, however, that involved every person at the Home in some form of activity. In 1933, Recreation Supervisor Joe Hoffer described the scope of his work for the *Home Review*:

It is obvious that no one person can provide recreation for every available hour. Hence we must first attempt to develop activities that do not require supervision and use our available supervisors to best advantage.

The program at the Home can be divided under three headings: Physical Education, involving all activities during school hours; Athletics, of interscholastic character; and Recreation dealing with the leisure time of children and adults after school and work.

We must keep in mind that one of the best methods of developing character and the spiritual nature of the child is by encouraging his play instinct through proper channels...If we can only partially stimulate their interest in the mastery of things and increase their power to actively participate in some form of recreation throughout life,

The bandshell, which went up in 1936, became another identifying Home icon.

we will save them from the drab and uninteresting routine of the average individual.

In 1957, an Ohio sportswriter named Allen White compiled a statistical history of Ohio high school athletic competition. On his list of all-time sports achievements, the Ohio Soldiers and Sailors Orphans Home led all Class A schools with five state track and field championships as well as most points scored in the state meets. During the late 1930s and early 1940s, the Cadets established a winning tradition in track, football and basketball that would continue in the decades to follow. Ex-Pupil Richard Moffat surmised that "the Cadets may have had some advantage in physical training due to the military program, a regular schedule, its closer bonds of 'brotherhood' from its more intimate 'family' life, and the faculty's closer control over student life than outside schools." But Moffat also pointed out that the opposition often had "superior numbers" of athletes and coaches—and fans, too. "The Home [had] a small field of loyal teachers and a few ex-pupils who could get back occasionally to bolster the . . . cheering section. If anything, the unknown factor that built a winning record would have to be 'spirit,' instilled over many years until it became a tradition, a spirit that refused to acknowledge odds or superior numbers."

The Home's first full season in football was 1926. The Cadets were coached by Professor Harold Seall—the same Harold Seall who was principal instructor of the band and orchestra. Seall also played amateur football and was a self-taught football strategist and coach. Opposing teams had bigger rosters, but Coach Seall liked to remind his players that on any given play there were no more than "eleven guys out there just like you—only they can't beat you."

One of Seall's last games as coach of the Cadets was also probably the most memorable game in the early history of football at the Home—a 7-0 victory over Xenia Central in 1933. According to one report, "The lone touchdown was made by R. Jones, who early in the first quarter grabbed a short pass aimed at a Xenia Central Buccaneer and started down the sidelines. Alert Cadet players immediately sprang up for interference and Jones crossed the goal line to terminate an 80-yard run for the first score. Badel circled right end to add the extra point."

The victory was the Cadets' first over their crosstown rivals, who had recorded six shutouts in the seven previous games between the schools. The football team initiated the 1933-1934 school year with the standard that made it the most successful athletic year in the history of the Home to that point. The basketball team completed a record of ten wins and five losses, including a win in tournament play. To complete the year, the track team placed second in the state meet. The star of the track team was Eddie Harris, and the team trophy was only the first of many track trophies the Cadets would win.

George Woerlein became head coach in 1934. Like Professor Seall, it took a while for Woerlein to build winning teams. He won three games his first season, four games in 1935, and six games in 1936. In the late 1930s, the Home joined the Little Six League and its football teams won twenty-six consecutive games. Clarence "Mike" Ford remembered those successful seasons. "We had the first team there that went through there that was never scored on. Nobody ever crossed the goal line, and that was in 1937. I played center. The only reason the coach wanted me to be the center was because I was one of the few that could remember the numbers. He always kidded about that. Oh, Coach Woerlein, he was quite a boy."

In 1937, Professor Seall, at the request of the *Home Review*, named his All-Time Home Team:

Left End—Carl (Jerry) Reynolds
Left Tackle—Dan Bolden, Kenneth Massie
Left Guard—Lawrence Redding
Center—George Wolf
Right Guard—Fred (Head) Franks
Right Tackle—William (Freddie) Lee

Rise of the Cadets
Coach Woerlein's decade

It was the decade when the Home program came into its own, notably with football. The Cadets and Xenia Central began playing each other in 1926, and the Cadets didn't score on their crosstown opponents until 1932, a game in which the two teams were tied until the final minutes when Central eked out a 12-6 win.

This lone—but metaphorically mighty—score was what the Cadets called their "New Deal," and they made good on their assertion in 1933—7-0. The key play was the 80-yard interception by R. Jones, which the *Home Review* called "a historic gallop that eclipsed Paul Revere's ride."

The outweighed Cadet line sank hopeful Central backs time after time, played with only one substitution, and for a brief moment in time, the Great Depression was held at bay. The Cadets outgained Central 143-26.

The two tied in 1934 and 1935 (0-0, 19-19), then the Home won 7-0. There was another tie in 1937, which was still a good year because the Home had William Dezarn, a speedy halfback who—during Field Day in the spring before—set the school record in the 100-yard dash by running 10.1, a blazing time for the day.

Central won in 1938, 27-0, then in 1939, the Home won, 13-0, en route to a 7-1 season.

By the time Coach Woerlein departed for the Navy in the spring of 1942, he'd won four Little Six titles, compiled a record of 47-12-4, with a 4-1-3 mark against powerful Xenia Central.

The orphans always played their archrivals on Central's turf, but by the time Woerlein was finished, the Home boys had almost made Central feel homeless.

These are the gridiron warriors of the fall of 1934, just as the athletic fortunes of the Cadets began to rise.

The Lady Cadets of 1930. Do not be fooled by the winsome countenances of the ladies. They were not to be trifled with.

Right End—Charles Tyrell
Quarterback—Warren Yowell, Jas. Shriner
Left Halfback—George Sharpe, Glendon French
Right Halfback—Everett Hickman
Fullback—Ivan (Pig) McCord

George Woerlein was also the track and field coach. From 1937 until Woerlein left the Home to serve in World War II, the Home's track teams won every league meet, four district championships, and two state championships. By the end of the decade, the Home had become an athletic powerhouse. In 1940, the Cadets won the state track title, and the football team won all of its games. The basketball team won eighteen games and lost only five, capturing its first district title. Many of these teams consisted of the same young men—but in different uniforms.

Times to Remember

Almost everyone at the Home, it seems, had a nickname. A new kid was called a "Newkie." The Home's publications regularly carried features on the new classes of "Newkies" as well as group portraits of them. After awhile, the new kids got their own nicknames. In 1939, the *Home Review* published a list of no less than sixty pupils and monikers, which tell us something about how the children saw themselves in the years of the Great Depression.

First, the boys—Speed, Blue Goofus, Gunner, Governor, Ruby, Shadow, Parson, Klank, Cascade, Snipe Shooter, Casanova, Blah, Thunder, Brute, and Spooey.

A few of the girls—Gypsy, Snore, Fuzzy Flossie, Happy, Phoebe, Grimmy, Bud, Brick, Bow-Wow, Dead Eye, Bumpy, Slewfoot, Oats, Loony, Beefy and Slats.

Once bestowed, nicknames tend to stick and become part of the permanent collective memory of the OSSO Home.

"We were the pride of Ohio. I'm just thankful I was raised there. I think every child should have a childhood like mine. Can you imagine that I went out into the world on my own, not knowing anybody, and made a business without having any idea what to do? I just did it, because I had faith in myself. The pride in ourselves that the Home gave us was what did it." — Dorothy Cox Skelly, Class of 1937

Marilyn Flickinger-Green
Class of 1950

"Beds were lined up, side-by-side along the walls. Ladies in long white dresses and wearing funny fly-away hats shook little glass tubes with quick snaps of their wrists. A man with a big silver eye peered into my mouth and ears. I was poked, prodded, and stuck with long needles. *What are they doing to me? Where is my family?*

"I didn't understand what was happening. My mother died when I was only 2, and I had just celebrated my 4th birthday. In time, it would become a place familiar to me—where I was cared for when sick, had measles, had my tonsils removed, my severely lacerated foot stitched up after I jumped from a fence onto a broken bottle.

For a time, I even worked as a student nurse. I wanted to be like those ladies in the long white dresses and fly-away hats. I wanted to learn to snap my wrist and shake down the mercury in the thermometers just as they did.

"It mattered little that what I actually did was wash down beds, clean hospital stands, run errands, and clean up the sun rooms. It seemed enough to me that I was in such an important place, doing important work. In early 1936, though, I was disoriented, frightened, and alone.

"Soon, I was assigned to Peter Pan, a low, sprawling, U-shaped building adjacent to the hospital. There were so many kids, so much noise! I was impressed with all the beds, all lined up side-by-side, extending out from the walls. They seemed quite large when I was so little. *Would anyone sing me to sleep? Would anyone ever hug me?*

"Later, I discovered I could jump on the big beds, as high as the sky! This was not acceptable, though, and as punishment, I spent the remainder of one night closed up in a linen closet across the hall. I cried and vowed never to be caught again. Even more traumatizing than a night in the closet was my introduction to the monster, institution-sized cockroaches. *And they could fly!*

"In the bathroom, I was intrigued by the high bathtub. It had steps to climb into it. There was a chart on the wall in the bathroom where the supervisors kept a record of each girl's bowel movements—or lack thereof. The antidote for missing one was nasty. And there were the little pieces of bread soaked in dreadful cod liver oil that we were required to swallow daily.

"It was as an impressible child in Peter Pan that I first heard about the tunnel walk. Was it only a wonderfully creepy story? Sometimes, even years later, if I was alone, late, on a particularly dark and damp night, the thought of it could still make me shudder.

"Everyone seemed to whisper about it. Each day before school, we were admonished to stay off the grass and use the walk. We did but we skirted the manholes; they were in the center of the walk and we tried to run around them. The tunnel breathed out its putrid air from the sinister interior— through the holes in the manhole covers. On an occasional windy day, the tunnel expressed its threats with an eerie whistle *through those same breathing holes!*

"I understood that if I didn't run faster, something might reach up through the holes, grab my ankle, and I would disappear down into the darkness of the tunnel. The whispered secret— *which we knew was true*—was this: all the Home children who sickened and died from diphtheria during the late 1800s were carried underground from the hospital, through the tunnel, on their way to the cemetery. This journey isolated the epidemic germs from the other children, you see.

"We understood later that the Home's heating pipes ran through the tunnel, but could it also have been used to transport the victims to the cemetery? That was what was whispered. If we chanced to go by way of the tunnel walk, especially on a dark night, was there any wonder why our heart beat a little faster and something raised the hair on the back of our neck? And what was that acrid smell emanating from the tunnel?

"Adjusting to life in the Home was not easy. Many kids had at least one parent who could visit for a few hours every month. But many of us didn't. Mr. J. Harley Waldron, the supervisor of Academic Education, was the man most influential in my life, a constant the whole time I was in the Home. He treated us gently and with compassion as we learned to live without our parents, and I have a special place in my heart for this man who loved us and helped fill the void in our lives with his care and encouragement.

"Once, he arranged for me to be excused from classes in order to get a permanent. I was very young, totally lacking in self-confidence, and I knew absolutely that a permanent would solve all my problems. *Imagine! A perm for me!* Until that time, all I had known was the institutional Dutch-boy haircut. I loved Mr. Waldron for understanding my need. And as a result of getting the perm, I *did* stand a little straighter and taller, though I must have been a sight to behold.

"When I was 7 or 8, Mr. Waldron recognized my love for music. He introduced me to Mr. Tague, the music teacher. I was thrilled beyond words. But when Mr. Tague lost patience with me and hit my hands with a ruler because of my incorrect hand positions, I ran tearfully to Mr. Waldron. He allowed me to discontinue my lessons until the next year when there was a new piano teacher. As a result, I accompanied the Home Choir, played the organ at chapel services, played violin in the girls' orchestra, and piano in the jazz band.

"When I was a senior, he arranged a piano audition for me at Miami University where I earned a scholarship, and he acquired room and board for me in a professor's home, in exchange for work and baby-sitting. This is when our relationship changed. Mr. Waldron was no longer my educator-mentor. He was a beloved friend. He was my substitute father, and he gave me away at my wedding in Collier Chapel at the Home.

"I was still a student at Miami and had no money. He served the rehearsal dinner in his own home, bought the wedding flowers, and even got his daughter's permission for me to wear her long, satin wedding gown.

"After all these years, I have continued to imagine my old friend sitting at his desk by the window. Busy at work, helping Sammy, or Dorothy, or Anthony, and listening to me across the hall practicing the piano. Now he's gone. The Home is gone. Change is never easy and almost never welcome. But I can still imagine that Mr. Waldron would put his arms around me, wipe my tears away, and say, 'There, there, Marilyn. Everything will be all right. You'll see....'"

A fine place and a real home (1940-1963)

At the Home in the mid-1930s, the Depression was moderated by Peter Pan's wading pool.

A look at the Home, c. 1940

It was never simply an orphanage. The 682 children living at the Ohio Soldiers and Sailors Orphans Home in 1940 enjoyed better food and accommodations, even nicer clothes, than a lot of children in traditional family settings. Their schools were equal to and, in some cases, better than the public schools. The Home's General Barnett Vocational School, in particular, was first-rate. The Home was a place founded on excellence—not to simply provide charity to the needy. Rather the Home was repayment for part of the debt owed by a grateful state to the families of the men who had served it.

In an article for the *Home Review* in 1941, ex-pupil Denver Hill took inventory of the improvements made to the campus over the previous fifteen years: *even new buildings have been put up . . . since 1926-1927. All of these are very large and modern. The largest of these buildings, the children's dining room was built in 1932. This provides a larger and better dining room for the children as well as the employees. What used to be the old dining room was turned into offices, a cafeteria and several small dining rooms for employees. The new dining room has the space so the meal groups will be smaller. This allows brothers and sisters to eat together...*

Another big improvement for the grounds as well as the children is the General Barnett Vocational School. . . . [It] is the largest state-owned vocational school in the state. There are four shops on the ground floor for the main vocations for boys. The girls have five trade rooms on the second floor, where they receive their vocational training. . . . This building alone contains many good reasons why children benefit by going to school at the Home.

The Home Hospital has provided this institution with a good medical backing. . . . It has a large x-ray room, a sterilizing room, a modern operating room, a small laboratory, a dentist's office, a two-room clinic, a loud speaking system with two main stations and five substations, four wards and four private rooms.

The little tots are the luckiest of the children on the grounds. A large and beautiful nursery was constructed at the side of the hospital for children between the ages of four and nine. The nursery, which is named Peter Pan Cottages, has seven cottages all joined, one of which serves as the dining room and kitchen. All cottages are named after a nursery rhyme, such as Little Bo Peep. The entire building is equipped with miniature beds, wash bowls, toilets, bath tubs, dining tables and chairs, and many other articles of furniture, with the exception of the supervisor's own room. There is a wading pool and a large area in the back for a playground.

The Woodruff Transition (1940-1942)

The Depression years had been good years, relatively speaking, at the Home. New buildings were built, as Denver Hill reminded *Home Review* readers. New programs established. A new open lifestyle had been adopted by the adults and children. The board of trustees and staff were justifiably proud of their accomplishments during the Thirties. Despite the scarce resources and budget cuts, the high levels of service and training had been maintained and the Home's reputation as a fine place to live and learn had been enhanced. If anything, the liberalization of dress and deportment made the institution even more attractive to both visitors and residents. Still, there was much to do.

In January of 1940, Francis R. Woodruff, former principal of Xenia's Central

An early portrait of the young men of Peter Pan taken in the late 1940s: Tommy Leonard, Terry Wallace, Paul Corcoran, Ron Frazier, and Tony Polino.

High School, was hired as the new superintendent, succeeding the popular and long-serving Harold Hays. Woodruff, who was married with a child of his own, had been chosen from more than forty candidates. In addition to his ten years at Xenia Central, he had taught in the Fremont and Bellevue public schools and specialized in vocational and industrial education while earning his bachelor's and master's degrees from Miami University, making him—on paper anyway—a great fit.

Like the Home's previous superintendents, Woodruff also came to the job with military experience, having served overseas in World War I. He was a lieutenant in the Ohio National Guard company under Harold Hays's command and became leader of the unit when Hays returned to active duty. "The students and employees . . . are very glad that Mr. Woodruff has been selected for the position and feel very fortunate that they have such a capable man," noted the *Home Review*. "Everyone is confident that Mr. Woodruff will fill Captain Hays's shoes, and wish him all the luck possible." Captain Woodruff would need it.

First came the departures of several long-time employees. Nancy Spencer had been the Home's finance officer for more than fourteen years when she died suddenly in February. Chaplain Cecil Hankins took a six-month sabbatical to

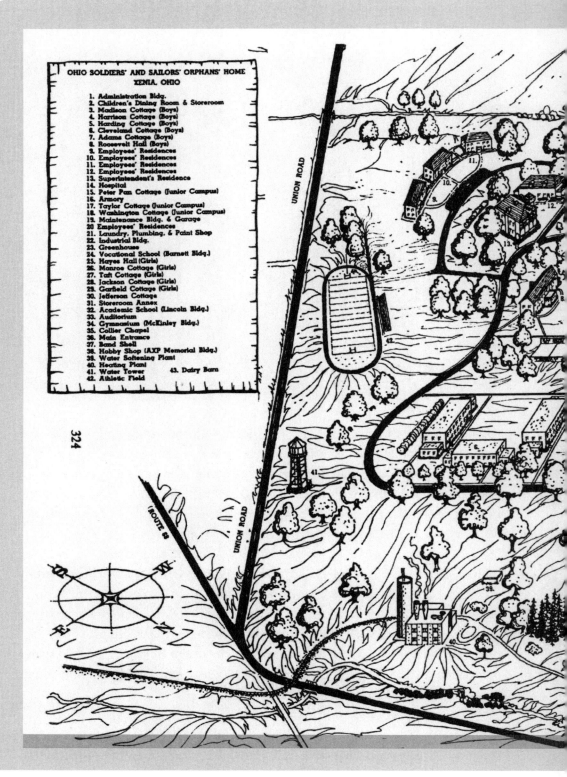

OHIO SOLDIERS' AND SAILORS' ORPHANS' HOME
XENIA, OHIO

1. Administration Bldg.
2. Children's Dining Room & Storeroom
3. Madison Cottage (Boys)
4. Harrison Cottage (Boys)
5. Harding Cottage (Boys)
6. Cleveland Cottage (Boys)
7. Adams Cottage (Boys)
8. Roosevelt Hall (Boys)
9. Employees' Residences
10. Employees' Residences
11. Employees' Residences
12. Employees' Residences
13. Superintendent's Residence
14. Hospital
15. Peter Pan Cottage (Junior Campus)
16. Armory
17. Taylor Cottage (Junior Campus)
18. Washington Cottage (Junior Campus)
19. Maintenance Bldg. & Garage
20. Employees' Residences
21. Laundry, Plumbing, & Paint Shop
22. Industrial Bldg.
23. Greenhouse
24. Vocational School (Barnett Bldg.)
25. Hayes Hall (Girls)
26. Monroe Cottage (Girls)
27. Taft Cottage (Girls)
28. Jackson Cottage (Girls)
29. Garfield Cottage (Girls)
30. Jefferson Cottage
31. Storeroom Annex
32. Academic School (Lincoln Bldg.)
33. Auditorium
34. Gymnasium (McKinley Bldg.)
35. Collier Chapel
36. Main Entrance
37. Band Shell
38. Hobby Shop (AXP Memorial Bldg.)
39. Water Softening Plant
40. Heating Plant
41. Water Tower   43. Dairy Barn
42. Athletic Field

324

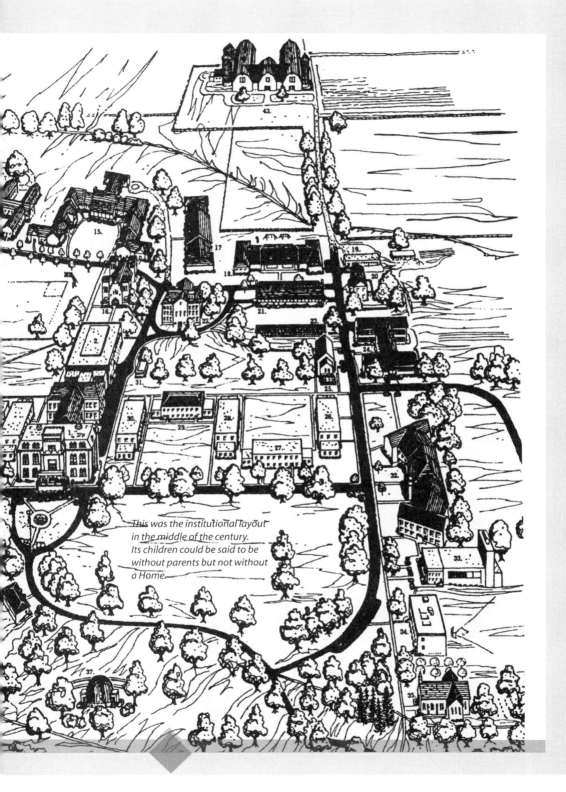

This was the institutional layout in the middle of the century. Its children could be said to be without parents but not without a Home.

develop religious education programs for the Home. Harold Seall planned to step down from his coaching and music positions.

Then the Home again underwent the scrutiny of Dr. T.C. Holy and the Bureau of Educational Research at Ohio State University, who were asked by the board of trustees to do a follow-up analysis of the bureau's 1933 survey and take a fresh look at the current operation. Dr. Holy and his team had concluded their original study with 109 recommendations for improving the physical plant, the education programs, and the children's quality of life. This time, the researchers made eighty-three recommendations, including the following proposal: "Three cottages are now seventy-one years old and [twenty] are more than sixty-eight years old. The board of trustees of the Home should plan a program of replacement of the older cottages and begin this program of rebuilding in the near future. . . ."

One long-awaited project finally got underway after the General Assembly finally released $150,000 for construction of a new school to replace the Home's seventy-year-old Woodrow Wilson building, where the top floor was closed and classes were being held in the basement.

In another positive development, the Home acquired an eleven-acre tract near John Bryan State Park for use as a camp for eight weeks in the summer and for Boy Scout and Girl Scout outings during the winter. "Camp Scribes" described some of the activities and adventures at Camp Cooper:

In the morning bright and early everyone is out to see the flag up and do calisthenics. You could usually find Chazz Lamb hidden under the bed. It took the calisthenics to wake some of the boys for breakfast. . . .

Who was it that went over to the 4-H camp (there were girls there) every night after taps? We won't mention any names but everyone knows it was. . . . You should have seen the honest thieves out in camp. They wouldn't swipe anything unless you were gone. . . . You should hear Billie B. murder those bugle calls! Gads! . . . There was quite a contest as to who could snore loudest in camp, but E. Jackson was awarded the prize. Maybe it was because he got the most practice. . . .

Here's one of the Boy Scouts' overnighters described in the *Home Review*:

I know of another instance when some scouts were out camping and having built their lean-tos to sleep in, they were just preparing for the night when it began to rain . . . A certain scout dug a trench around his lean-to and feeling very secure, turned in for the night. About midnight, he was rudely awakened by a trickling of

The Home boys lived the good life at Camp Cooper.

cold water down his back. He found his shelter full of water. The following morning he was told the next time he dug a trench, not to forget to make an outlet for it. Such is the life of a scout on an overnight hike.

Clean-Up Day was usually held in late April. Teams of children and employees fanned out across the campus, following the age-old army adage: "If it moves, salute it or pick it up. If it doesn't move, bury it or give it a coat of paint." In 1940, a committee came up with a new name: "Home Beautiful Day." In addition to sprucing up the place, there would be a poster contest, an essay contest, a grab-bag drawing, and a picnic. The first Home Beautiful Day was a great success, according to the *Home Review*.

April 30, the day set for clean-up, was cloudy and a little damp outside, but everyone was going on with the job, so old clothes were taken from their hiding places and adults as well as students went to work. No women or girls were assigned to work outside this year. Instead, girls were assigned to help women teachers clean their school rooms. Their working hours were from 8:30 to 11 a.m. Boys were assigned to

Ms. Kerwin, supervisor of Roosevelt Hall, and J.R. Rooney, the drama teacher, share a good picnic laugh.

outdoors [and] worked . . . until approximately 3 p.m. in the afternoon.

At the picnic, more than 150 prizes provided by the Xenia Post of the American Legion were awarded to students for their essays and posters. A supper of wieners, potato chips, pickles, lemonade, ice cream, and marshmallows was held in the Home woods and residents of each cottage sat together in groups.

In his winning essay, sixth grader Garland Hughes showed himself to be a young man with honorable intentions. "I could ask to have some flowers planted around where they are needed mostly. . . . I can remember to keep off the grass and remind others to do so too. I can help to keep the sidewalks clean and wash them when they need to be clean. I can remember not to throw orange peels and banana skins on them. I am sure I'll try to do all of these things that I have mentioned, and not disobey the rules of the Home and have this [be] the best Home in the whole United States."

Peter Pan

Bob Carter, a 1957 graduate, remembered his earliest days in Peter Pan. "We had to polish the floors in Peter Pan," he said. "First, we rubbed them with a rag. Then we found that by having someone sit on a blanket and pull them up and down the hallway, you polished it just as fine, and the job got done, and you kind of enjoyed doing it, all at the same time . . . .

"If you were bad, they sent you up to the dining hall and you had to shell peas. That was one of the worst jobs I ever had. You sat there and shelled five or six big baskets, bushel baskets full of peas and it took hours. The same with green beans. You sat there stringing green beans, bushels of them, and everyone else was out playing . . . ."

Marjorie Balside arrived at the Home from Zanesville in 1943, one of thirteen children in her family, so poor that she and her sister ate leftovers from the school cafeteria, and used soap box tops in their shoes so they could walk to school in the snow.

When she and two of her sisters came to the home, her mother told them they were going on a vacation.

"The first impression I got when I got to the Home was, boy, what a big vacation place. But they took us right to the hospital and that was no vacation. But we had good food . . . ."

Soon, she was in Cottage 5, learning to live by the whistle, which blew for every occurrence in the day.

"We never carried a watch; we knew what time it was when the whistle blew . . . ."

Occasionally, there were fights, most of them broken up by the night watchman, except the time the boys turned on the night watchman and tied him to a tree.

"We got dessert at lunch and supper, cakes and pies and puddings and fruit and cookies. We thought this was a really good vacation but then when we had stayed there a long time, I began to wonder how long a vacation could actually last . . . ."

Nancy Hoover, who graduated in 1960, remembered the scale of Peter Pan: "Everything in Peter Pan was little. Little toilets, little beds, little tables in our dining hall. I remember going to the dining hall in Peter Pan and we always had fish on Friday, but I hated fish, so I sat there. They made you sit there until you finished. I found out that the boys had cuffs in their pants and they were sticking fish in their cuffs and walking out . . . ."

And Millie Flannery, who was at the Home from 1942 to

Ms. Brennan, one of the Peter Pan supervisors, risks her decorum by helping her boys fly a kite.

1951, once sat in the Peter Pan dining room until bedtime because she refused to eat parsnips. Parsnips made her gag and her stomach roll.

"When the dining room closed I was told to go back to Pan 7. At breakfast, my supervisor told the dining room ladies to bring my parsnips. Finally, the director came and told me they decided I did not have to eat the parsnips, but I would get no dessert for a week. That was okay with me. I was glad it was resolved. Later, I learned from the girls who had been there awhile how to dispose of food I could not eat. Dresses went to the laundry with food in the pockets, and there was lots of coughing and sneezing into napkins, which had to be taken to the bathroom trash immediately so we could wash our hands . . . ."

These Peter Pan boys provide a poster portrait for the children not otherwise taken care of.

The folks on the farm apparently did their part to improve the Home's appearance as well. An article in the 1941 *Home Review* noted that the hog lots in front of the dairy barn had been converted to cattle pastures. "The cows have been dehorned so they will be more docile when turned out into the exercise lots. Their horns were taken off to help prevent accidents." As for the dairy operation, "an average of 51 cows in the herd produced an average of 11,880 pounds of milk with 3.42 fat test and 406 pounds of butter fat. The dairymen aren't planning to attend as many fairs as they did last summer. The first show they will attend is the little red and white show in Springfield. The date for this occasion is not known as yet."

One date that was well known by early 1941 was March 28—the day of the dedication of the cornerstone of the new school building. Several hundred guests, including former superintendents Thomas Andrews and Harold Hays, attended the ceremony. After the presentation of the colors by the Home's battalion and the introduction of dignitaries, the cornerstone was put in place. Lieutenant Governor Paul Herbert delivered the principal address. "Let us be perfectly frank," said Herbert. "Were it not for the constant efforts of the veterans of the Spanish War and of the World War, those of the Civil War having passed on, it is doubtful whether this school could claim the remarkable progress that it has today. Do not make a mistake: do not infer that our government is not sympathetic. But there are so many demands on the money of the state that were it not for the constant presence of those veterans of the last two wars, I fear that we would not be here today nor would we have this splendid building that is now yours."

Some of the events that the children had most anticipated and would remember long after they left the Home—parties during the holidays, movies on the weekends, and so on—were held in the schools. Just as moving from the Peter Pan Cottages to the cottages on the main campus marked a rite of passage, so did graduation from grade school to junior high school to high school. An event that marked the end of their journey through the grades was the senior class trip to Columbus.

In April of 1941, the seniors left Xenia by bus at eight o'clock in the morning for a full day of activities that began with a visit to Columbus City Hall and a meeting with Mayor Floyd Green. At the Statehouse, each student shook hands with Governor Bricker. After visits to the city jail, the Ohio Penitentiary, the Kroger Bakery, and the Moore and Ross Dairy, some of seniors visited the Ohio State University museum while the rest watched the Buckeye football team in spring practice. The whole group then toured the Columbus Zoo, had dinner at Sunshine Park, and danced to the music of two local pianists. Everyone arrived back in Xenia at 9:45 p.m.

The seniors that year were the first class to take driver's training at the Home, after which they applied for temporary permits and took a final examination in May to secure their permanent licenses.

The rifle team, which practiced on the rifle range in the basement of the Gettysburg Armory, continued to bring home the hardware. Three Cadet teams, including an all-girls team, placed in the 1941 Ohio Rifle and Pistol Association junior matches, while the Home's "first team" placed 38th out of 270 teams in the second series of the national bi-weekly matches.

In high school sports during the Forties, the Home was a powerhouse. Coach George Woerlein and his assistant S.L. "Pete" Stephan assembled winning teams in basketball, football, and track. Woerlein, a native of Groveport, Ohio, came to the Home with a master's in physical education from Ohio State. His football and basketball teams had only one losing season from 1934 to 1942. Over that remarkable eight-year span in the Little Six League, the Cadets won four football championships (1937, '38, '40 and '41), and two of those teams were undefeated and unscored on.

The 1937 team had two 0-0 ties but the 1941 team was undefeated and unscored on with eight wins and no losses, scoring 359 points. The Home won two basketball titles (1937 and '42). They were district basketball champs in '41 and '42 and twice advanced to the "Sweet Sixteen" in the state tournament, where they were a state semi-finalist in 1941. The Cadets were even more dominant in track and field, winning five Little Six League meets (1937, '38, '39, '40, and '41) and back-to-back state championships in 1940 and 1941.

The 1941 football team was regarded as one of the great teams in the history of the Home. Kenneth Pitzer, a 180-pound end, earned All-Ohio honors. Tackle John Downs, quarterback Don Polaski, and fullback Granuel McKinney was named all-league, along with Pitzer, while halfback Tom West and center Carl (Popeye) Norris were chosen for the second team. Willard Colby on the 1940 football team won a place on the All-Ohio grid team, becoming the first class B school player to receive such an honor. Linemen Kenneth Pitzer and Harvey Mallory were named on the All-Ohio reserve team.

Unfortunately, assistant coach "Pete" Stephan didn't get to stick around for the celebration. In early 1940, the Roosevelt Administration responded to the outbreak of war in Europe by re-instituting the military draft—for the first time ever in peacetime. Officers and members of military reserve units—Coach Stephan among them—saw themselves restored to active duty as well. He returned to the Marines, while other men at the Home also were called up or drafted.

Kenny Pitzer was one of the best athletes in Ohio during his time at the Home and likely the finest all-around Cadet athlete ever.

ONE OF OHIO'S FINEST ATHLETES, A CONTRIBUTION OF THE CLASS OF 1942

Kenneth Pitzer, a member of this year's graduating class, who has made such an outstanding record in athletes while in the Home High School. Kenny was the first boy in Home history to earn four letters in each of three sports. He starred in football, basketball and track.

In addition to his athletic achievements, Kenny made an enviable record in his studies, and also in other activities. He was Cadet Major in the battalion, one of the highest positions to which a student can climb. Kenny became recognized throughout the state to the extent that he made the all-Ohio teams in both football and basketball. In the State track meet on May 23, he vaulted 12 ft. 3 in., to set a new Home record, and missing the state record by a mere 1/4 in.

Champions

WON 8, LOST 0 * * POINTS—Cadets 359, O[

he Miami Valley

WIN STREAK EXTENDED TO 18 STRAIGHT GAMES

The 1941 Home football team might have been the single greatest team in the history of Home sports: unbeaten, unscored upon, one All-Stater, and six All-League players.

It was the greatest year in athletics in the Home's history. It began in the winter of 1940-1941 when the basketball team won the district for the first time in its history and reached the final four of the state tournament, where they lost to the eventual state "B" champions, Glenford, 45-35. Dick Shrider, the Home's big All-Ohio center, staged a deadeye one-man show, scoring 31 points, most from the center of the floor.

Then before track began, there was a brief moment of levity between the Cadets and a new military instructor who had just arrived from Culver, bringing with him an excess of military spit-and-polish.

The instructor liked morning calisthenics; the boys, of course, did not. A battle of wills (and wiles) ensued, culminating in the instructor having himself built an enormous platform from which he led the physical exercises. Then one morning he came out for his drills and found his platform in the lake. (If he'd only thought: it took more exercise to get the platform in the lake than the Cadets ever expended in the drills.)

In the spring came track and another state title on the heels of the previous year's state title. The Home boys of 1940 were Ohio Wesleyan Relay champs, Field Day champs, Little Six champs, district champs and state champs.

In May, Patterson, Pitzer, Impson, Hecker, Colby, Spears, Brooks, Steberl, Strunk, and Wyne went to Columbus where they broke old Home records in pole vault (11' 10"), 880-yard relay (1:34.9), mile relay (3:39.8), and rolled

up 38 and a half points, more than twice what runnerup Oak Harbor could muster. Patterson and Pitzer alone scored 19 and a half points.

The boys did it with virtuosity, and teamwork— Pitzer and his pole vault scored a first, and so did Patterson with the discus (145, 7 and a half), and both the mile relay team and the 880-yard relay team. Then there were four third-place finishes, and a fourth.

In total: ten new trophies were added to the Cadets' growing collection.

In 1941, the Cadets placed in seven of the state's 13 events, and won four of them:

1—The sprint relay team ran the half mile in 1:34.1 to erase its former mark of 1:34.9 set at the state meet the year before.

2—In the 440-yard run, Jake Steberl smashed his own mark of 53.4 by running a 52.4.

3—Robert Impson won the high hurdles in 15.6.

4—And Willard Colby won

Bob Impson and Willard Colby were just boys when they became part of one of Ohio's all-time track dynasties. And no girlie synthetic rubber surfaces for these guys, either.

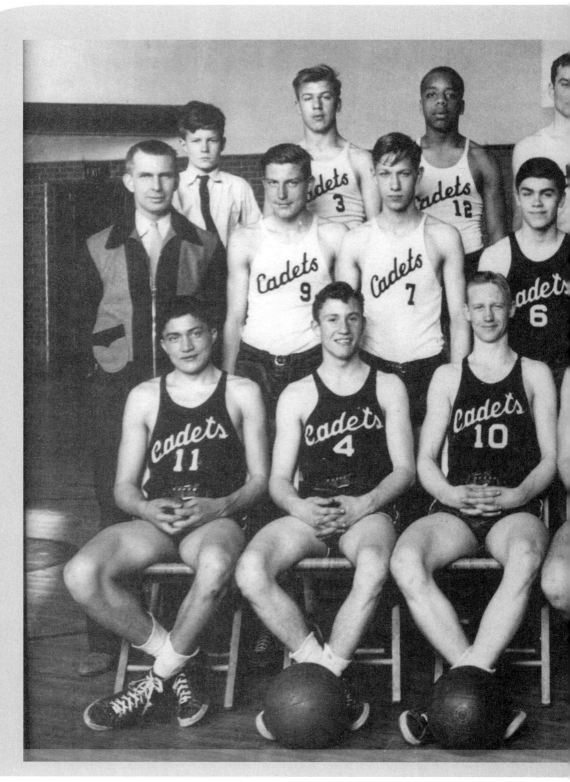

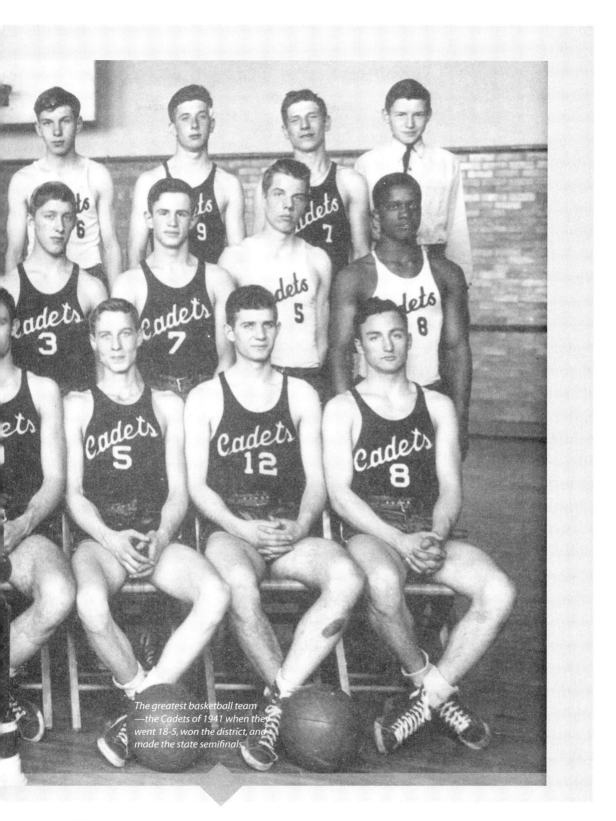

The greatest basketball team
—the Cadets of 1941 when they
went 18-5, won the district, and
made the state semifinals.

the 220-low hurdles in 26.4.

In the autumn, the Cadet football team accomplished the near-impossible—they were unbeaten (8-0), untied, unscored upon (359-0). Only one team claimed the distinction of getting inside the Cadet 5-yard line, and that was the Cadets' own second team, in a scrimmage. The second-teamers got to the 2-yard line, but four plays later they were still at the 2-yard line, and that was that.

The gridders opened their season by dedicating a new football field for Coach Woerlein's hometown of Groveport—71-0. Obviously, no quarter was given to relatives. The Groveport offense set cleated foot into Cadet territory only once in the entire game, when a pass to the Cadet 45 was halted by the gun sounding the end of the game.

Some of the other outlandish scores of the season: Franklin, 53-0; Lebanon, 77-0; Ohio Deaf, 60-0. The squeaker of the year was across town with arch-rival Xenia Central, which the Cadets won 7-0 after Kenny Pitzer, one of the Home's greatest athletes, blocked a punt and fell on it in the end zone. The kick hit Kenny in the face and he played the rest of the game without remembering what had happened.

The stars that year were Willard Colby, ace halfback, first Home boy, as well as the first Class B athlete in Ohio, to be named on the All-Ohio team. (Colby, in the season, scored 143 points, and in two games scored ten TDs). Two Home boys, guard Harvey Mallory and end Kenneth Pitzer made honorable mention. (Pitzer became the first Home boy to earn four letters in each of three sports (football, basketball, and track), and was All-Ohio in two sports, as well. In track his pole vault of 12-3 in 1942 missed the state mark by a quarter of an inch).

The place wasn't the same when Pitzer graduated, but he left a little brother—Ray—who made All-Ohio in 1942 when the Cadets were once again undefeated, running their string to 26 games.

The Home's dynamic sports duo was Mousie Eisenhut (left) and George Woerlein (right). Neither much liked losing, and so they didn't.

In August of 1941, the Home got a new shop teacher and Coach Woerlein got a new assistant: Warren B. Eisenhut. Eisenhut played football and baseball at Miami University and served as a paid coaching assistant for one year, graduating with an education degree in 1940. At Shaw High School in East Cleveland, his football teammates called him "Mouse," which later became "Mousie." Eisenhut stood 5-5 and weighed 124 pounds, but to his son Tod (and presumably his players as well), he was an "absolute giant."

"When you called him 'Mousie,' you called him 'Mousie' out of respect," said Tod Eisenhut. "The thing that he represented more than anything else was equality. . . . I was the youngest of three brothers but I watched my dad all the time. He treated every kid equal. . . . He would just find something. You know, there was no written agenda for this. It was just something about the kid's background that he would bring out. When he brought this out, the kid starts thinking. 'Yeah, I really am a person. I've got something. I am somebody.'"

In October of 1941, the Home's children did some shopping at the annual Christmas Store in the Gettysburg Armory, sponsored by various service and veterans organizations. They selected gifts to open on Christmas morning. Despite the news from overseas of war and destruction, everyone looked forward to the holidays. It would be a holiday season like few others.

"We had these bright uniforms, 'OSSO' across the front. That was intimidation in itself. See, we had such a history and when we got on the field or the court or the track, we had a step on 'em right from the start—because of our history. I met this guy from Wilmington years later, down 68 south, and we got to talking and he says, 'OSSO' was one school we hated to play.'

"We take off that warm-up jacket and they see that 'OSSO', you can hear them talk. Guy who's new says. 'What is that?' And the other guy, who's played us before, he says, 'You'll find out.'

"I remember playing Fairborn and they shot us with B-B guns. Brought up a big welt. It just made us play harder." —Austin Washington, Class of 1956

The cadets and the band perform on the parade grounds, circa early 1940s.

Another picture of the Home cadets on the march, this time in downtown Xenia.

War Comes to the Home (1941-1945)

It was a cold, clear morning in Xenia on Sunday, December 7, 1941. Sundays were special at the Ohio Soldiers and Sailors Orphans Home. Everyone could sleep a bit later and their duties, other than attendance at chapel, were limited—especially during the winter. By early afternoon, most of the children and staff had eaten lunch and were preparing for afternoon activities. Then, shortly after 1 p.m., the world changed with the Japanese attack on the U.S. naval base at Pearl Harbor, Hawaii—the deadliest attack on American soil by a foreign enemy since the British burned Washington in the War of 1812.

The following day, President Franklin Roosevelt appeared before a joint session of Congress, where he asked the senators and representatives to declare that "since yesterday December 7, 1941, a state of war has existed between the United States and the Empire of Japan." War with Germany and Italy would follow shortly. The United States was about to engage in what many people at the time called "The War to Save the World," and the Home would be involved every step of the way.

Perhaps realizing the country's participation in the war would be long, difficult, and painful, the staff made every effort to keep things normal over the upcoming Christmas holiday. Christmas Day began at six o'clock in the morning. "The beautiful strains of the Christmas carols broke the early morning stillness," reported the *Home Review*, "and the long columns of carolers wound their way around the Home, through the hospital and Peter Pan, instilling in all the distinctive feeling characteristic only of the Yuletide season—the Christmas spirit. From the main building the carolers proceeded to the candle-lit children's dining room for the traditional singing of the Home Christmas Carol."

Wish you Merry Christmas! Hark the Joyous Song,
How the cheerful voices roll the notes along,
Happy Hearts responding to the welcome call,
Wish you Merry Christmas. Merry Christmas all.

Let your sweetest numbers flow,
Wake the heavenly songs again,
Sung by angels long ago,
"Peace on earth, good will to men."

Wish you Merry Christmas, Merry Christmas all!
May the richest blessing ever on you fall
Every year be brighter than the one before.
And your Christmas mornings many, many more.

Let your sweetest numbers flow
Wake the heavenly songs again,
Sung by angels long ago,
"Peace on earth, good will to men."

Merry, merry, merry, merry, merry, merry,
Merry, merry, merry, merry, Christmas all!
Merry, merry, merry, merry, merry, merry,
Merry, merry, merry, merry, Christmas all!

"After breakfast," continued the *Home Review*, "the children hurried home to open their presents and clean the cottages in preparation for the day's flow of guests. The remainder of the day was spent in looking at trees and decorations in the cottages and showing gifts to friends. Time was taken out at noon for the Christmas dinner of delicious turkey, cranberry sauce, and all the makings of a blue plate special. Many [ex-pupils] and boys on furlough were here for the day [and] added much to the pleasant time had by all."

The New Year's Eve dance was canceled in deference to the country's declaration of war, but that didn't stop the traditional celebration. "Most everyone on the grounds stayed up to welcome the New Year, so at 12:00 the whistle was blown and everyone who could find anything to make noise with, made it. All in all, New Year's Eve was quite an occasion at the Home and most everyone enjoyed it."

Joy turned to sadness, however, when word arrived that Durward Laney of the Class of 1936 had been killed in action. Laney had been class president, student council president, a major in the cadet battalion and active in a number of sports. At the time of his death he was serving as a pharmacist's mate in the United States Navy. Laney was the first ex-pupil from the Home to die in World War II, but he would not be the last. By the end of the war, eight ex-pupils had died in the service of their country. And in time, eight marble benches—provided by the discharge classes of 1942, 1944, 1945 and 1947—would be placed on the parade ground.

> RALPH ASH—killed in action in Belgium
> CARL LAKES—killed in action in Belgium
> DURWARD LANEY—killed in action at Pearl Harbor
> FREDERICK MERRELL—killed in action in Italy
> JOHN MORREL—killed in action on Corregidor
> ANNON YEAZELL—killed in action in Belgium
> JAMES RAMSER—died in service
> WARREN VANDEVIER—died in service

In all, 415 former residents of the Home would serve in World War II. After Coach Stephan re-joined the Marines, other staff members departed for military duty in 1942. Band Director John Rutledge left in March and was replaced by Pearson Bailey of Springfield. In June, George Woerlein returned to the Navy and "Mousie" Eisenhut took his place as coach of the Home's sports teams. J. Robert Rooney, the Home's beloved dramatics teacher, left in July. Superintendent Francis Woodruff announced that he, too, was leaving. Captain Woodruff would serve as

In Christmas of 1887, the Sons of Veterans of Ohio had given a full set of band instruments to the Home. A year later, the band got the gift of uniforms. At this time, it became what many believe to be the first high school band in the country, and if so, the Home had an instrumental music organization, a fife and drum corps even earlier, in 1870.

A half century or so onward, Christmas at the Home had become highly ritualized—and the favorite of most children. There was, for instance, the impressive Christmas breakfast: the dining room was festive with six trees and a large manger scene on the stage, and a tree with what seemed to be a million lights.

Imagine the huge room, with skylights, big enough to seat 700 children. The hall would be darkened and the children filed in carrying lighted candles and singing the Home's own Christmas carol, written by music teacher Sarah Collins and first sung during the Christmas of 1887.

Sometimes, the carolers were joined by returning ex-pupils, and the voices grew in intensity until it seemed as though they would burst through the skylights on their way to heaven.

A music student named Marilyn was moved beyond words. She wished the ceremony could go on forever. On around the room the carolers slowly marched, completing their circle and moving toward the opposite door. Gradually they exited and the music diminished.

"There remained a sort of religious quiet in the dining hall which added to the sadness we felt," she would write years later. "What we had anticipated for so long was over and much too soon…"

And then there was breakfast, a service in the chapel, followed by turkey in the dining hall. After the Christmas Day meal, most of the kids went off to private homes for the rest of the holidays.

On one such Christmas late in the 1940s, the music student named Marilyn was faced with a Christmas dilemma. She had a picture of herself, and she entered into a lengthy debate about whom she would give it to for a Christmas gift.

Maybe Carl? she thought. *Yes, probably Carl. But maybe it should be* Jimmy. *I like*

Jimmy. I like Jimmy a lot. But then I think I like Carl better. I'll give it to Carl.

Back and forth it went in her mind until finally she decided: She would give it to her brother.

Problem solved.

At Thanksgiving of 1949, Mabel Ryan Kilpatrick started a collection to buy an artificial limb for an ex-pupil. She raised $84, and in November, the woman and her husband, who made up the additional amount, went to Fidelity Medical Supply Company in Dayton to be fitted. The woman had her new limb on Christmas.

That was perhaps the oddest Christmas gift connected to the Home, since in most cases, gifts ranged from pen and pencil sets, puzzles, candy and cosmetics, toys, and cork guns.

In 1973, there were as many as sixty Christmas trees on the Home campus—one in every cottage, six in the dining hall, and several outdoors. Many were grown on the Home grounds from seedlings planted by the boys.

There were two Santas on the roof of the administration building, a sleigh in front of the Peter Pan cottages, a lighted fountain, candy wreaths hung on lampposts, and poinsettias from the greenhouse everywhere.

Years afterward, ask almost any ex-pupil about Christmas and watch his or her eyes light up, a reflection of childhood Christmas at the Home.

Mrs. Harris, houseparent, poses under the tree with her Christmas girls, Mary Birkel, Marianne Rickman, and Patty Louthan.

an Army instructor in chemical warfare methods during the war. Upon his return, he became director of the Montgomery County Children's Home before retiring in Lebanon.

Woodruff's successor as the Home's superintendent was Floyd Hartpence, immediate past commander of the American Legion in Ohio. The Morrow County native and Army veteran had spent sixteen years teaching American history and world history at Linden McKinley High School in Columbus after graduating from Ohio State in 1917. Married with two daughters, Hartpence reported for work in October of 1942.

> "We didn't know we weren't supposed to like black people. There were black students there, the same as me, and I didn't know we weren't supposed to like them until I got out and I saw somebody I went to school with. I stopped and talked to him and the girl I was with said, 'What are you talking to him for?' And I said, 'I know him,' and she said, 'Don't you know you're not supposed to do that?' And I said no, I didn't know . . ."
> — Mary Bissey, Class of 1944

Homefront

The U.S. government spent more than $33 billion trying to solve the problems of the Great Depression. It was not enough. But the $330 billion the government spent to fight World War II proved to be an immense economic stimulus that lifted the country out of the abyss. Many existing factories stopped making cars, or radios, or washing machines, and began making war materials. New factories were built. In Ohio, the Parma Tank Plant near Cleveland employed 90,000 people. Curtiss Wright Aviation near Columbus employed 25,000. Large numbers of unemployed people—black and white—would leave rural America and the upper South, in particular, to find new jobs in new industries in the North. It was the greatest mass migration in America since the opening of the Great West. Ohio's cities were populated by recent arrivals from Appalachia. The state became more industrialized and more urban. It also became more racially diverse.

In 1942, Governor John Bricker had received the following petition, signed by approximately eighty people in Cincinnati and Xenia:

The girls of what is believed to be the class of 1945 pose handsomely in front of Hayes Hall, the senior cottage.

1. We beg to call your attention to the fact that in this institution there are three units to which colored children are not admitted: Roosevelt Cottage for last year boys, Hayes Cottage for last year girls, Peter Pan unit for children under ten.

2. We submit that whatever the reason for the maintenance and conduct of these special units, it should apply with equal force to all children.

Unlike many other institutions in the North—and especially across the South—the Ohio Soldiers and Sailors Orphans Home had never excluded black children from admission; if their fathers had served in the military, they were eligible to live at the Home. In fact, the last pupil to leave as a child of a Civil War veteran was Lucinda Dole, an African-American who graduated in 1942—the same year the petition was sent to Governor Bricker. Black children and white children had lived together in the cottages and participated in the same classes and activities since the early days of the Home. But since the early part of the twentieth century, black children had lived apart and had more recently been excluded from the Peter Pan Cottages and the two senior cottages—Roosevelt for boys and Hayes for girls.

It took almost forty years for the South to develop a fully repressive system of legalized segregation that came to be called "Jim Crow." But by 1900, it was well in place. Just as slowly but just as certainly, a de facto system of cultural segregation spread across much of the rest of the country as schools, hospitals, and other institutions were recognized as "separate but equal." Social customs separating white people from black people in restaurants, theaters, and public transportation also evolved. Long-time teacher and wife of Home superintendent, Jane Stephan, recalled an incident from that era. "One time I remember when the team went out someplace and had a football game. Afterwards they stopped on the way home to eat. The waiter said that one boy on our team was black and couldn't eat in the restaurant. He had to come and eat in the kitchen. So he went and ate in the kitchen and some of the rest of them went and ate with him."

The petitioners asked the governor to order a "return to the fine and democratic manner in which this institution was until fairly recently run." But by December of 1944, there was still no change in the housing situation, so a committee from the prominent local African-American institution, Wilberforce University, took up the matter with Superintendent Hartpence. "They are requesting four specific changes, namely, colored children should be admitted to Peter Pan, Roosevelt Hall, Hayes Hall and the beauty culture course," Hartpence informed the Home's board of trustees. "My statement that the colored children are not accepted in those four places because of administrative difficulties was not accepted. . . . We

Lester Anderson
Class of 1956

"Upon arriving at the Home with my five brothers, our heads were shaved and we took a bath. No more walking along the river looking for wood to build a fire in the stove. No more walking out of the house to go to the outhouse. For the first time in my life I had a bed to myself. I loved this strange but wonderful place. Our family status of being poor had suddenly become upper middle class.

"We lived in segregated cottages but the rest of our campus life was totally integrated. We were given a lecture by the older boys who told us how we were expected to react to how whites might treat us. We were to use violence only as a last resort, but we were not to be bullied by anyone. Be tough, they said, stand up for yourselves, but in a nice, gentle way. I guessed this to mean you had to smile while defending yourself.

"There was a game we played: We took turns hitting each other on the shoulder to see how hard a punch we could take without crying out. It helped us in playing sports, as well as adjusting to the pain of living in a segregated country where Negroes were treated as second-class citizens. Being in the Home lessened this reality.

"Xenia was a segregated city, just as all of America was: Negroes on one end of town, whites on the other end. Many stores in the downtown did not permit the Negro to shop or eat at their facilities. Certain parts of town were off-limits to us. The Home was not the real world, Xenia was.

"Most of the prejudice at the Home came from the older students and supervisors, a result of how they were brought up. It scared them to see that Negroes were as smart—or smarter—than they were. As the older students left and younger kids replaced them, the prejudice eased. By the early 1950s, there was very little prejudice at the Home. In spite of the racial turmoil outside the Home, the Home kids got along with each other amazingly well.

"The group living was an absolute positive influence on my life. I accepted the fact that no matter how smart I was, how good I was at sports, how much I tried to please, there would always be someone who hated my guts simply because of the color of my skin. I did not let this bother me. Life would go on without their love.

"Life at the OSSO Home was ahead of the outside public. We were all living, working, and playing under the same rules. With the Negro as part of the Home teams, the Home was dominant in sports.

Lester Anderson: "It was almost like a country club...."

1956

195

When one team refused to play us because we had Negro players, we simply reloaded the bus, turned around, and headed home. I admired the Negro athletes who got up before breakfast to go to the track to exercise or practice. Sometimes they'd sneak out after curfew to run the track.

"Most of the public looked at the Home children as poor orphan kids. Most of us were from poor backgrounds and broken homes, but in reality we had more than most of the kids outside the Home. The Home was wonderfully structured, based on a military theme while still maintaining a family atmosphere. It was almost like a country club. The Home was also a showcase of everything that was right about integration. Racially motivated altercations were rare, and the daily interrelationships at school, work, and play helped both Negro and whites realize that we were all the same.

"And all of us were blessed to have been part of the big family known as The Ohio Soldiers' and Sailors' Orphans' Home."

Here's a photograph of some of the Home cadets from school year 1955-1956, looking trim and fit.

parted on apparently friendly terms, but with the committee indicating that it might be necessary for them to take their case to the newspapers. . . . My contention hinged upon the word 'discrimination.' I maintained that we were using different definitions of the word, but was unable to convince them that my definition was the correct one."

No further action was taken by the Wilberforce committee, leaving the issue unresolved—for the time being.

Meanwhile, the Home continued to cope with changes caused by the war. Staff members found many items in short supply after rationing was introduced in 1942 to ensure that critical supplies were made available to the armed services. Sulfa and penicillin were almost impossible to obtain, as was silk. Gasoline, rubber tires, sugar, and coffee were heavily rationed. The 1943 reunion of the Association of Ex-Pupils was only permitted to go forward with the understanding that each returning ex-pupil family would be asked to bring a pound of coffee, a pound of butter, and a pound of sugar.

Americans held scrap drives during the war years to provide finished metal to the metal products industries. The OSSO Home gathered fourteen tons of scrap metal in 1942, arranging the material in a "V" for victory in front of the Grant Hall administration building. To further aid the war effort, the board re-invested the Home's guardianship funds. Most, but not all, of the children admitted to the Home over the years had been legally placed under the guardianship of the institution. Many arrived with some amount of money, which was placed in a savings account until they left the home. Rather than continue to keep the money in a local bank, the board used the funds to buy war bonds that were given to the children when they graduated.

Under "Mousie" Eisenhut, the football, basketball, and track teams continued their winning ways. The Cadet football team went undefeated in 1943 for the third straight season and extended its winning streak to twenty-six games. The track team, which won three consecutive state championships from 1940 to 1942, would place among the top five teams at the state meets throughout the 1940s. But as the war dragged on, the loss of staff and pupils to military service began to be felt in the Home's athletic program and its "golden age" of sports slowly came to an end. After the Navy called Coach Eisenhut to active duty in March of 1944, Frank Higham of Chagrin Falls was hired to coach the sports teams. Higham, a Bowling Green graduate, had recently been discharged from the Army.

Some aspects of Home life remained unchanged.

The boys went on their annual Thanksgiving rabbit hunt in 1942. "Throughout

The long view in the deeps of another Ohio winter. The savvy Home boy—on the cottage porch at left—could give pointers to the others as to where heat might lurk in an Ohio February.

The Home's teen hangout was the Orfenz Den, where in this candid snapshot Roger Hill and Sarah Smart test their feet on what appears to be a slow number.

the Thanksgiving vacation, a visitor to the Home would not have missed seeing groups or gangs of boys armed to the teeth with clubs, a handful of rocks or even sling shots," reported the *Home Review*. "Upon inquiring just what they were doing and where they were going, the visitor would be told that this was hunting season and they were going out to try their luck. . . . One person stopped a group of boys and asked them what fun they got out of hunting with a club. They also asked if they ever caught anything. The answer they got was something like this: 'When we run across a guy with a good gun and a dog but no rabbits, well, we get a big kick out of it. We also get a lot of fun out of trying to outsmart the rabbit and run it down.'

In October of 1943, a chapter of the Grande Voiture of the 40 & 8—a service society of World War I veterans—donated money for prizes and refreshments for the annual Halloween Party. "The Peter Pan boys and girls besides participating in the parade, had parties of their own, complete with donuts, cider and apples. Ghosts, tramps, Hawaiian girls, zoot suiters, prisoners and many others crowded the floor of the auditorium Saturday, October 30, to enjoy a dance which was open to all boys and girls of 14 and over. . . . The Home Orchestra, the 'Starvation Stooges,' furnished music for the occasion." The 40 & 8 provided more prizes and refreshments on the Saturday after Thanksgiving as the children played games in the afternoon and an evening dance for those 14 and older was held in the auditorium.

In May of 1943, Lieutenant Governor Paul Herbert returned to dedicate the new school building whose cornerstone he helped lay a few years earlier. "What a splendid tradition this school has," Herbert said. "What a fine list of successful men and women has graduated from this school. . . . No school anywhere has a tradition such as this one. The leadership of the world, of whatever quality it may be, has taken care of the future of this school. World War II has taken care of that. And the State of Ohio will not fail in its obligation to the fathers in this war. The tendency is for people soon to forget the obligations toward the veterans of a war. The State of Ohio will not forget its obligations to those men and their children."

In December of 1944, just as the lieutenant governor promised, the Home received a visit from the Ohio Postwar Planning Commission, looking into possible changes and improvements to the campus to accommodate children after the war. The number of pupils at the Home had declined during World War II and now stood at 478, but the Xenia institution could easily handle up to 750. And with new cottages, two new dormitories, and a new grade school building, perhaps as many as 1,500 children could be boarded there. The Planning Commission submitted an ambitious plan to outgoing Governor John Bricker and his successor, Governor-elect Frank Lausche, recommending that the state build an entire new campus for fourth, fifth and sixth graders and spend approximately $4 million for new construction as well as rehabilitation and repair of existing facilities.

Some of the high school boys at the Home apparently had postwar plans of their own. With Mr. Higham in charge, they opened a club called the "Orfenz Den" in the basement of the main building. "This club will be similar to those that have been formed in many other communities throughout the country to give high school boys and girls a place to get together and find recreation," reported the *Home Review.* "Those in other places have adopted such names as 'student center' and 'hangout.' It is open to all boys fifteen years of age and over and each boy has to have a membership card for which a charge of fifty cents is made. The boys are not to come stag and there is no smoking in the rooms. They also have to put in ten hours of work each on the Den."

The Orfenz Den, with its booths and a juke box, would become an institution within the institution. "[It was] a place to meet with girls and have a soda, candy bar, popcorn or some snack," recalled the ex-pupil Edward Michael, "but usually you went to meet with your girlfriend. You could dance, but I had two left feet." Long-time teacher and school principal Em Whilding saw a change in relations between the Home's boys and girls after the Orfenz Den opened. "One time there was just no contact, period. Boys stayed on their side and girls stayed on their side.

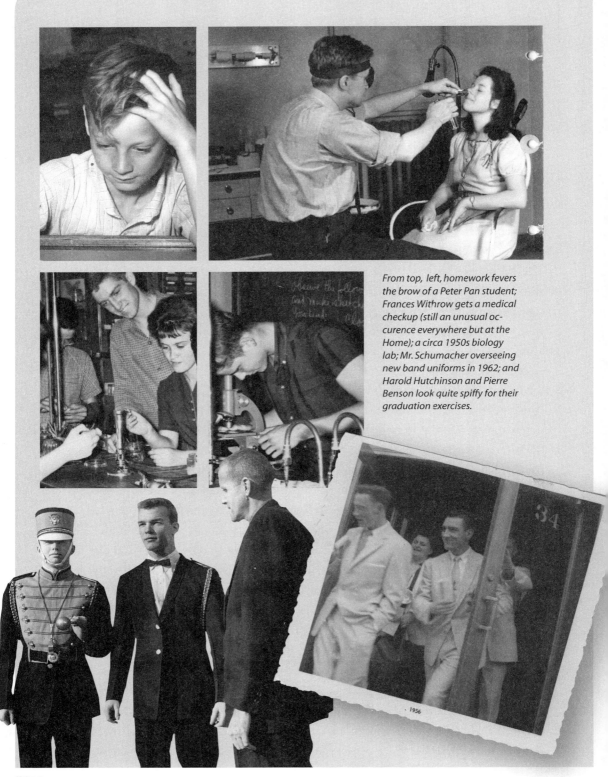

From top, left, homework fevers the brow of a Peter Pan student; Frances Withrow gets a medical checkup (still an unusual occurence everywhere but at the Home); a circa 1950s biology lab; Mr. Schumacher overseeing new band uniforms in 1962; and Harold Hutchinson and Pierre Benson look quite spiffy for their graduation exercises.

Ruth Beyer Long
Class of 1942

"When we were seniors, we went to Hayes Hall and Florence Melvin was our supervisor. This gives you a little idea of Melvy's flexibility with the senior girls: My roommate, Shirley Bruce, and I went to a movie in town one afternoon and on the way back, we passed a grocery store and Shirley said, 'Let's get a can of beer.'

"So we went in and bought some cigarettes and a beer. We came home, we tucked the beer under the heater in our room. Saturday night after the show in the auditorium and all the other girls had gone to bed, we slipped into Melvy's room and said, 'Melvy, we brought you something…'

"We went in the kitchen, opened that warm beer, and it went all over the kitchen. What was left, mostly bubbles, we divided up and drank it with Melvy. It tasted terrible, and then she lit up a cigarette with us, and she wasn't horrified, she satisfied our curiosity, and she did it with us.

"The next day, we spent all Sunday afternoon after church scrubbing down the kitchen to get the beer smell out…"

In front of Hayes Hall in 1953, Miss McConnell and Miss Melvin show off Sweetie Pie, another well-fed Home bedfellow.

Then things relaxed. . . . They could date on weekends. . . . They could go down in the Den and maybe [play] a jukebox, radio or records, and they could dance. . . ."

The children took a hayride into town and joined the spontaneous celebration after the Japanese surrendered in August of 1945. George Laypoole remembered "dancing and yelling in the streets until midnight."

In the spring of 1948, Joe Morris, former pupil wrote to say that, no, he had not married. Explained Morris, "No gal ever proposed and promised to protect and provide for me till death do us part. I am a very unselfish person, you see, so how could I select one gem from so many? Polygamy is illegal, therefore I decided I could not deprive some fine gal of a wonderful husband so I started running and drifting. . . ."

The Home after the War (1945-1950)

After four years of war and a decade of economic depression, many people felt the last half of the decade would be a time of unmitigated peace and prosperity. They were wrong. Jobs were scarce in the late 1940s. Positions either had been eliminated as war-time production ended or had been filled by people who sought work during the conflict, such as "Rosie the Riveter." Most of the women had left the industrial work force, but some still remained on the job. Ohio, though, was a good place to be in the years following the war. Its economy had improved significantly and for the first time in a generation, workers were optimistic about their future prospects. Under the GI Bill of Rights, returning veterans went back to school and earned high school diplomas and college degrees.

The Home had proceeded with plans for a massive, unprecedented expansion under the assumption that hundreds, if not thousands, of children would be left in need as a result of the hundreds of thousands of soldiers killed or disabled in action overseas. But state legislators balked at the $4 million investment in the institution recommended by the Postwar Planning Commission, so the board of trustees trimmed their request to $1 million for "additions and betterments," with the money to be used to replace the old cottages with ten double cottages, a new auditorium, and steam and utility tunnels connecting the facilities. Confident that lawmakers would make the funds available, the board dispatched Superintendent

No one felt much like sleeping on V-J Day, when Japan surrendered and the war finally ended. The kids celebrated with a hayride into town.

Hartpence to Pennsylvania and Michigan in the summer of 1945 to visit large children's homes in search of new ideas and better ways of providing care.

These preparations, however, turned out to be a bit premature. The first World War II orphans arrived at the Home in March, 1946, in the persons of Anna May Leach and Arlene, Glenn, and Kenneth Pearson. They soon would be followed by more children, but not as many as expected. A lot of families and individuals who might have been desperate for help in hard times did not need any assistance in the booming postwar economy. Aid to Families with Dependent Children also offered an alternative to losing one's children, and local social service organizations were more certain than ever that foster care was superior to institutional care for the average child in need. Thus the fiscally conservative Ohio General Assembly and Democratic Governor Frank Lausche, who was as tight as most Republicans, decided to approve the reconstruction of the Home but at a slower pace than proposed.

The board selected Dan Carmichael as the project's architect. Carmichael reported in September of 1947 that water from nearby Lake McDowell was draining into the basement of the new auditorium. Perhaps remembering that yet another child had drowned in Lake McDowell in May, the trustees approved Carmichael's request to drain the basin. "The lake has been drained," reported the *Home Review* in October, "and its future is in doubt. . . . The valves were opened on September 25 to let out the water. On the 29th, state game officials, headed by Elwood Stroup, district game commissioner, began taking out the fish. . . . Thousands of small blue gills, catfish and sun fish were removed and taken to the hatchery. . . . Also taken from the lake were several large catfish and black bass up to fifteen inches in length. The largest bass weighed 3¾ pounds."

Ex-Pupil O. E. Hacker remembered the lake and the winter fun:

How about sledding on the hill and the skating on the gas pond, the creek and the lake behind the school? Remember the fine sleds we used to make by taking a tongue and grooved piece of flooring for runners, turning the grooved side down, curving the front and putting a piece of quarter-inch rod in the groove. It was a simple matter to put a floor on top. With a piece of rope to pull it we had a good sled that would hold three or four kids piled on top of each other. We "belly-gutted" down the hill from the water tower to the falls at the end of the creek.

We remember how Jim Wones and his gang cut ice on the lake and stored it in the ice house which stood at the edge of the lake. Skating on the "rubber ice" was a thrill too. I guess it's a sign of old age when we reminisce about the good times we had when we were kids. We kids at the Home were doubly blessed as we had a lot of good times and friends.

The board suggested in 1947 that Lake McDowell might be refilled, but the basin eventually was plowed and planted with grass.

As the new buildings neared completion in October of 1948, the trustees named the high school after Woodrow Wilson and the cottages after American presidents Monroe, Taft, Jackson, Madison, Harrison, Harding, Garfield, Cleveland, Adams, and Jefferson. The auditorium, which would be dedicated on May 8, 1949—the fourth anniversary of the end of World War II—was described in detail in the *Home Review*.

"[It] is a fireproof building of modern design. The arrangement of 844 seats and the inclined floor give the audience a clear view of the stage. The large windows on each side of the building will be equipped with curtains to permit the showing of motion pictures during daylight hours. The basement is designed to serve as a recreation center. Plans to move the Orfenz Den to this location are under

Donna Meadows
Class of 1957

"I went to the Home when I was 4. The first thing I remember about the Home was looking out of the window at the hospital at night and seeing all the lights on at the big building next door. I remember thinking, *I'm gonna go see if they know where my mother and daddy are.* So I walked over there, it was Mr. Hartpence's house, the superintendent. He told me later that he opened the door and there I was, this little girl, barefooted, in pajamas, from the hospital. 'Who on earth are you?' he said. And I said, 'I'm Donna and I wanna go with my mother.'

"I didn't remember anything after that, but it was a big thing for me, seeing that big house, and I thought, *I bet my mother and dad's in that big place over there and they aren't letting me see them…*

"From the hospital, I could see the kids from Peter Pan playing on the swings. I thought, *Wow, that looks nice.* And then they took me down there, Peter Pan 6. Mrs. Hilty was the head of it. She was a little midget. I'd never seen anything like that before, and I just thought she was my friend, my playmate. She got all these kids in their boots and told me, 'Just sit there in your locker, I'll be right with you, Donna.' These kids all had to go to school. So off they went and I was so excited, I was going to see all these kids every day, and I had a new little friend. She talked almost as much as I did, and she said, 'We're going to have to get you sheets,' and I remember that she was going to get me this and get me that. And she says, 'Now it's time for you to lie down,' and I didn't pay any attention to her because I thought she was just one of the kids. She wasn't much bigger than me, and she was trying to

get me to take a nap. Well, there was no way I was going to take a nap when she's up. She told me later I ran her ragged: 'Let's do this, let's do this…' I was into everything, and banging on the piano.

"Then the kids came through the door and she was saying, 'Hang up your coats where they belong and don't forget to put your mittens over here so they dry, take your boots and turn them upside down…' She was talking individually to different ones and they were all paying attention to her, and they were saying, 'Yes, Ms. Hilty, yes, m'am.'

"And my fun was over. Suddenly, I knew this was not my little playmate. This person was in charge. Then she turned around and said, 'I'm Ms. Hilty, now see how these children listen? That's how you'll listen. Now, do you understand, Donna?'

And I did. 'Yes,' I said.

Supervisors Hilty and Armstrong on the steps of Pan 6 in 1951.

"And that was it. My little friend was gone and here was this supervisor who was nice, and I loved her…

"I remember most the clean beds, because before I came to the Home I slept on a roof. There was a roof that went out one side of the house and we kids slept out there because my parents would fight and they pushed us out the window so we wouldn't hear.

"Dad coughed and coughed, from being gassed. My sisters and I would go get my mother out of this place where she would sing and dance on the bar. She was always in and out of jail, and I was in this little crib and Daddy was reading the newspaper and he was coughing and coughing.

"I was waiting for him to finish coughing and he went off the side of the bed, and I never saw him again. My mother is in jail, I am in my crib and can't get out, and I'm crying, Where did my dad go? I couldn't see on the other side of the bed where he rolled. He had a massive heart attack, and after my brother Bill came home from school, everything was chaos. I don't remember anymore about that part of my life. Then I remember only being at the Home, and it was clean, and I had my own clean bed.

The kids of Miss McKenzie's fifth grade geography class were locally famous for writing Clark Gable, who sent them fruit from his California ranch. This is one of her third grade classes.

consideration. Recreation equipment, including ping pong tables, will be provided and a pit has been built for the installation of bowling alleys." (As they had done in the past, veterans organizations came to the Home's assistance, purchasing new pianos and motion picture equipment for the auditorium.)

Governor Lausche was invited to the dedication, but had to decline at the last moment and was represented by his wife and Carl Smith, commander of the Ohio Department of the American Legion. In his remarks, Smith praised both the Home and the new building. "This is a beautiful auditorium in one of the outstanding schools in the country. So long as the children of this country receive the type of training they receive here, our form of government is secure." Ohio's first lady spoke directly to the children of the Home. "This world will soon be your world, and you will soon be running it. You can add so much to it if you use the training you are getting here."

The Home began to return to normal after the war. Several former instructors and coaches returned from their military jobs in 1946, including George Woerlein, "Mousie" Eisenhut, J. Robert Rooney, and Perry Swindler. Coach Woerlein returned to his coaching position in March, but left after four months to pursue other opportunities and was replaced by Eisenhut. Swindler's return was short-lived as well; he stepped down as head of military instruction in August, replaced by his former assistant, Herman Gill. Rooney was back for good, however, after a one-year stint at the University of Vermont as an instructor in public speaking. Here's how a *Home Review* contributor and several of Rooney's pupils portrayed the popular dramatics instructor:

"Show the audience your face. Now don't steal the scene." These are the same to Mr. J. Robert Rooney, the Home's dramatic teacher, as milk and sugar are to us. Why? Because in a personal interview "Bob" (as he is called on the Home grounds) said, "Acting has always meant a great deal to me since I was doing plays in backyards, charging two pins for admission."

As a writer, he has written approximately twenty-four plays, one of which was a centennial pageant for the State School for the Blind. He also wrote a couple for the Columbus Players Club. He had two presented on the radio. The rest have been written while he has been at the Home and several of them have been given by the students here.

All of us have our habits, but most of us only tell the good ones. Mr. Rooney was asked, not about good habits, but what his worst one is. In reply he said, "My worst habit is losing my temper." Well naturally I asked him how he was trying to break it.

He then made the unwavering jest, "Who said I was going to quit?" I'll bet some of the students in the Home wish he would change his mind.

Marilyn Mercer on her former teacher: "I think I learned more from [Mr. Rooney] about life in general because he was just a kind man. He taught English and he taught math. But you know, if you didn't understand it, he took the time to tell you. And if you had something you wanted to talk about, he would listen and you could always talk to him."

Ken Carpenter: "I was in drama probably from the time I was in the seventh grade until I graduated. We put on plays and he was very strict with us. You really had to learn the thing. He taught English and Literature and Drama and he put on all the plays. He was a great leader in that area. His programs were strong. And often, the Home did well in statewide competition for short plays."

The Neighbors, a one-act play given by Rooney's young dramatists in 1947, won first place at state that year and was the only school production to receive

In the late 1940s, budding student starlets such as Miss Ramona Hill brought recognition to the Home.

a "superior" rating. Two actors, Lee Carter and Ramona Hill, received certificates for their performances. Other cast members included Milford Isaacs, Barbara Ensor, Wilhelmina Balside, Thelma Plummer, Rose Meadows, and Minnie Bennett.

"The play deals with several families in a neighborhood, and their efforts to help each other as well as others in need," explained the *Home Review*. "A romance is brought in between a pretty daughter played by Thelma Plummer and a shy suitor played by Lee Carter."

The Cadet band, under the direction of Mr. Schumacher, also earned a "superior" rating in the Ohio district contest in Columbus. "The Home band played 'Aurora Overture' by Yoder, the 'Footlifter March' by Fillmore and

The young actors of the Home won state honors for this play, "I Shall be Waiting."

The maestro of the Home stage, Mr. Rooney, bringing back more hardware.

'Sohrab and Justum' by Johnson," reported the *Home Review*. "The judges praised the band as being the best on the stage that day."

An all-girls orchestra was formed in March of 1947. The Home also revived the annual high school class trips and resumed a few of the popular vocational classes that had been discontinued or scaled back during the war, including driver's training, cooking for boys, home mechanics for girls, and a course in social relations for all freshman boys. (The purpose of the social relations class was to teach "proper social procedure on the dance floor, at meals, at home and elsewhere.")

The Ohio Board of Education examined the Home's education program in early 1949 and found it up to par. "Few have achieved as much as this school has—both in the academic and the vocational," said the state supervisor.

The end of the decade also became the end of an era as the few remaining Civil War veterans gathered in Alliance, Ohio, in July, 1949, for what would be their last encampment. One final time, the Cadet band played for the men who founded the Ohio Soldiers and Sailors Orphans Home in 1870 and supported it over the next eight decades. A few months later, Lieutenant Colonel Herman Gill convinced the Home to invest in new uniforms of blue and gray.

> Come on you kids, get ready,
> Perry and James and Teddie,
> Bass section, clarinet, drums and fife,
> Watch the downbeat, play for your life . . .
> —Fred Engle's ode to the band

Old Values and New — The Home from 1950 to 1963

The Fifties began with Americans involved in another foreign conflict, this time on the Korean peninsula. The fighting lasted three years and among the casualties were two ex-pupils—William Steele and Ralph Littler—both killed in action in 1951.

Back at the Home, the girls' physical education department put on their annual water show in March of 1951—a show that surely would have shocked their forebears. "As daylight slowly fades into the horizon and the calm of night settles over the peaceful world," said the program description, "we see eight girls swimming to the forever haunting strains of 'Serenade in Blue.' . . . For this number the girls were dressed in blue bathing suits with pink plastic ruffling and flowers."

The forebears might have been even more flabbergasted by the recommendation of the Medical Advisory Board in April that a proposed program of sex education "disseminate most efficiently the correct information and guidance about a very basic aspect of living that should not be left to chance. . . . Mere regulations governing boy-girl relationships cannot be effective in raising the moral standards of children unless a sane and sound educational program is effected."

The board of trustees decided that no cottage could have a television of its

Memorial Day
a recollection by Marilyn Flickinger

"The muted drums, muffled and monotonous, leading. Next, the Color Guard. Then Mr. Hartpence, the Home superintendent. Other dignitaries and ex-pupils follow at a respectful distance. Then two little girls in white dresses carrying the traditional *Lest We Forget* banner. So began the annual Memorial Day parade.

"Like a ballet, everyone was in an assigned place. Next came the Home Cadet Band and the companies of the Cadet Battalion in their smart uniforms, marching in a much-practiced and slow-motion cadence. The procession moved slowly in front of Woodrow Wilson High School, past the girls' cottages, the parade grounds, the main building, the museum, the bandshell, and on toward Collier Chapel and the cemetery.

"Suddenly the band, alert to the bandleader's silent gestures, began to play the dirge-like music. The sound carried back along the parade route and ascended up into the threatening sky. Was that thunder or merely the rumbling drums?

"The battalions of cadets separated to line both sides of the road approaching the chapel, their rifles at parade rest. Contingents of older girls in their white dresses marched in perfect step, four abreast, between the lines. Then came the companies of little children, boy and girl partners. The boys wore white pants, white shirts, and black ties, carrying small American flags on their right shoulders. The little girls, wearing white dresses and white shoes, carried metal baskets that held beautiful, fragrant peonies. (They were grown in a field behind the Barnett Trades Building for just this purpose.) The baskets were made especially with points on the bottoms so they could be pressed firmly in the ground and still stand upright. Miss McKenzie, who choreographed the parade, cast a nervous glance at the darkening sky.

"On and on, with measured step to the solemn music, the participants made their way to their destination— the cemetery behind Collier Chapel. This was the annual Memorial Day parade at the OSSO Home, one of the most poignant and meaningful of all its traditions. Around to the back of the chapel everyone marched, dignitaries, speakers, choir, the cadet band and cadet battalions. At a signal from the bandleader, the drums became quiet and an expectant hush fell over all.

"A prayer was followed by a recitation of the Gettysburg Address, and one of *In Flander's Fields*. Someone important gave a speech that brought tears from many of the adults. The choir sang *Lest We Forget*.

"Then it was time for the special part we were all anticipating. As the drums again performed the muffled drum roll, the children moved slowly and carefully up the little grade into the cemetery, the girls on one side of the graves and the boys opposite. We stood expectantly. Then we sang the haunting strains of music for which I can no longer recall all the words.

These are but a token
They are cherished still:
Who in sleep unbroken
These narrow houses fill…

"The little girls pushed their baskets

Perhaps it was because almost everyone participated in the careful ceremony that was Memorial Day at the Home, but for whatever reason, the observances carried a particular resonance that most of them never forgot.

of peonies into the soil beside the graves and the little boys placed their flags on the opposite side. The music went on to its conclusion, and before we knew it, we were processing in an orderly fashion to the chapel, away from the hundreds of fluttering flags and the fragrance of the flowers. At the door, we were met with the trumpet introduction to the hymn, *God of Our Fathers*, and with goose pimples, we took our seats.

"Miss McKenzie looked on with quiet satisfaction. Another poignant tradition observed with respect, dignity—and no rain. I knew some of the people who now lie in cemetery behind Collier Chapel. Ruthie Meadows, a classmate, Smokey Holmes who died too young and my brother's good friend, and Mousie Eisen-hut, the Home boys' coach.

"Memorial Day never passes but that I remember how we observed this special occasion from my childhood.

Here's another view of Memorial Day, an almost ethereally ghostly shot of the Home's young ladies wending their way through the trees.

The girls of 1955 on Hayes Hall steps: Roberta Todd, Rose Kantz, Marlene Weber, Marjorie Telatco, Lucinda Massie, Audrey Flick, Amanda Keith, and Geraldine Miller.

own until TVs were available to all of the cottages, but throughout the Fifties, the children would see their world changing through the newspapers, films, music, and styles of dress. Profound demographic change, of course, came with the passage of the National Interstate and Defense Highways Act of 1956, which led to the development of a $300 billion highway system that people used to travel to new homes in suburban subdivisions near America's larger cities, segregating rich from poor, young from old, and black from white.

Veterans organizations had always been strong supporters of the OSSO Home. Now, with the institution nurturing a new generation of children in the wake of World War II, groups like the Grande Voiture of the 40 & 8 began to fade into the background. The Ohio chapters of the Grande Voiture sought a permanent home for an automotive replica of the boxcar for forty men or eight horses that gave the organization its name after World War I and was told by the board of trustees that they could keep the boxcar at the Home if they so desired. In June of 1953, Dorothy Hertzler became the last child of a United Spanish War veteran to graduate from the Home.

The American Legion and the Veterans of Foreign Wars—the largest of current veterans organizations—maintained their close ties with the Home and participated in many of the annual events, holidays and events on campus. They also continued to lend their support when obstinate legislatures or governors occasionally delayed or withheld funding for the Home. After the new auditorium was completed, the VFW provided new motion picture equipment for the facility.

The Home also remained closely associated with the regular army. Although the boys did not wear uniforms all the time as they once had, the battalion and the band still practiced regularly and received high marks in the annual military inspection. In 1956, the rifle team won the Hearst Trophy for the seventh time since 1933 as the best team in the Second United States Army area.

A strong windstorm passed through Xenia in September of 1952. It didn't cause any major structural damage at the Home, but more than forty trees—some of them older than the institution itself—were blown down and had to be removed. Although new trees were planted, the campus was not as green as it was before Mother Nature's pruning.

The board convinced the Ohio General Assembly that McKinley Gymnasium needed to be remodeled and that new housing was needed for some of the Home's staff, but the legislature only provided about half of the funds requested for the construction project. The trustees proceeded with the repairs to the gymnasium, but the staff housing would not be completed for more than a decade.

The Home began to lose its economy of scale during the Fifties. Built to house and educate as many as 750 children, the institution had accommodated more than 900 at various times. Now those numbers were declining as more families were able to keep their children at home with government support, other institutions became more acceptable, and foster care was increasingly promoted by the social service sector. In 1940, the Home cared for 673 children and spent, on average, $608.67 per child. In 1950, there were 415 children in residence and the average cost per child was $1,798.99. By 1960, the Home's population hadn't changed much, but the average cost per child was $2,975.83.

There were several reasons for the higher cost of care. Trained, experienced staff members were paid higher salaries. Inflation drove up the price of food, clothing and other supplies, as well as the costs of construction and maintenance. The most significant cost factor, though, was the dwindling number of children at the Home. The governor, the state's lawmakers, and other political leaders looked at the cost per child, saw that it was higher than reported by other children's homes, and became more cautious in their funding, especially after 1957 when the country slid into a recession that lasted for several months.

The staff and trustees of the Home had been planning to build a new junior high residential campus for fourth through sixth graders since the end of World War II. It would be 1956, however, before the first unit—Taylor Hall—was completed. The second unit—Washington Hall—opened in 1962. Part of the reason for the delay was the board's decision to spend more than $600,000 in the late 1950s to build a new heating system for the Home. But there were also concerns about the economic efficiency of the institution. And there was controversy.

"If you were good and had some money, you could apply for a town pass and there was a theater downtown called the Orpheum, and I thought it was the theater for orphans." — Minnie Jordan, Class of 1957

Defining Discrimination

Home officials had confronted the issue of racial separation on several previous occasions, always contending that there was no discrimination in the institution's admission process and that all of the children took the same classes, attended the same events, and participated in the same activities. There had been no housing segregation in its early years, but since the turn of the century, as the Home began admitting more black children and the North and South became increasingly racially segregated, black boys and girls had been quartered in separate cottages—a practice the board and superintendent did not consider to be discriminatory.

Protests began in the 1930s after the new Peter Pan and Senior Discharge cottages were built, but the hot-button issue then had been the integration of the small children and graduating pupils—not the continuing residential segregation of blacks and whites on the main campus. When the Wilberforce committee raised the issue of separate cottages with Home administrators in 1944, both parties had agreed to disagree and little was heard publicly about the matter until a new generation of black leadership emerged following the war. Largely educated in the historically black colleges and universities and closely tied to the religious mainstream of black America, the new leaders began to take forceful action for change. In 1948, President Truman ordered the desegregation of the armed forces and the U.S. Supreme Court declared racially restrictive covenants in real estate sales to be unconstitutional. In 1954, the concept of "separate but equal" education was found to be unconstitutional as well.

As the Civil Rights movement began to make itself felt across much of America in the early Fifties, a lady named Ruby Pettiford sat down at the Ohio Soldiers and Sailors Orphans Home on August 25, 1952, and wrote a letter to Frank Lausche, seeking an audience with the governor:

After expressing my appreciation of the splendid and fair administration you are giving us, I wish to ask a favor. I have for almost eight years been supervisor of the Negro girls at this home. During this entire period there has existed a grossly unjust condition of a discriminatory nature that is depriving the Negro girls of the much needed training to prepare them for responsibility when they are discharged. . . . May I have an appointment with you this week if possible?"

Lausche was well into the third of his five terms in the Ohio governor's office. A fiscally conservative Democrat, he had a reputation as no-nonsense, law-and-order advocate and supporter of a strong national defense. He also had been a war-time mayor of Cleveland and understood, quite well, that the large numbers of black Americans now living in Ohio as a result of war-time economic growth were a political block not to be ignored. In the left-hand column of Ruby Pettiford's letter, Lausche simply wrote, "Yes."

After their meeting in August, 1952, Pettiford continued to correspond with the governor. On June 24, 1953, Lausche sent her a copy of a letter he had sent to the president of the board of trustees of the Home. In it he said, "You do understand that by the spirit of our government, we are obligated to give equality of treatment to the wards entrusted to the care of our state. We cannot ask the people to be considerate and free from racial prejudices if the governmental agencies do not adopt that concept of life."

After no change was forthcoming, Pettiford addressed another letter to the governor. On September 14, 1953, Lausche's secretary wrote back, stating that "the Governor will not attempt to impose his judgment upon that of the Board of Trustees and the persons in charge."

As Ruby Pettiford stepped aside, a number of other people stepped forward. In February, 1954, the Woman's Culture Club of Xenia sent Lausche a petition signed by twenty-four of its members, asking the governor to "take some action . . . relative to the segregation in Hayes Hall, Roosevelt Hall and the Peter Pan Cottages." Between the months of March and May, the governor's office received twenty copies of the same petition signed by 244 people in southwest Ohio representing social, religious and public service organizations.

Edward Michael
Class of 1958

"The day my brother and I came to the Home was a cold, rainy, dreary day. We were too confused to ask questions. We were in this ward and there were no toys and we can't go outside and play. All we could do was sit on the chairs and cry, hoping things would get better because to this point it had not been one of our best days.

"About suppertime, a girl came to ask what we wanted for supper. I remember how pretty and nice she was. She hugged me and told me things would get better. She and another girl brought supper to my brother and me and sat with us. She said she was a student at the Home, just like we were, and that working at the hospital was her chore.

She came to our room that night and tucked us into bed. She said she would be back the next morning, and I stayed up all night to make sure she came back.

"How kind she was to us during our two weeks of quarantine! She explained the quarantine, and she told us about the school, and made sure we had a radio. I have always remembered her name—Ramona Tabor. When she graduated I cried because I could no longer see her.

"I spent a year in Peter Pan 1 and couldn't wait until I got to the main campus. There, you learned fast that you were on the bottom of the totem pole. The older boys ran the campus and the pecking order was established on the main campus. It was determined by a fistfight by the water tower.

"You would challenge, or be challenged, by a person about your age and then you fought. If you lost, you were one step lower than the winner. If you won, you challenged the next person and so forth. By the time you got out of the sixth grade, the pecking order was established, and you just went about your business.

"When school was not in session and we didn't have a work detail, we sneaked off campus, to town, and played around in the junkyard at the viaduct, or went up to the farm and played in the haymow. We had to be back by 3 p.m., and we ran the dean of men crazy trying to catch us.

"The game was between the employees and the kids. If you attempted to sneak back on campus by the regular routes, you usually got caught. If you came through the woods by the farm, then acted like you were coming from the farm, you were okay.

"Detention meant you didn't get to see the Saturday night movie. I didn't see a movie for about five years. I was always on detention. I had a cottage supervisor named Harriet Miller and we didn't see eye-to-eye. She would tell me to clean my room, I slopped my way through and left, then she gave me demerits. Ole Harriet issued the demerits by 20 and 25, and you had to work them off doing chores for 10 or 15. I didn't have to take my shoes off for that kind of math. I was *never* going to work off my demerits. That's why I became a good ballplayer; if I was on a team, I was going to get off campus. To this day, I don't see too many movies.

"I never understood what ole Harriet was trying to teach me until I went to college. Any business student knew about the law of diminishing returns. Ole Harriet had been trying to teach me the law of diminishing returns...."

Another concert in the Home's band shell, always an occasion, for how many kids lived in a house that had an outdoor concert amphitheatre in the backyard?

*H*A *ome* of their own

In August, a committee of representatives from the NAACP and the Veterans of Foreign Wars met with a representative of Governor Lausche and informed him that that the Home's board of trustees "had not acted to eliminate segregation." Seemingly unable to move Home officials to take further action but also unwilling to order changes, Lausche took a different approach. On September 16, 1954, he appointed L. Pearl Mitchell to the board. The daughter of a former president of Wilberforce University and graduate of the historically African-American school, Mitchell had worked in Cleveland as a probation officer for a number of years until her retirement for health reasons. In 1923, she joined the Cleveland NAACP and led protests against discrimination in the city's schools and public housing projects, eventually becoming a national vice president of the NAACP in 1959. According to the minutes of her first board meeting, "Miss Mitchell called the attention of the Board to various statements made to her in the matter of racial segregation. The other members of the board assured her that they did not know of any instances whatsoever. . . . They invited Miss Mitchell to make a complete investigation."

Investigate, Miss Mitchell did. The minutes from the February, 1955, meeting stated that she "asked the board to consider her request that the complete integration of colored and white children in living quarters be started by moving eligible children into Peter Pan and the Senior cottages. After full and careful discussion of the question, considering it from all angles, the board voted to make no change at this time. Miss Mitchell is recorded as dissenting from this decision."

Over the next eighteen months Mitchell appealed to the other board members to begin the process of racial integration in the Home's living quarters. At the same time, she was in frequent communication with Governor Lausche. On July 31, 1956, Lausche sent a letter to each trustee, stating, "It is not enough to have equal but separate quarters. That practice does not conform with what the Supreme Court of the United States declared the Constitution of our country to mean."

On September 14, "the Board by unanimous action directed that all children eight years of age and under, and children over eight years to the extent of the availability of rooms, to be housed on the junior campus consisting of Peter Pan and Taylor A & B. . . ."

Lausche responded with a letter to Mitchell. "I can't tell you how pleased I was to receive your letter of October 19th, stating that 'at long last . . . colored children, age 4 yrs to 8 yrs are now permitted to live in Peter Pan cottages.' . . . That I had any part in achieving that justice makes me very happy. The credit, however, for what was done, must go to you."

Over the next several years, L. Pearl Mitchell continued to wage her campaign to

Formation work by the cadets of Company A on Field Day of 1953.

fully de-segregate all aspects of residential life at the Home. Her efforts to persuade the board to act were largely ineffectual, but working with the Ohio NAACP she managed to get the attention of Republican Governor C. William O'Neill. On October 29, 1958, O'Neill wrote to board president Frank Hilliard, reminding him that "under the law and Supreme Court decisions there can be no segregation in this state. If there is any at the Home, I am asking that it be discontinued."

Mitchell and the NAACP kept the issue in front of O'Neill's successor, Democrat Michael DiSalle. Governor DiSalle took office as the leaders of the Civil Rights movement were in full stride. The Reverend Martin Luther King Jr. and others had brought about significant change in the formerly segregated South. After meeting with the Home's board and NAACP representatives on May 15, 1959, DiSalle appointed a committee of disinterested third parties to advise him about the situation. Up to this point, the debate over housing at the Home had not been widely reported in the press. DiSalle's new committee, however, received a lot of news coverage. Newspapers across the state carried the July 10, 1959, announcement that the committee had concluded "that segregation of children by races does exist" at the Home, and the United Press wire service reported, "The committee's recommendation for an immediate halt to separation of Negro and White children in chapel and dining halls was ordered put into effect by the Governor."

Two weeks later, Mitchell was appointed to another term on the board. Over the next year, the trustees and staff worked with the Ohio Civil Rights Commission to implement the further desegregation of the Home. By the summer of 1960, the process was completed. Mitchell resigned from the board in 1961 and was replaced by A.A. Andrews, president of the Canton NAACP and former head of the Ohio

NAACP Conference of Branches. At their December 1, 1961 meeting, the board of trustees adopted the following resolution: "By unanimous action, the secretary was directed to express to Miss L. Pearl Mitchell, resigned, the appreciation of the Board for her years of service to the Home and the children in its care." She returned to East Cleveland and continued to work with social and service organizations until her death in 1974.

> *At our school we have a team*
> *That's really rough and on the beam*
> *And the boys they rarely seem*
> *To have a lack of pep or steam*
> *And if you know just what I mean*
> *They play it hard but very clean*
> *Maybe it's because their lady dean*
> *Makes them tough but feeds them cream.*
> *——poem by Paul Boykin*

Home Life in Changing Times (1950-1963)

People familiar with the Home's sports teams sometimes refer to the 1950s as the "Boykin Years." There were twenty-one children in the Boykin family. Many of them did not come to the Home, but the ones who did were wonders to behold, beginning with the quarter-miler and four-time state track champion Paul Boykin. In 1951, Boykin won the 440 and placed second in the 220-yard dash at the state track meet; in 1952, he won the 440 and placed second in the 100-yard and 220-yard dashes; and in 1953, he won both the 440 and the 220 and placed second in the 100.

Many years later, Paul Boykin recalled the day his great sports career began.

I came into the Home when I was twelve years old. I was as tall as I am now, and I weighed 180 pounds. I was bigger than everybody. I was just bigger than life. And I had never played sports before. I couldn't play basketball. I didn't know nothing about football. So when the kids saw me when I come down on campus, they led me right over to the armory and put a football uniform on me.

A Home of their own

Tom Boykin hands out equipment to three younger members of the Boykin dynasty—Shep, David, and Randall.

I said, 'What do you want me to do?'

They said, 'All you got to do is knock down the guy in front of you.' So I did that for awhile.

I was bigger than everybody, so boom, they were knocked down. But the other guys got to run the ball. They were always getting all the glory and all the touchdowns, and I'm doing all the work! I said, 'Wait a minute, I can outrun all you guys. Let me run the ball for a minute!'

Then I found out I could run. I was pretty fast. I just practiced all the time. The whole time I was in the Home, I ran every morning before they got up for breakfast. I done my two miles. And I never got beat in high school in the quarter mile because I practiced all the time. I ran against the World Champion and he only beat me by a step.

The budding young warriors of the mid-1950s, the Home's junior high team, featuring a young man on his way up, Tom Boykin (center of back row).

The 1952 Cadet football team went undefeated and ranked third in the state being led by quarterback Earl Montgomery and halfbacks Paul Boykin and the hard-charging Napoleon Reid. Both Boykin and Reid were named to the All-State team. In the spring of 1953, Boykin led the Home to a second-place finish at the state track meet. Beside the points scored by Boykin, the Anderson brothers of Clifford, Irwin and Lester were joined by Gene Olsen to placed fourth in the mile relay.

In 1953, Paul was voted to a halfback spot on a mythical Ohio high school All-State "dream team" selected by a committee of some 600 coaches, officials, sportswriters, and sportscasters.

That was also the year the Home got a new football yell, "The O.S.S.O. Chant:"

Oooo, Ssss, Ssss, Oooo (Done slowly and drawn out).
FIGHT! (Fast)
Oooo, Wil—son—High (Slowly and drawn out).
FIGHT! (Fast)
Oooo, Ca—det Teammmmm (Slowly and drawn out).
FIGHT! FIGHT! FIGHT! (Fast)
And HEAVE HO
Heaveeeee—Ho! (Hold the Heave until the cheerleader hits the ground).
Heaveeeee—Ho!
Get that ball (done quickly with lots of pep) and let's go!

During the decade of the 1950s, the Home track teams would win league titles, five Ohio Wesleyan Relays titles, eight district titles, and three state championships, as well as one second-place finish at state and one third-place. The Boykins were important in all of them.

Paul Boykin would return to the OSSO Home as a teacher. His brothers Tom, Dave, Shep, and Randall continued the family's athletic legacy at the institution. In the 1955 state meet, Tom Boykin took second in the 100-yard and 220-yard dashes and third in the discus throw; the mile relay team and quarter-miler Lester Anderson had first-place finishes; and the Home's Woodrow Wilson High School track team became the first school in Ohio to win four state championships. The Cadets won the team title again in 1956 as Tom Boykin finished first in the 220 and the mile relay team of Austin Washington, Henry Gordon, Marv Barbour, and Lester Anderson broke a ten-year-old state record by more than two seconds.

Four members of the 1956 football team were voted to the All-League team

and one of the players—David Raimey—became an All-American at the University of Michigan in 1962. Raimey was a kid from the Dayton projects who had never played football until he arrived at the Home and played as a junior only because the Home required that everyone participate in sports. He was inspired by his coach, "Mousie" Eisenhut, as well as by teammate Tom Boykin, and he went on to become Michigan's MVP in 1962. He played one season with the Cleveland Browns and finished his pro career in Canada with Winnipeg and Toronto. He was an All-Star each of his four years at Winnipeg and was inducted into the Canadian Football Hall of Fame in 2000.

In 1957, the basketball team won the Mid-Miami League championship—the first league title since 1942—and Tom Boykin was voted on the All-State team, in addition to being named the United Press Class B Player of the Year. He averaged 16.9 points that season, and he scored 1,096 career points at the Home. Upon graduation, the number of his trophies and medals approached fifty. And yet in addition to his athletic ability, he was a good musician (he played clarinet in the school band) and he was known for his unassuming manner.

Tom recalled developing his shooting eye by breaking into the armory. "Yeah, we busted in, in there playing ball and Mr. Hayes pulls up in that big long Chevy. Somebody said, 'Here comes Hayes!' And everybody hit the balconies. Mr. Hayes walks in. 'I know you're in here,' he said. Balls still bouncing in the middle of the floor. See, they had two stairs on each balcony, and he come up one and everybody run down the other one . . . ."

The last Boykin to graduate from the Home was Randall. An All-League player in both basketball and football, he continued the Boykin track tradition of winning events in the 100- and 220-yard dashes and the field events of shot and discus. Local coaches were glad to see the thirteen-year Boykin era come to an end.

Robert Carter—Class of 1957—recalled his playing days on the baseball field: "There was a pecking order, yes, and you knew who you could outrun, who you could outfight and who you could outplay. . . . Everyone pretty well knew the skills and the abilities of each other. Those who were chubby, or weak, or something, were always the last ones picked. I was fast. I was aggressive. . . . One thing really helped me. I made a set of weights. I got some [No. 10] cans . . . and poured some concrete in them. I would go home and . . . lift those weights. I developed bigger arms and chest and became one of the best batters we had. I could score very well. I was in demand for that."

The Home's basketball teams had a lot of success in the early 1960s. The *Dayton Daily News* and the *Dayton Journal-Herald* recognized the talents of 6-7

Lloyd Buck, naming the Cadet to their All-Mid Miami League Team in 1961. Buck led the league with a 26.6-point scoring average.

"This poll is not an official League poll," acknowledged the *Home Review*, "but that of the sportswriters of the *Dayton Daily News* and the *Dayton Journal Herald*. This poll carries a lot of 'glory' with it."

1959—The male lead of the class play, Denny Bosworth, broke his leg in the football game with Beavercreek, and was disabled from both the gridiron and the stage. The name of the production was, ironically, at least for someone, was . . . "The Victim."
The play, along with Mr. Bosworth, was postponed.

Change and more change

The Home underwent an identity change in the 1950s as graduating pupils began receiving diplomas from "Woodrow Wilson High School" and class rings were engraved with the letters WWHS as well as OS&SO. Two long-time staffers retired: J.E. Balmer, in June of 1957, after twenty-seven years as vocational education supervisor; and two years later, J. Harley Waldron, after twenty-four years as principal of academic education.

There were always a few employees like "Johnnie" Trunnel, though, for whom retirement was not an option. Trunnel arrived in 1932. In addition to being the shoe shop instructor, he was the Home's scoutmaster. Shortly before his unexpected death in 1958, he received the Silver Beaver award—the highest award a scout leader can achieve.

"For twenty-five years, this kind and understanding teacher, shoe expert, scoutmaster and substitute parent was a counselor to hundreds of boys and girls," wrote J.E. Balmer in a tribute to his departed colleague. "His death is a tragic loss to the Home and to those who sought his advice. Johnnie, you were a grand person to know. You were unassuming, sincere, loyal to your admirers, and charitable to those who did not agree with you. No one can replace you in the hearts and lives of your co-workers and Home children."

In December of 1952, the dairy barn caught fire. By the time the blaze was extinguished, the west wing of the massive structure, known as the "hospital barn,"

In 1951, John Trunnel and his Explorer Scouts built themselves a boat. The boys pronounced it seaworthy even if John seemed a bit unsure.

had been substantially destroyed. The sick livestock and veterinary records were saved, thanks to the prompt action taken by pupils and staff, but the damage to the barn, built in 1933, was estimated at over $75,000. A cigarette carelessly tossed into a haymow was listed by the arson bureau of the State Fire Marshal's Office as the probable cause of the fire.

The Home celebrated the holidays as usual. A *Home Review* article describing an Easter Sunday in the late 1940s noted that services for the children and staff were held in the chapel, with a sermon delivered by the chaplain and a musical program presented by the choir. The Ohio American Legion Auxiliary also sponsored an egg-decorating contest with prizes awarded to the first four winners in each cottage.

"The [Auxiliary] committee arrived early on Saturday morning and set to work with a will. Presents which had been arriving for three weeks from over 200 auxiliary units were wrapped and made ready for distribution. In the evening the children's dining room, Peter Pan and Hayes Hall were decorated for Easter morning breakfast. The decorations consisted of balloons, favors and beautiful flowers. In the egg decorating contest, many unusual and highly artistic eggs were entered, and considerable artistic ability was shown."

Field Day was held each May 1st. "The boys did their ROTC and their track events," recalled Dolores Cottle, while she and the other girls had spent the entire month of April cleaning the cottages and waxing floors so that everything was spotless on Field Day. "They came and inspected the whole cottage and wiped them with a white glove, you know, the floors and the desks and everything."

The unique and memorable Memorial Day Service was complemented by the annual reunion of the Association of Ex-Pupils on the weekend nearest the Fourth of July. Many children at the Home often passed the summer with relatives or in summer school and camp. After returning in the fall, they looked forward to Halloween, which was followed by the Thanksgiving and Christmas celebrations. Christmas was always special. Children might leave during the afternoon on Christmas Day to be with relatives or friends, but Christmas morning always belonged, in the words of one ex-pupil, "to one's real family—the family of the Home."

In 1961, all of the children at the Home were immunized with the Sabin oral polio vaccine. The crippling disease had been checked by the Salk vaccine in the 1950s and now was virtually eradicated with the new strain.

The long anticipated Washington Hall opened in July of 1962 as the Home moved forward with the original plan for a junior campus that had been proposed two decades earlier.

In the fall of 1962, James A. Rhodes was elected governor of Ohio. Rhodes had served as mayor of Columbus and state auditor before winning the '62 gubernatorial race.

Floyd Hartpence announced his retirement in 1963 as the Home's longest serving superintendent. "I feel the time has come for someone else to take up the challenge—a man with new ideas and fresh enthusiasm, one who will continue to work for progress and development in making the Home the finest of its kind," Hartpence said. The board adopted a resolution stating that "throughout his entire service he was devoted to duty, interested and concerned for the welfare of the children and employees, and faithful in every respect to the responsibilities that were his. . . . The Board of Trustees of the Ohio Soldiers and Sailors Orphans Home on its own behalf and on behalf of the children of the Home who have benefited by his counsel, express to Mr. Hartpence their deep appreciation for his outstanding service as Superintendent of the Home." Floyd Hartpence retired to Westerville, Ohio, where he and his wife lived quietly until both were killed in an automobile accident in 1969. Hartpence was 74 years old.

Colonel Stephan retired from the Marines to take the superintendent's job in

1963. Colonel Stephan had been an instructor at the Home from 1936 to 1941. His wife had served on the teaching staff as well from 1936 to 1941 and again from 1943 to 1945.

In 1963, the Association of Ex-Pupils published the first history of the Home. Originally begun by Edward Wakefield Hughes (Class of 1880) and continued by William Clyde McCracken (1877), *Pride of Ohio* was completed under the editorship of McCracken, McKinley Warth (1914), and Lloyd Brewster (1923). The following words from Governor Rhodes appear on the last page of the book: "This great Home has long served the wishes of President Abraham Lincoln who called upon the nation to bind up its wounds and care for the widows and orphans of its servicemen. It was a cause dear to his heart and Ohio has long honored that cause. It is significant therefore that this history should be completed just a century after Abraham Lincoln voiced his sentiments. The world has turned many times since then, and monumental changes have taken place, but the spirit of man's concern for man, manifested through the years at the Ohio Soldiers and Sailors Orphans Home, gives us pause to remember that such goodness is unchanged and unchanging."

1943— "The first impression I got when I got to the Home was, boy, what a big vacation place. Then they took us right to the hospital and that was no vacation. But we had good food. We got dessert at lunch and supper, cakes and pies and puddings and fruit and cookies. We thought this was a really good vacation but then when we had stayed there a long time, I began to wonder how long a vacation could actually last. . . ." —Marjorie Balside

$\mathcal{T}$ransition comes to the Home (1963-1978)

$\mathcal{A}$ look at the $\mathcal{H}$ome, circa 1963

A traveler arriving in Xenia for the first time on a pleasant spring day in 1963 might have wondered about the buildings atop the ridge on the south end of town. Driving up the winding driveway past the two cannons and reaching the crest of the hill, the traveler would no longer be curious. He or she would simply be impressed—impressed by the well-tended lawns, wooded drives, and dozens of buildings of the Ohio Soldiers and Sailors Orphans Home.

The campus no longer looked quite as quaint as it appeared when the original carpenter gothic cottages stood in a row facing the parade ground. But the new cottages, with two children to a room, made for much nicer (and

237

Who better to run the Home, with its military traditions, than an old Marine like Colonel Pete Stephan?

more comfortable) living quarters. Retiring Supertintendent Hartpence had overseen the razing of twenty-five dormitories, filling in of Lake McDowell, extensive street repaving and the construction of a dozen buildings including the new auditorium and the remodeling of the gymnasium. Also during the Hartpence tenure he and his wife, Dawn, encouraged and supported the cultural life of the Home. No school the Home's size had so extensive a fine arts program in art, music, and drama.

After almost a century of effort, the OSSO Home had become an extraordinarily efficient, self-sustaining institution, caring for upwards of 500 children at a cost of $2,600 per child for the year. In 1963, its farm slaughtered 408 hogs and produced almost 74,000 gallons of milk and 700 bushels of vegetables for the Home's kitchens. The farm, along with the power plant and the laundry and the other industrial facilities on-site, also doubled as a "laboratory," if you will, in the Home's highly-regarded vocational training program. The Home's long and successful life span as a state-sponsored institution could be attributed, in large part, to the two-pronged program of education the children received. The founders recognized the importance of vocational training as well as scholarly achievement, and by 1963 the OSSO Home arguably had one of the best vo-ed programs in the state.

The Home continued to observe its traditions and rituals. One hundred and twenty-one young men conducted military drills each day at noon. Most Sundays, the battalion drilled in full uniform on the parade grounds. The Cadet band still played regular concerts in the band shell and performed at commencement, the annual reunion of the Association of Ex-Pupils, and other Home events. As it had done in the past, the band also played at several conventions of veterans organizations.

The Association of Ex-Pupils held its eighty-third annual gathering on July 5,

1963. One hundred and ninety former students registered for the event and many more came informally. That year, the ex-pupils used monies from the Association's "Loyalty Fund" to buy new uniforms for the Home's cheerleaders and a camera for the print shop.

A Changing Time 1963-1969

The man who would lead the institution into the new decade, Colonel S.L. "Pete" Stephan, was returning to a place he knew pretty well after a lengthy career in the Marines. The colonel and his wife Jane had previously worked at the Home— she as a teacher, he as an assistant coach and teacher prior to World War II. It was still the relatively quiet, peaceful place that Stephan remembered, but the world around the Home was anything but tranquil.

But as Colonel Stephan took charge of an institution caring for nearly 500 children with traditions and buildings going back almost one hundred years, he had with him a large group of teachers, house parents, and administrators whose careers were dedicated to both the Home and the children. Some of the almost thirty employees had been there since the 1930s, and all had been there since 1950. A forty-hour week was not standard; all freely gave extra time with the children.

Teachers who directed them in both their school and personal issues were Emlyn Whilding, Lenora Mart, Richard Might, Charles Minch, Marcella Mootz, George Schumacher, Frances Baird, James Beaver, Foy Coffect, Dorothy Paxton, Ruth Lampe, Jack Newhouse, and Warren Eisenhut.

Special house parents were Nora Binkley, Merle Fitzpatrick, Mary Moore, and Thelma Brooks.

Long term administrators were Dorothy Hilty, Mildred Blair, Jay Bernett, Harold Whit, Glen Howard, and Mary Neville. These people set a tone of excellence at the Home.

Ohio in the 1960s

In the Sixties, a variety of historical forces would come together, creating a kind of perfect "cultural" storm. There was the great Civil Rights struggle, which had begun in the South and now continued in the North. While the Home had become fully desegregated by the early 1960s, racial separation remained firmly in place

One of the aims of the Home was to keep families, such as the Daulbaughs, together. Shown here are Ricky, Jerry, Janice, and Jean.

in many institutions. Other forces were at work as well, many of them stemming from the unpopular war in Vietnam. Baby boomers questioned America's cultural values, clashing with the older generation over styles of dress, language, and music.

In 1960, Aid to Dependent Children, the government program established in the depths of the Depression, was re-named Aid to "Families" with Dependent Children, reflecting new eligibility requirements that would have an impact on Home admissions. Families could continue living together under difficult circumstances and still receive assistance—including families of Ohio veterans with children eligible for entry into the OSSO Home.

Admissions also would be affected by foster care. Since the White House Conference of 1909, foster care advocates in the social services community had extolled the virtues of the nuclear family while disparaging orphanages and children's homes as dehumanizing environments. Defenders of institutional care argued that properly managed facilities like the OSSO Home were equal—or even superior—to family settings in which the foster care parents sometimes proved to be less-than-competent providers.

Many institutions, including Ohio's prisons and mental treatment facilities, operated under severe budget restrictions during the Sixties as Governor James A.

Rhodes, elected in 1962, took steps to slow the loss of jobs to the Sun Belt and the West and stabilize the state's economy. The Home experienced significant budget cuts. Its annual budget for salaries, maintenance and equipment provided by the State of Ohio was just under $1.3 million in 1963. By 1970, the budget was slightly over $2 million, but inflation and new expenses had driven the costs of operating the institution relentlessly higher. The Home was only able to live within its means by paying careful attention to operations and by receiving support from its friends.

Veterans saw their organizations shrink in numbers and influence in the years following World War I, but the math changed after World War II with the return of sixteen million potential new members and friends. By 1950, The American Legion, The Veterans of Foreign Wars and the Disabled American Veterans were political forces to be reckoned with in American life. Their support became important to the Home's operation in tight economic times.

Programming for Young People in Need

The Schools of the Home

Early on in Colonel Stephan's administration, he and the trustees asked themselves a tricky question: Who should we admit to the Home? By law, they were required to accept the children of Ohio veterans, but the board had always been permitted to set reasonable standards for admission. Stephan and the trustees decided that the Home's eligibility requirements should be "flexibly interpreted in keeping with changes in social conditions affecting dependency." Nevertheless, to be eligible for admission, children had to be at least four years old, healthy enough "to be able to compete" in sports and recreational activities, have a measurable IQ of at least 75, and possess reasonable emotional stability and self-discipline. The board also noted that "the freedom permitted in the Home makes it undesirable to admit the seriously delinquent" and warned that "an imbalance in behavioral problems may result in a pervasive destructive attitude."

In May of 1964, the trustees authorized Superintendent Stephan to work with the Ohio Board of Education on possible changes in the Home's education program. Stephan and the state board would continue their efforts for a number of years. In 1972, the *Home Review* reported on the status and success of the vocational education program:

The older Home band soon gave way to a more martial look in the 1960s when it began wearing military dress. Here, bandsmen are forming on the parade ground.

The . . . program offers a remarkably thorough curriculum. It is divided into ten departments – Business Education, Print Shop, Cosmetology, Sewing Department, Cooking Department, Shoe Shop, Electric Shop, Metal Shop, Wood Shop and Auto Shop. Altogether there are approximately 115 students enrolled in the morning classes. It is during the morning classes that the upper class students receive their vocational training. Members of the junior high classes participate in various degrees of elementary preparatory training in each of the different departments during the afternoon.

In years past the enrollment in the [Print] Shop has been limited to boys. But recently, some members of the fair sex have joined the ranks. The first of these female pioneers were Sandy Morris, Debbie Wray and Nancy Keeton.

The definition of home economics had changed as well.

Recently, Mrs. Wessell, [a] Red Cross worker, instructed all of the eighth grade girls . . . in Home Economics in a two-week course in sex education. She also repeated this course for the eighth grade boys enrolled in Industrial Arts.

In December, the board attempted to address a growing concern that the public no longer identified the institution as the Ohio Soldiers and Sailors Orphans Home, but simply as Woodrow Wilson High School. The trustees instructed Colonel Stephan to include the words "OSSO Home" on the diploma given to each graduating senior and on "all correspondence, transcripts, and reports which emanate from our schools—the purpose being to identify the Woodrow Wilson High School as a unit of the Ohio Soldiers and Sailors Orphans Home." Class rings also were to be engraved with both the letters "WWHS" and "OSSO."

Traditional Ties

The Military Program

No matter how contentious the war in Vietnam and other military matters became in the 1960s, the Home remained a model of patriotism and tradition. Its battalion held daily drills and marched in full uniform on Sundays on the parade ground, accompanied by the band. The Annual Federal Inspection—a day of drills and activities, culminating with an evening military ball—continued as usual.

But there also were noticeable changes.

The farm had always sustained the Home but by the 1960s, there were questions about its purpose.

Since 1937, the Home's academic curriculum had included a National Defense Cadet Corps program. In 1966, the Home began offering Junior Reserve Officers' Training Corps, better known as ROTC—a federal program that provides books, uniforms and weapons at U.S. Army expense. One hundred and twenty-five boys in grades 9 through 12 were enrolled in the Home's first ROTC course, and sixty boys in grades 7 and 8 took pre-ROTC. The Home also began offering a Girls Reserve Officers' Training Corps course in 1969. Twenty-six high school girls signed up and twelve were chosen to start the program.

Along with the transition from the National Defense Cadet Corps military training program to ROTC came a change in uniforms. The traditional blue and gray dress uniforms were replaced with Army green uniforms with blue lapels.

The Farm

The Home's farm had always sustained everyone who lived at the institution, putting food on the table and providing pupils with valuable vocational training. "My husband makes fun of me because I always told him how good the milk was," said Denise English Armbruster. "It was ice cold and fresh since it probably had just come out of one of the cows that morning. Haven't tasted milk like it since." Kathy Berry Figgins remembered her 4-H days, when she showed one of the farm's cows at the Greene County Fair. After Wendy's Foundation of Columbus purchased her beefy 4-H project, Figgins named the cow "Wendy." "I didn't know what he [founder Dave Thomas) wanted that old steer for," she said, "but . . . he got it."

In the years after World War II, the Home began to buy more food. By the 1960s, the board sometimes questioned whether the farm was needed at all. But Colonel Stephan reminded trustees in August of 1969 that the Home still needed its

pigs, and not just for the money they might bring or the food they might provide. The pigs devoured most of the Home's garbage. "To find another means would be very expensive," the superintendent said. So for the foreseeable future, the pigs—and the farm—would stay.

A 1964 report in the *Home Review* revealed something of the scale of the farm:

One hundred and fifteen head of cattle were raised on the Home farm this year, fifty-two of which are milking cows. Two hundred and fifty gallons of milk are produced . . . each day. Of the five hundred and forty-one animals raised at the farm, two hundred and eighty-seven are swine of three different breeds. . . .

"Spring planting will begin . . . as soon as the weather will permit. Clover, alfalfa and pasture hay will be planted first. Later in April the farm garden will be planted. . . .

"Nine people are employed at the Home farm under the supervision of Mr. Harold Wilt.

There was a time when the farm not only fed the Home population, but the kids—initiated into the rural processes early and often—had a real insight into the agricultural processes. This photograph was taken in the hayfields at mid-century.

Sports, band, and drama

Three programs that brought recognition, pride and success to the Home school would lose their long-time leaders to retirement during the 1970s. The retirement of J. R. Rooney, drama coach; Warren "Mousie" Eisenhut, all-sports coach; and George Schumacher, band director, came at a time when the Home began to lose student population. Change would follow in their excellent programs.

"Mousie" would continue to coach football, basketball, and track until 1970 when he would give up football and basketball and focus on his first love—track. He would retire in the mid-1970s with impressive accomplishments, including 1960s' team successes in basketball with stars Randall Boykin, Tom Hanson, and Lloyd Buck. He also had several winning football seasons in the 1960s. Track at the Home, however, continued to dominate—seven consecutive district championships, and at the state meet, a second- and a fourth-place finish. The runner-up finish in 1968

The cheerleaders, circa 1967, pose at the field. From left, Pat Srofe, Renee Hemenway, and Jean Daulbaugh.

was the third time the Home had finished second and starred the mile relay team of Robert Cox , Jack Porter, Rusty Winters, and Charles Burns. The three second-place finishes were in addition to the six firsts won by the Home since 1940.

In the 1970s, successful sports gradually changed to soccer and cross country, but football had one last undefeated season in 1972. New coach John Davis was named coach of the year with his 9–0 team, and two-way back Ernie Sheeler was selected first team all-defensive back by the Associated Press. In four years of play, Sheeler gained 2,500 yards for the Cadets.

The first years of soccer produced only two winning seasons, but in 1977 the team lost only one game and were league champs. Mr. Might's cross country team also had its successes. Formed in 1960, the 1965 team had a 7-0 record and the 1967 team—after losing its opener—won eleven straight meets. The Cadets also finished second in the league and second in the district. In 1968 the team won the Lowell Thomas Invitational and the district championship and again finished second in the league. Top runners for the Cadets were Dennis Fought, Bill Boivin, Willie Focht, Wayne Wells, and Mike Hryonak.

Mr. Rooney's retirement in early 1970 left a large gap to be filled in the drama program. During his thirty-plus years directing the drama program, he produced

Mousie
Coach, Hall of Fame

In 1972, Athletic Director Warren Eisenhut received Miami University's prized Bishop Medal, in recognition of community service by an alumnus.

He was a 1939 Miami graduate, taught and coached at the Home for thirty-one years, and was selected in 1970 to the Ohio Association of Track and Cross Country Coaches Hall of Fame.

Nicknamed "Mousie," his sobriquet arose after Eisenhut as a 124-pound sophomore ran back a kickoff for a Cleveland Shaw High touchdown.

"Why, Eisey," said one of his teammates, "you were running around like a little mouse out there."

As a prepster, observers wrote, he was "second cheese only to the great Jesse Owens."

The name followed him to Miami, where he was a collegiate scatback, and subsequently, in 1941, to the Home where he was called "a diminutive fireball, a triple-threat mentor."

The word "firebrand" stuck to Mousie, because he was impatient when he sensed his kids might perform better. There's a classic Mousie story: one of the students had a stutter. One day, Mousie pinned the kid with his impenetrable coaching stare and said, "Don't ever do that around me again." And although the kid stuttered elsewhere, many attest to the fact that whenever he found himself in Mousie's presence, his debility completely vanished.

At the Home, Mousie produced champions in all three varsity sports he coached. His basketball team was unbeaten in 1959, and his track teams won four state titles, were runnerup twice, and won sixteen district titles and 130 dual/tri meets.

He produced some of the Home's greatest athletes: the Boykin brothers, Archie Estes, and John Day.

Even after the turn of the new century, there were Boykins around, and when one might surface—such as a kid playing for Centerville in 2009—the oldtimers would ask if his grandfather was one of the Boykins from the Home.

"Is he from that long line of Boykins at old Woodrow Wilson?" they asked.

"I have my favorites," Eisenhut said once, "but I'll never tell."

There was one other thing that Mousie liked to say, particularly when people asked him why he'd never wanted to coach anywhere else. "Coaching here, at the Home, isn't just a job," he'd say. "It's a way of life."

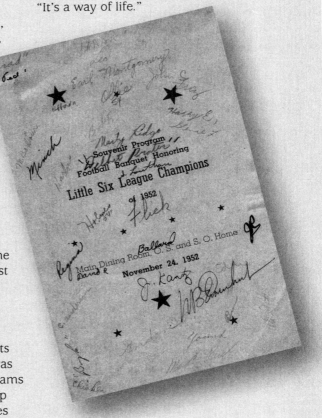

The front entrance in later years, almost as it had always been, and as if the cannons could actually hold off the bureaucratic forces massing outside.

some three plays each year. His one-act plays and the actors in them often won awards. During the 1960s some of his plays were: *Arsenic and Old Lace*, *The Man Who Came to Dinner*, *My Sister Eileen*, *A Midsummer Night's Dream*, *You Can't Take It With You*, and *A Mayor for a Day*. Hundreds of students benefited from his teaching and enjoyed being in his plays or being a part of the stage crew.

When George Schumacher retired in 1975 he had directed the marching band, orchestra, and dance band of the Home for over thirty years. As they would in the 1960s and 1970s, the marching band performed each summer for veteran groups at conventions and other events. As the 1960s started, the American Legion gave the band new uniforms to replace ones that had been in use since 1940. And then the Women Relief Corps donated a new flute, clarinet, and saxophone.

Summers were filled with parades across Ohio from Cleveland to Cincinnati to Dayton, Springfield, and Xenia. The dance band was sought-after by several organizations, as well as the Home students.

The Senior band always had a least two concerts a year—Christmas and spring. They were popular events on the campus, the public was welcome and attended both. Student talent was often recognized at these events. In the 1963 spring concert senior Warren Smart was asked to stand in for Mr. Schumacher and conduct two numbers—"Totem Pole" and "Stella Polaris." In other concerts, student solos and trios were featured.

Glen Shaw replaced Schumacher as band director and at his 1977 Christmas concert the band played his rendition of the Home Christmas Carol.

Health

Since its modest beginnings, when the superintendent of the institution also served as staff physician, the Ohio Soldiers and Sailors Orphans Home had developed an extraordinary network of advisory medical professionals. One family—the Messengers—provided more than 100 years of care to the children and employees. Dr. Asa Clay Messenger served as a physician at the Home for forty-six years until his death in 1938. His son Harold, a member of the consulting staff from 1927 until his death in 1954, played a key role in the establishment of General J. Warren Keifer Hospital and the procurement of modern medical equipment for the on-campus treatment center.

Harold Messenger's son, Dr. H. Clay Messenger, joined the Home's Medical Advisory Group in 1951. Meeting regularly since 1903, the group made recommendations that led to improvements in the hospital and the employment of an increasing number of doctors, dentists, and nurses. The needs of the children were quite extensive, judging from the annual report by the Home's medical director in 1968. A total of 26,818 visits were made to the hospital's clinic that year. There were 951 hospital admissions, 467 physical examinations, 346 x-rays, and a large number of immunizations and vaccinations. The report also noted that "eight fractures were treated, nine tonsillectomies and a dozen other surgical procedures were performed. Four other cases required sutures. One thousand seven hundred and nine children were treated in the dental clinic. . . .

The Medical Advisory Group continued to meet through the 1960s and among its recommendations were fluoridation of the Home's water—a highly controversial proposal at the time—and the administration of the Sabin polio vaccine to the children. The consulting staff also identified a need for more psychological and psychiatric resources to deal with an increasing number of children coming to the Home with emotional and other behavioral problems. "If they had a fever we would put them in bed," said Madeline Prindle, a nurse at the Home in the Sixties. "Normally with colds and scratches and things like that, we just treated them in the clinic. But we saw the children three times a day—and four times if they had to come back in the evening for medication. Our plan was more preventive medicine to keep the children well. At Christmas time they set up about seven Christmas trees in the hospital alone, which was a lot, and we had a party for the staff and the children [who] helped work [there]."

Building, Rebuilding and Removal

Joseph E. Balmer was supervisor of vocational education from 1929 until his retirement in 1957. During his tenure at the Home, he had been a vigorous advocate of vocational training and education. Many improvements to the "trades and shops," as they were known, were due to Balmer's efforts.

In the years after his retirement, it had become increasingly clear that the industrial building, built in 1909, needed to be replaced. Plans for a new $264,000 building, to be named for Joseph Balmer, were approved in December of 1966.

"He was a man of vision, and during [his] twenty-eight years he developed our vocational education program, was in charge of grounds and maintenance, and was instrumental in introducing high grade breeding for our dairy herd so that it became one of the finest in the state," noted the board of trustees.

The Joseph Balmer Building was dedicated in the presence of his family and friends on March 11, 1968, and was long regarded as one of the finest vocational training facilities in the nation.

After fire destroyed the old domestic building in the summer of 1965, the Home erected a new $334,000 domestic building with offices, dining halls, storage rooms, and eight one-bedroom apartments. It was opened in June of 1967 and named for the man who did the honors at the ribbon-cutting ceremony—Herbert R. Mooney. Mooney, a former director of public welfare for the State of Ohio and past commander of the Ohio Department of the American Legion, had served as a member of the Home's board of trustees from 1929 to 1949.

In the early 1960s, the Ohio Department of Transportation announced plans to widen and improve its major highways, including a four-lane roadway allowing through-traffic on Route 35 to bypass Xenia to the south. The highway department, however, would have to acquire more than thirty-five acres of the Home's property to build the bypass. After a long negotiation, the land was sold to the state for more than $70,000 in 1967. The board approved two other subsequent requests for additional Home acreage, allowing transportation officials to put up a garage and the State Highway Patrol to build a command post near the access ramp to the new Route 35 bypass.

Special Times

Each year, New Year's Eve was celebrated with a dance for the older students in the Orfenz Den recreation room. Here's the *Home Review*'s account of the 1963 celebration:

The music began spinning from Mr. Might's tape recorder and the couples started dancing. Of course there was "twisting" music for all the "twisters" in the group! At 10:30, the Bunny Hop was done with Ronald Coleman and Betty Gibson leading the hoppers. Quite naturally, after all that hopping around the den, everyone was hungry. But that little matter was quickly solved by the serving of pizza and cokes. . . . The New Year was finally here and it was time to head for home and get some sleep.

Another major celebration without a great deal of public notice took place at Halloween. As a substitute for traditional door-to-door "trick or treating," the Home staged a series of other events for the children:

Halloween tended to bring out a previously unheralded creativity in the Home students. Treats, however, were usually preferable to tricks.

Masked and costumed marchers competed for prizes October 31 in the annual Halloween Parade. The band led the way to the circle in front of the Main Building and the paraders proudly began the display of costumes. As winners were selected by the judges, they were taken out of the line of march to the winners' circle.

On the night that witches and goblins were flying high, the students in grades 9-12 and teachers were in the gymnasium from 8:00 to 10 PM celebrating "All Fools Day" with a carnival. Before the two hours were gone many pupils had won stuffed animals, canes, felt hats, straw hats and cakes from the "cake walk." . . . The swimming pool "dunker" was run by Mr. Emlyn Whilding and Mr. Charles Joslin. They took turns sitting on the "dunking machine." Separate parties for the younger children were held in the evening in the various cottages of the Home with food, games and prizes as well.

Ninth-grader Patty Griffin remembered another special occasion with far less fanfare, but for Griffin, just as memorable as all the big holiday events:

Two nights in the second-to-last week in January, Monroe B, a favorite cottage of

In the last years of the Home, the chapel was a mainstay, always a comforting presence, as it had been for almost the entirety of the Home itself.

mine, had snow ice cream. The first night Joysan Barker and Beverly Long got snow off the roof. The girls got the milk out of the dining room in a gallon jar. Mrs. Winnard had the vanilla flavoring and sugar. After study hour was over, Mrs. Winnard mixed the ingredients together. All the girls had at least two bowls of snow ice cream.

The second night Joysan Barker and Darlene Pence got the snow off the roof again. . . . We had chocolate-flavored snow ice cream. . . . Let it snow, let it snow, let it snow.

The Home celebrated its 100th anniversary in 1969. Copies of a specially-designed centennial seal were sold for $1 on the streets of Xenia, as well as to members of the Association of Ex-Pupils and friends of the Home. The formal centennial ceremony took place in July during the annual reunion of the Association of Ex-Pupils, where a resolution of the Ohio House of Representatives was read. It stated, in part: "Resolved, that we, the members of the 108th General Assembly of the State of Ohio . . . proudly express our congratulations to the Ohio Soldiers and Sailors Orphans Home upon the attainment of its Centennial—an unsurpassed one hundred years of service and progress in the interest of the sons and daughters of the veterans of our armed forces—and tender to its Board of Trustees our gratitude for the Home's great contribution to the citizens of Ohio."

There were many people to thank, of course, including all of the children and staff members who had lived and worked at the institution during its first one hundred years, the Association of Ex-Pupils, the Ohio General Assembly, and several governors, beginning with Rutherford B. Hayes in 1867. But no group had been more important to the Home's continued existence than the veterans organizations representing the men and women of Ohio who had served their country in peace and war in the armed services of the United States. Beginning with the Home's founders—the Grand Army of the Republic—and the various groups that followed the GAR, the veterans became sponsors of virtually every aspect of the Home.

At seemingly every meeting of the board of trustees, a local chapter of a veterans organization would be recognized as a new cottage sponsor. The old soldiers visited their sponsored cottage on a regular basis, often bearing gifts and providing food and supplies. Some groups sponsored specific events. For many years, the Halloween celebration was underwritten by the Veterans of Foreign Wars. The American Legion Auxiliary sponsored Field Day and Thanksgiving Day events. Virtually every group contributed to the annual Christmas celebration. "At Christmas," recalled ex-pupil Carla Budd Dean, "each auxiliary would adopt a cottage and buy gifts for the kids. I had never had that many presents in my life. Their love came through. One year a couple gave me a screwdriver with the name and address of their hardware store on it. I have it today . . . thirty-three years later. They really cared."

Home officials showed their appreciation by holding annual visitation days for many of the sponsors. The *Home Review* covered AMVETS Visitation Day, September 29, 1974:

Sixty-one visitors, including members and their families, registered in the auditorium at 9:30 that morning. The chapel service was conducted by Reverend Roger Wolff and was the first item on the agenda. . . . Following the service, the visitors were encouraged to go to the Main Campus cottages. . . . At noon, dinner was served in the Children's Dining Room. . . . A program was held in the auditorium at 2:00 PM. . . . A check was presented to the Home on behalf of the visitors. . . . Following this portion of the program, a 4-H style show was conducted. The girls modeled the clothes they made for the competition at the Greene County Fair. . . . Then a procession of primary students made their way from the back of the auditorium playing a variety of instruments. . . . The children from the kindergarten, first and second grade classes marched to the stage singing a collection of songs and dancing jauntily around the stage area.

In its centennial year of 1969, the Home recognized the American Legion Auxiliary:

Two hundred and thirty-nine members . . . and their families, the largest Visitation Day turnout to date, attended the sixth annual American Legion Visitation Day held at the Home on Sunday, October 19. . . . Following church services, the guests visited the various cottages. At noon the Auxiliary members and their friends joined the students for dinner in the Children's Dining Room. Following the meal they were conducted on tours of Peter Pan and the Hospital with students acting as escorts.

An entertainment program in the auditorium featured songs and a one-act play given by the senior drama class. The Auxiliary presented the Home with a check for $1,971 to pay for a new carpet for the auditorium. After tours of some of the other buildings, the Legionnaires ended their day, fittingly, on the parade grounds—the spot where, one hundred years earlier, more than a hundred children had gathered in a few cottages and a temporary administration building and made themselves at home on Poverty Knoll.

The parade grounds was also where the Home's battalion held its military drills on Sunday afternoons. The *Xenia Gazette* recommended the "stirring cadet corps review and flag retreat" to its readers in 1963. "It is exciting and heart-lifting to witness the cadet battalion marching onto the campus in front of the Administration Building to the cadence provided by the institution military band," said the local newspaper. "Here the young military trainees stand at attention while the band plays, the flag is lowered, a salute is fired and bugler plays taps. The event is enhanced by the autumn scene. As the late afternoon sun shines through the shade trees with their emblazoned end-of-summer coloring, there is engendered a warm feeling of pride in our country and comfort for the future."

A Time of Transition (1970-1978)

Ahead lay new and formidable challenges for the OSSO Home, which, even during the economic good times of the 1960s, had its share of doubters in the Ohio General Assembly and social services community. Many of the oldest buildings on campus that had been constructed in the 1870s and rehabilitated several times now required more renovation. The cottages built in the 1950s also needed major repairs. In 1971, improvements were made to the Children's Dining Room, the main kitchen, and the steam tunnels serving the Home. There were plans for other major capital improvements, including new kitchenettes in several cottages, an art and media center, and a mental health treatment wing on the hospital. But the projects remained on the drawing board until late in the decade, due to budget cutbacks experienced by all state agencies.

One budget problem that wouldn't go away was the declining number of children presenting themselves for admission to the Home. With 400 boys and girls in 1969, the Home had roughly 25 percent fewer children under its care than it had in residence at the beginning of the decade. This downward spiral was accompanied by an equally disturbing upward trend in children admitted with emotional problems, learning disabilities, and behavioral adjustment problems. While Home officials continued to defend the institution against claims that admission standards had been relaxed, no one disputed the fact that more money was needed to deal with these problems. Money, though, was a problem itself.

A Search for Answers

Superintendent Stephan spent much of his time addressing financial and operational problems, but he would get some help from another colonel, Edwin Freakley, initially hired as senior military instructor in 1970. Colonel Freakley, an army veteran, had served in the same job capacity at the Massanutten Military Academy in Virginia, but after demonstrating exceptional administrative and fiscal skills in his new teaching post, he was made chief fiscal officer and personnel director at the Home in 1971. Freakley suffered a heart attack shortly after assuming his stressful new duties. However, he would make a full recovery and return to the Home as assistant superintendent, involved in most major decisions for the next several years.

The board adopted a new "Statement of Purpose" in 1970, which read: "The purpose of the Home is to provide a home-like situation for eligible children of Ohio veterans to develop them mentally, physically, morally, and socially to become well-adjusted and productive members of society." The trustees and staff members began looking for people both inside and outside the institution who might be able to help them solve the problems facing the Home. Their search took them back to another institution that had helped the OSSO Home many times in the past: the College of Education at The Ohio State University.

In 1972, the board hired Dr. Ray Nystrand of the OSU College of Education to undertake a survey of the Home and its educational programs. One of the most important recommendations in the survey team's final report focused on the treatment of children with emotional or other behavioral problems. In 1973, four Home staff members visited several institutions in North Carolina, including Group Child Care Services in Chapel Hill, "for the purpose of obtaining assistance in the establishment of a treatment unit." Over the next several years, Group Child Care Services provided a variety of consultant services, made site visits, and held in-service training for Home employees. It was hoped that a two-fold approach—providing traditional care for most of the children in the Home and individualized care for those with special needs—not only would be more helpful to all of the residents but also drive up admission rates.

In his report to the board in August of 1973, Colonel Stephan pegged the Home's enrollment at 282, down from 500 in the previous fiscal year. He noted that five cottages had to be closed. "Turnover has been considerable in the past several years," he said. The implications of Stephan's report were ominous. Shrinking enrollment meant fewer students were available for a variety of programs, both within the school and in interscholastic competition. Shorter stays meant the children had less time to adapt to, and benefit from, the Home's programs. Hoping to reverse the trend in admissions, the board of trustees revised the Statement of Purpose yet again in 1974: "The purpose of the Home is to provide care, education and treatment for eligible children of Ohio veterans . . . so that they may be prepared for return to a family setting or able to care for themselves in independent living." The board also received a copy of a pilot program designed "to provide residential treatment and individualized care" at the Home.

For the Home's schools, smaller numbers led to consolidation of academic classes and abbreviated training in vocational fields. Surely more unsettling than any changes made to the education program, however, was the retirement of long-time dramatics instructor J. Robert Rooney in 1971 and his passing a year later. The board re-named the Home's auditorium in his honor. A trust fund also was established in his memory for scholarship aid to ex-pupils and their children and for other charitable purposes. The Rooney Fund was started with a donation from Rooney's widow, Florence Melvin, another popular and long-time staff member. "Melvie," as the children affectionately referred to her, retired in 1974 after thirty-seven years at the Home and was recognized by Governor John Gilligan as "State Employee of the Month." Ex-Pupil Donald Grimshaw of the Class of 1941 shared some of his memories of Mrs. Rooney with the *Home Review*:

Volleyball girls: Brenda Derexson, Rachelle Harris (front), and Barb Collins, Vicki Winn, Penny Ward, and Charmaine Sheller.

Those of us who were in the Home in the late '30s and early '40s reserve a special place in our hearts for "Melvie." During World War II she must have written thousands of letters to Home boys and girls who were serving in the armed forces. She was the center of communications for us. . . . It was from "Melvie" that I first heard of the courage of Colonel Pete Stephan on a faraway island in the Pacific; from her also that Paul Green was flying in Italy; and from her that I first learned of the deaths of Doug Yeazel and Carl Lakes.

She wrote of her strolls around Lake McDowell (long since filled in) and of her converse with the denizens of that entreating body of water. . . . She wrote of weddings and of the singing of the Carol at Christmas. . . . And those of us who were fortunate enough to have received her letters were able to forget for a brief moment the meanness of our circumstances and recall a better time and place. . . . God must have had a great compassion for Ohio's orphans to have steered "Melvie" to the Home; she has left an indelible imprint on our minds.

Lester Anderson, a Rooney Fund trustee, praised the efforts of his 1956 classmate, Morrison Gilbert, who together with Mrs. Rooney created the trust fund. "Morrison begged, cajoled, threatened and strong-armed folks into entering raffles or donating money," recalled Anderson. "I must admit. I always resisted, just to hear his sales pitch! . . . I remember the hundreds of ex-pupils who received monies from the Trust expressing their gratitude for the financial aid they were awarded to help them achieve a better quality of life."

The Home was rocked by another retirement in 1972. "Mousie" Eisenhut retired shortly after receiving the Bishop Medal from Miami University for outstanding community service. He coached championship teams in basketball, football, and track during his thirty-one-year career at the Home, but it was his track teams that made him a Hall of Famer. Woodrow Wilson won four state titles and sixteen district championships, including the aforementioned streak of seven in a row.

The Home's sports program had been in transition even before "Mousie's" retirement. In 1967, Woodrow Wilson left the Mid-Miami League and joined the Dayton Suburban League. After disappointing results on the gridiron in the late 1960s, John Davis rebuilt the football team and won the Suburban League title in 1972 with a team that went undefeated. But in April of 1975, Superintendent Stephan forewarned the board that the Home's athletic program might have to be restructured because of "the increased transient type of student and the number of students (or lack of) we have at the present time." Specifically, Stephan suggested that the Home might be forced to leave the Suburban League and become an independent school. In some sports—such as football—future competition would be on a reserve level rather than varsity level.

One sport on the rise was soccer, which the children had played on an intramural level in the years following World War II. The Home began fielding an interscholastic team in the mid-1970s and quickly found success with an undefeated 1976 team.

Another set of challenges—as well as opportunities—arose over the issue of unionization of the employees of the Home. In early 1971, a representative of the American Federation of State, County and Municipal Employees (AFSCME) came to the Home and requested permission to speak to the staff. Shortly thereafter, a representative of the Ohio Civil Service Employees Association (OCSEA) also showed up on campus, seeking to become the sole bargaining agent for the Home's employees. Superintendent Stephan shared the requests of both unions with the Home's trustees, and over the next several months the ambitions of the contending labor organizations sorted themselves out, with the OCSEA emerging as the sole bargaining agent. The outcome was not unexpected, given the fact that a rather large number of Home's employees were members of the OCSEA. In April of 1972, the board reached the first of what would become a succession of collective bargaining agreements with the OCSEA.

The tornado
Xenia, 1974

This was the year of the Xenia tornado—Wednesday, April 3 and all the clocks at the Home stopped at 4:40 p.m.

The boys at the gym having baseball practice watched the storm through a basement window. They didn't understand what had happened because the path of the tornado was on the other side of town. The Home was spared except for the loss of several trees and some roof damage.

Bob Goody, a 9th grader, spent part of the night near a manhole cover, and saw the dead people being transported into the armory.

Soon National Guard helicopters were landing on the Home football field, and a temporary morgue was set up at the armory. All through the night and into the next day, distraught people were filing through, identifying the bodies of their loved ones.

Many townspeople stayed in their basements all night.

A severe thunderstorm warning was issued around 8:30 p.m. that first night and one of the senior boys ran from cottage to cottage warning sleeping inhabitants of yet another tornado.

Fifteen of the homes of employees were damaged and all school at the Home was curtailed.

Someone at the Home snapped this picture just before the tornado veered away, sparing all but some trees and roofs.

The Return of the Winds

The devastating tornado that struck Xenia on April 3, 1974, touched down about nine miles southwest of the city at 4:30 in the afternoon. It roared into downtown a few minutes later, flattening everything in its path. Trees. Buildings. Businesses. Homes. . . . The powerful wind picked up a tractor trailer rig and deposited the big truck on the roof of a bowling alley before continuing on its 32-mile path through Wilberforce, finally lifting away nine miles north of South Charleston. Thirty-two people were left dead and hundreds more injured. More than half the buildings in Xenia had been damaged and more than three hundred homes and nine churches destroyed. The roof was blown off the Greene County Courthouse.

The tornado missed the Ohio Soldiers and Sailors Orphans Home—but not by much. According to a board report, the wind did about $2,400 damage to the campus, mostly to the roofs of some the buildings. "The biggest effect is the disruption of certain programs and the after-effects of the tornado on both employees and children," stated the report. Patty Thomas was a ninth grader when the deadly storm blew through town:

At 4:00 I went to the farm with Patty Canida. Sonia Montgomery was already there. We rode one of the horses. After awhile the wind started blowing fairly hard, then it started to rain. Pretty soon it started pouring, so we turned the horses loose in the pasture. We ran for shelter. Soon one of the farmers said he saw something twisting in the sky. I thought he was kidding, but wasn't. We all looked outside and sure enough, there was the tornado's funnel. We watched it for a long time. It looked like it was heading straight for us in the barn. And just when we all thought it was going to hit us, it turned. Sonia started worrying about her boyfriend, Don. She started to cry. I was really scared. Then, in the background we saw a house lifted into the air and carried away. As soon as the wind died down we headed back to the cottage in Dale's truck.

Jay Davis described what happened next in the *Home Review*:

At 4:40 p.m., Xenia, Home and surrounding area clocks all stopped and then it hit. Rescue squads, police cars and many other authorities were surprisingly fast to the call for help. All through the night, sirens were heard and there was a mass confusion of cars and sightseers trying to get into Xenia. National Guard troops from Springfield, Ohio, were on the scene . . . to keep looters and camera bugs away from town and to

help people find their loved ones. Many Guard helicopters landed at the Home football field to help speed up the rescue mission. . . .

The National Guard stayed on the scene for three weeks, and Governor Gilligan and President Nixon each toured the devastation. Thousands of people provided food, shelter and other necessities to the people of Xenia. The memory of that day still lingers. Two years removed from the catastrophic event, Jay Davis reflected on its repercussions in a 1976 editorial published by the *Home Review*:

Did Xenia really get destroyed? Maybe this is the beginning of a new and better town. Sure, people lost their homes, their friends and other possessions, but the backbone of Xenia wasn't demolished. . . . In the back of everyone's mind there is a little compartment which contains the words love, loyalty and togetherness. This was opened in Xenia on that terrible April day. "Xenia Lives" is the motto for the city and that is just what we are going to do. To the people of Xenia this is a new beginning.

Looking Ahead

The OSSO Home returned to normal in the weeks after the tornado and began to implement the dual program of treatment and traditional care recommended two years earlier by the Ohio State survey team. With the state operating on a tight budget, Home officials decided to launch the program on a small scale. Washington Cottage was dedicated to the new individualized treatment program and the Home's teachers, house parents and other employees attended in-service training at Wright State University, Clark Technical College, and Kent State University.

In 1975, administrators decided it would be helpful to have a profile of the Home's graduates as a reference tool, whether for planning new programs of treatment and care or for adjusting its traditional programs. A random survey was taken at the annual reunion of the Association of Ex-Pupils and the principal author of the final report was Morrison Gilbert. In his introduction, the 1956 graduate "heartily thanks the Home administration for their complete cooperation and assistance in the conceptualization and planning of this survey questionnaire. A very special mention of Ms. Dorothy Hilty's guidance is made at this time. Her content input was significant and her ideas helpful in the design style. She is a special lady."

A convocation of young biologists meet in their classroom for this Home photograph taken in 1977. Jack Newhouse was the Home's longstanding biology teacher.

Ms. Hilty was a special person indeed. She came to the Home in 1941 with a psychology degree from Ohio University and a master's in clinical psychology from Ohio State. After serving as a cottage supervisor, she was named assistant psychologist at the Home in 1951 and two years later became head psychologist. Dorothy Hilty was diminutive in size, but her evaluations of the children, always made with a warm, personal touch and a genuine concern for their well-being, loomed large. Ms. Hilty not only made important recommendations about applicants, she often suggested steps the Home might want to take to make a particular child's life more positive and fulfilling. She retired in July of 1975, shortly after the completion the Association of Ex-Pupils survey.

The survey provided portraits of some of the children who passed through the Home. It was also a snapshot, if you will, of how well the Home had done its work. Only one hundred ex-pupils responded to the questionnaire, and although that number of respondents was not a statistically valid measure of opinion, the results were still interesting, if not valuable. The average ex-pupil was 47 years old with 2.97 children and presently living in a metropolitan center in Ohio. He or she voted regularly, but generally did not participate in school, community, civic or professional organizations, and did not attend church frequently. The ex-pupils did model their own family's discipline on the training they had received at the Home. They also expressed a willingness to help other recent graduates in their adjustment to independent living. Of the ex-pupils who said they were employed, a sizeable majority described their income as "average."

The average stay at the Home was approximately nine years, with roughly two-thirds of the respondents having graduated from the high school. Extracurricular activities had been important, with one-quarter of the ex-pupils surveyed indicating that they had served as class officers, while 30 percent had participated in Scouting, 30 percent in dramatic arts, 41 percent in music, and 51 percent in athletics.

Some of the more important findings dealt with the Home's vocational training. Eighty-two percent of the ex-pupils surveyed felt that no Home trade was obsolete, yet 43 percent also felt that no Home trade had prepared them for their job. Sixty-one percent said they acquired the technical skills through on-the-job training, 16 percent received specialized instruction from their employer, and 46 percent developed a skill unavailable to them during their time at the Home.

Their favorite Home trades were auto mechanics, business, print shop, wood shop, tailor/sewing, cosmetology, electric shop, cooking, switchboard and metal shop. Their favorite academic subjects, in order of preference, were mathematics, English, music, science, history, biology and, in last place with 1 percent of the vote, geography. The survey summary also noted that the opinions of pupils diverged regarding the success of the Home in preparing pupils for life after their discharge. "A majority of ex-pupils felt that the Home did not prepare them well in social adjustment, understanding ethnic groups, and developing a healthy relationship with the opposite sex." On the other hand, "a majority felt that the Home prepared them well in personal adjustment, citizenship responsibilities, and realizing a purpose in life."

On a different upbeat note, the Home received a generous donation from the Grand Voiture of the 40 & 8 for construction of an outdoor swimming pool. The pool was completed in time for the annual 40 & 8 Field Day celebration on May 1,

$\mathcal{H}$ A
$\mathcal{H}$ome
of their own

268

This photograph of the Home band was believed to have been taken in the 1960s, a shadow of the large touring bands the Home once had.

A trio of intent clarinetists take direction from the longtime Home band director, George Schumacher.

1976, attended by Grand Voiture veterans as well as representatives of the AMVETS, the American Legion, the American Legion Auxiliary, and the Association of Ex-Pupils. It was to be one of the last major public appearances by Colonel "Pete" Stephan, who retired in September and was succeeded by his former assistant, Colonel Freakley.

The *Xenia Gazette* asked Stephan to assess his thirteen years at the helm. "I never realized the decisions the superintendent has to make until I began," he said. "This place isn't run by pushing a button and getting things done. It takes a lot of effort." Stephan had taken over an institution with about 400 residents and a $1 million budget that now served the same number of children—"both long-time residents and temporary charges"—on a $2 million budget. "Costs have gone up," he acknowledged, "and the students we have here now have many more problems. We're trying to do something to help them."

Stephan said that he would leave with many pleasant memories. "The loyalty of the ex-pupils . . . is something I never realized—the time and the effort they contribute for the good of the children at the Home. It's been most gratifying as it has continued through the years and I'm confident it will continue that way."

A Quiet Transformation

Edwin Freakley faced a formidable set of problems in his new job. But having previously worked at the Home for six years, much of that time spent on budget and personnel matters, the colonel felt up to the challenge. Almost immediately, he found himself in negotiations with the OCSEA on a new contractual agreement with the Home. He asked the board to shut down the Washington Cottage treatment facility in ninety days if administrators could not properly implement the program. He also made an appeal for something the trustees and administrators of the Home had never before thought necessary: public relations assistance.

While there were many factors cited for the Home's low admission rate, Colonel Freakly felt that either not enough people were aware of the benefits of the institution or they misunderstood its mission. Upon his recommendation, the board hired David Milenthal and Associates, a Columbus-based advertising and public relations firm, to advise the trustees and staff as to how the they might best present the Home's message through a slide program prepared by the consultants. If this program was shown to enough people, perhaps the image of the Xenia institution would be enhanced, thus causing a spike in admissions.

Superintendent Freakley and his staff took the slide show on the road, making a vigorous effort to sell the OSSO Home, but soon they would be faced with a more pressing problem: how to cut 2 percent from the Home's budget. Governor James Rhodes had not been able to secure support for a major bond package in 1975. With state revenues declining, Rhodes called for the 2 percent reduction in the budgets of all state agencies.

The Home had to find a way to save money—and a lot of it. At the February, 1977 meeting of the board of trustees, Colonel Freakley proposed closing three cottages, the Peter Pan dining rooms, the hospital kitchen, and the laundry, reducing farm operations, discontinuing ROTC if necessary, and ending the Washington Cottage treatment experiment. Twenty-five people also would be laid off, saving the Home approximately $314,000. The board agreed to shut down the Peter Pan and hospital kitchens and offer cafeteria-style food service in the children's dining room, but by April the Home had received more than $800,000 in supplemental funding from the state and many of the more drastic cost-cutting measures were postponed.

In March of 1977, the board was notified that the estate of Morrill "Hat" Noland of the Class of 1929 had left a substantial bequest to the Home. Noland, the owner of a successful paper company, was one of the institution's strongest supporters among the ranks of the Association of Ex-Pupils. For years, he had donated paper—literally by the boxcar load—to the print shop. His arrangement was simple: if the Home paid the freight, it could have the paper. Noland also underwrote much of the costs associated with the publication of *Pride of Ohio*, including donating the paper on which the history of the Home was printed. With Noland's bequest of 10,000 shares of stock in his paper company and donations from his friends totaling almost $2,000, the Home placed a memorial bench on campus in "Hat's" honor.

As fall approached, Colonel Freakley recommended that Milenthal and Associates be retained for another six months. As part of its consulting deal, the Columbus PR firm would prepare an occasional newsletter for widespread distribution, promoting the Home's facilities and services. Freakley also proposed a reorganization of the Home's Department of Student Life, which was approved by the board. Henceforth, the superintendent would directly administer the Peter Pan and Junior campus, while Assistant Superintendent James York would supervise the military department. The director of student life would oversee the main campus, as well as the religious and recreation departments.

In October of 1977, Colonel Freakley came to the board of trustees with good news and bad news. The good news was that a satisfactory contract had been negotiated with the OCSEA, which the board approved. The bad news was that despite the best efforts of the Home's staff and its consultants to publicize and promote the Xenia institution, admission levels remained unchanged. "The superintendent advised the board that in view of the current low enrollment of the Home and the fact that a public relations effort had failed, to date, to increase enrollment to a satisfactory level, a change in the admission requirements should be considered. The Home should be open to all children of Ohio residents, with first preference given to the children of Ohio veterans."

Over the next two months, Freakley discussed his proposal with the Association of Ex-Pupils and various veterans organizations around the state. He also suggested changing the name of the Home to the "Ohio Soldiers and Sailors Children's Home." Colonel Stephan had first proposed a name change in 1967, then again in 1970. This time, both the name change and Colonel Freakley's new admission policy had the support of the Home's trustees. The veterans organizations and Association of Ex-Pupils also agreed—reluctantly—to back the proposals.

The board was scheduled to vote on the changes at its January meeting in 1978, but Mother Nature, one might say, filed an objection. On January 26, Ohio was visited by the worst blizzard in the recorded history of the state. Winds in excess of

The blizzard

January, 1978

"January struck us with the ferocity of a bulldog shaking a rag doll," wrote the *Home Review*.

There were frigid temperatures in the cottages, and students shivering under extra blankets. There was glee at the prospect of no school, but no such student luck. For the maintenance men it was nothing but hard work and bitter cold. The students helped the supervisors dig their cars out and clear streets. Then the students vanished, reappearing on the front hills of the Home with their sleds, running into trees, slightly battered, and into the creek.

As for snowballs, "the Home has never had so many Major League prospects," reported the *Review*.

Roosevelt Hall became noted for its mammoth snow fort, able to hold off all comers.

The drifts were so high students lost shoes in them, staggering into buildings as though they'd stomped through the Klondike.

On January 14, when temperatures plunged to minus-twenty, the school was actually closed an hour early, the first time that had happened in nearly three decades, and poor Mr. Edwards, supervisor at the heating plant, was facing near insurmountable difficulties because of the frozen coal....

Belying the fact that the vocational ed department had no snowboarding courses, Home students, as usual, made out on their own.

sixty miles per hour dropped temperatures to a wind chill equivalent of minus-50 degrees and whipped ten inches of snow into drifts up to twenty feet high. With a death toll of fifty-one persons, it became one of the deadliest storms in Ohio history.

At its February meeting, the board decided to seek legislation changing the name of the OSSO Home to the "Ohio Veterans Children's Home." The trustees also agreed that the children of any Ohio resident, "destitute of means of support and education," should be eligible for admission to the Home, provided that "sufficient space" is available and that children of Ohio veterans in a similarly bad way be given first priority for placement in the institution. In April, in the presence of the trustees and representatives of the Association of Ex-Pupils, Governor Rhodes signed into law a bill authorizing these changes.

The name change ceremony was held at the Home on July 23. Among the 150 guests were Xenia mayor Walter Marshall, commanders of veterans organizations, former superintendent Stephan, and a number of ex-pupils. Battery C of the First Volunteer Light Artillery presented a Civil War artillery firing re-enactment that was followed by musical selections by a choral ensemble and the unveiling of a sign that read: "Ohio Veterans Children's Home."

The night watchman would let me walk around with him. I would ask him if he minded if my buddy and I took a midnight run, and he would just say, 'Stay off the girl side.' So we would sneak out and go up to the track and walk around, get some midnight running in . . . and we stayed off the girl's side. He had his rules, so we followed his rules and he let boys be boys.—Larry Tolle, Class of 1969

Board members Mary Lee and James Snyder flank Governor Rhodes as he signs the Home's name change into law. Superintendent Freakley and Senate clerk Bill Chavanne, an ex-Home pupil, look on.

So much
permanent
good (1978-1995)

Well into the 1970s, the Home's mission stayed consistent; it would take dramatic social currents to alter it.

A look at the Home, circa 1978

Any institution occupying the same place for more than one hundred years acquires a certain reliable familiarity to the people who pass by it from time to time. Thus, people driving by the main gates of the Ohio Soldiers and Sailors Orphans Home in the summer of 1978 might have experienced something of a shock. The OSSO Home was now—according to a newly prepared sign—the Ohio Veterans Children's Home. Even passers-by who knew the name had been changed probably would have wondered if anything was different up there on the ridge south of Xenia. People driving up the long lane to the Home to satisfy their curiosity would have been hard-pressed to find something out of the ordinary. Budget reductions had

For more than a century, the Home had been a singular American institution; of course, it would face changes. The question was how.

forced officials to postpone repairs and renovation to many of the older buildings, and the declining population of the Home had led to the closing of some of the residential cottages and staff layoffs. But the administration building still stood as a towering sentinel over the parade grounds. And life on campus appeared normal.

Officers of the United States Army showed up in April to conduct their annual inspection of the Home's JROTC battalion. The battalion had fewer numbers than in prior periods—the girls were as well represented in the ranks as the boys by the late 1970s—but as always the children in the unit were dressed in full uniform and stood in perfect formation across the parade grounds. The inspection of the ranks was immediately followed by the "Pass in Review," after which the visiting officers held an exit briefing and delivered their report to the superintendent of the Home.

A few weeks later, the Grand Voiture of the 40 & 8 returned to the Home for the fifty-first time to hold its Field Day activities. The veterans organization gave the children rides in vans that were adapted to look like the WWI boxcars that held forty men or eight horses. Drill competitions were held at the company, platoon, and squad levels. An individual drill competition was held for advanced students. There was a rookie competition for children who had not been assigned to the battalion or the band for more than a year. In the evening, most of the children on the campus attended the annual military ball in the McKinley Gymnasium.

During the remainder of his term as superintendent, Colonel Freakley did his best to keep things operating normally. That summer—as always—some children participated in a program of remedial learning, camping, and maintenance of the buildings and grounds. Some took vacations with their parents or guardians. Others assisted the farm staff. And in the last weeks of August, practice began in earnest for the football and soccer teams. But many of the children and staff going about their normal routines knew that it was just a matter of time before things were going to change.

The Home's problems hadn't magically disappeared just because it now went by a new name. It had been taking in fewer and fewer children for a number of years, while the costs of staffing and maintaining the grounds and buildings had escalated. The cost per child continued to go up because there were fewer residents to absorb the fixed costs. A place that had once prided itself on having to spend only a few hundred dollars a year on each child now found itself spending not hundreds of dollars but thousands of dollars per child—and, if anything, expenditures were likely to keep going up.

Although the Home now could admit children of any Ohioan in distress, the trustees, as well as the veterans organizations and other interested parties, assumed the Xenia institution would operate as it always had—taking in children of a wide variety of ages and backgrounds who would stay for a number of years in order to fully utilize the educational and training programs. Colonel Freakley and his staff, however, were not ready to make that assumption. Like most social workers and children's services administrators, they had known for some time that the use of what had once been called "orphanages" and now were called "children's residential treatment facilities" was becoming more and more limited. For more than forty years, federal and state assistance to single mothers with small children, allocated through the Aid to Families with Dependent Children program, had meant families once threatened with dissolution could stay together. Social workers argued that family life was the best life and that foster homes were greatly preferable to large institutions because of their smaller scale and because the children placed there could receive more individual attention and care. Foster homes also were reported to be up to ten times cheaper than places like the Home. What could not be accurately assessed, however, was the quality of life in a private home with far fewer resources than the Ohio Veterans Children's Home.

If Colonel Freakley wasn't as confident as some of his colleagues about the Home's future, maybe it was because the superintendent knew almost $4 million per year for the next two years would be required for maintenance and operations. The only answer seemed to be admitting more children, even if that meant accepting some with behavioral, social, or other problems. Freakley was not advocating admitting dangerously disturbed children; there were other facilities for those special cases. Rather, the Home would accept some children with mild emotional disorders or perhaps other psychiatric problems, trusting that their association with the Home's more permanent (and stable) residents would be beneficial to both. For the moment, it seemed that a middle way of treatment and care had been found—a way that would keep the Home alive.

Minutes of the August, 1978, meeting of the board of trustees reveal that Dr. Joe Cresci, the staff psychiatrist, "discussed the type of child being admitted and specific behavior patterns being demonstrated by the children." Earlier that summer, Colonel Freakley spent five days at a summer workshop in Chapel Hill, North Carolina, where his courses included "Character Disordered Youth in Group Care" and "Preparing Children for Independence." The superintendent returned with new ideas to implement, including an incentive program. Awards would be given each month for the "Best Cottage," "Best Cadet of the Term," "Best Company of ROTC," and "Best Citizen—Scholastic Achievement."

The staff also underwent rigorous training in the care of troubled youth.

Even with the current population of the Home, staff members sometimes became frustrated. (In July, the chaplain resigned, in the words of Colonel Freakley, "due to his inability to exercise patience and follow stated procedures in dealing with children.") A local social worker conducted in-service training, stressing "the development of relationships, feelings, maturity, motivation and vision." A second staff development program was offered by Wright State University. It focused on education both inside and outside the classroom, and included sessions on Student Motivation, Teacher Behavior, Disruptive Students, Classroom Atmosphere, and Frustration and Anxiety. Staff members also were offered the opportunity to earn a certificate in institutional child care, and some of the training was mandatory.

To reflect the Home's new mission, the board revised its statement of purpose to read: "The Ohio Veterans Children's Home is a residential care facility for children of Ohio residents with first priority for admission given to veterans' children as determined by the Board of Trustees. A multi-dimensional individual therapeutic program, including vocational and academic education is offered. A program of personal growth and awareness for meeting the physical, social and spiritual needs of the child is employed to help each child understand himself/herself prior to returning to family or independent living."

With the new training program in place and staff resignations and student incidents on the decline, Colonel Freakley announced his retirement in May of 1979, to be effective on or about September 1.

Life at the Home in the 1980s

The Seventies had not been one of America's more emotionally uplifting decades. The Eighties would be much more controversial and far more eventful, beginning with the election of Ronald Reagan. During his eight years in office, he limited the size and power of the federal government, affecting every agency and program that received government money, including Aid to Families with Dependent Children. Many people in the social services community supported foster care as the cheapest alternative to institutionalization. Democrat Richard Celeste, who served as Ohio's governor throughout most the decade, was willing to help institutions like the Ohio Veterans Children's Home as they struggled to re-invent themselves, but because of the harsh fiscal realities of the time, Celeste and his administration were not always able to provide the needed assistance.

*Memorial Day, past or present?
There was one ritual that never seemed
to change much at the Home, no matter
the social forces outside.*

The Schools

The Home began the decade with a new name, but its high school, named for President Woodrow Wilson, remained an important part of the institution's identity. The core courses taught at Woodrow Wilson had not changed much over the years, although curriculum planners in nearby Xenia and Greene County, as well as professional evaluators from the Ohio Department of Education, tried to keep the academic offerings fresh and relevant. It was the vocational program—as old as the Home itself—that continued to provide the children with unique learning opportunities. The program had changed with the times. Blacksmithing, for instance, no longer was offered as a standard course. But students still could choose from a broad range of occupations, according to a summary of classes in 1988 published in the *Home Review*:

"The Business Office Education class has been restructured this year. Each employee is an expert in one of four areas: Word Processing, Typing/Transcription, Business Machines, and Business Mathematics. Every ten days the employees rotate to a different area. First-year students in addition to the above areas are studying Accounting; second-year students, Business Law."

In carpentry, "topics covered this year will include interior and exterior finishing of houses. Included are dry wall and paneling installation, door and window installation, installing cabinets and applying trim board and exterior siding."

The Graphics Arts class was busy "printing 13,000 envelopes for the Home, as well as silkscreen printing, typesetting, layout and camera work," while the Cosmetology class made its "yearly trip to Vicki's Uniform Shop in Kettering. This year the students selected white skirts and grey and white shirts."

In the Horticulture class, the fall projects included raising "a crop of poinsettias" for sale to the staff of the Home at Christmas. "With cooler weather approaching, we will be working on the softball field and learning about turf grass management." The previous year had seen the horticulture students more occupied with floral pursuits. "Although the cemetery may be a place for sad occasions, on October 15, the Home cemetery witnessed a happy event. Mr. Jones's [Horticulture] class planted daffodils for spring blooming. The bulbs donated by Skeeter Baker were to be planted in the fall so they could be ready to bloom by next Easter. . . . The following day, October 16, found the Horticulture class busy once again selling plants which they had raised for Sweetest Day. With the plant came a card and a small balloon which said 'P.S. I Love You.' The money earned was put in the vocational fund. They earned $88. We all look forward to their next adventure."

"I was very shy, and the Home was overwhelming to me. On my first day, a girl in my cottage, Tonya, said, 'Why are you so introverted?' And I began to cry. But some of the other girls went to the senior girl in the cottage and said, 'Tonya made the new girl cry.' And the senior girl smacked Tonya. I felt guilty because maybe Tonya meant nothing by her remark, and I was just feeling overwhelmed. But I also felt good. Because this meant I had been *accepted*. My first day in a strange new place, and someone had taken up for me!

"In Bellefontaine, I was a good kid. I was a straight-A student. I had never even smoked a cigarette. But when my mother found some pot in my brother's room, she hauled us both down to the police station and filed charges. My brother took up for me, but no one listened. Suddenly, I'm on probation, and I have a new circle of friends.

"My brother said once, 'Laura, Mom thinks that when she sent you to the Home, she was sending you into lockup. But the Home changed your life, and it turned you around.' And maybe he's right, that if she'd understood the freedom I found, she would never have sent me there.

"I craved regimentation, although I didn't know it at the time. I needed that place so badly, but I didn't know that I needed it. The Home was a godsend.

"The girls in my cottage were like a family, even though each had her own experiences and background. Even Tonya was not angry with me after getting herself smacked. My shyness started to go away. I had to be in ROTC, and I found myself walking in front of the company, carrying the flag. I *couldn't* be shy. I was elected military ball queen.

"Being accepted was a new thing. The children of alcoholics have had little acceptance in their lives, and they're always insecure. My mother would say to me and my siblings, 'Giving birth to you kids was the worst thing I ever did.' We don't think much of ourselves, but then these people at the Home were seeing something in me that I didn't see.

"You could find friends at the Home. There was always someone to help. Our cottage had what we regarded as the strictest houseparent, Mrs. Saxton, but it was okay. We didn't mind because we had the feeling she cared about us. At first, she didn't understand the relationship between me and my mom. My mom was secretive and put up a good front. But one day after she had written me a horrible letter, I was terribly upset, and I showed it to Mrs. Saxton. She began to cry, too. 'Now I understand,' she said.

"My mother was such an influence in such a bad way. All of us struggled. When people look at me and say, 'How did you do so well?' I think to myself: *I didn't want to be her*. And I had the Home. I told someone that if it weren't for the Home, I don't think I'd be alive…

"The Home gave me work, too. All the students had to practice a craft of some kind, and while I went into the print shop because that's where my boyfriend was, I soon really liked it. I liked being creative but I couldn't paint, but soon I found that running the press helped me feel creative. There were so many things involved: the type, the camera, the press. When I run a job and everything comes together, the ink is perfect and the job looks good, I am proud. Not just everyone can start a press and make a job look good. Around my mother I never felt proud. We could never do things well enough.

"I still work for my old Home printing teacher, Brian Liming. He hired me after graduation. When I left the Home, I had nothing, and the staff members helped me. They gave me a table and a couch. They had always helped. For my prom, the superintendent's secretary took me shopping. They were people we could depend on, and when I arrived at the Home, I didn't have anybody like that in my life.

"I was a junior when I arrived, and the classes were a little rowdier than I was used to, and there were some disrespectful kids. The population of the Home was changing. It had kids who had been there since they were 4 or 5, and then short-timers like myself, who had just arrived and understood alcohol, drugs, and all the outside stuff. The long-term Home kids were probably isolated from a lot of this. If I'd had *their* childhood, I'd been great. I'd have taken their childhood over mine anytime. I *envied* their childhood.

"I was at the Home a short fifteen months, but it shaped my whole life. I still live and work in Xenia, and I drive past the Home twice a day. I see kids sledding on the hill and I think: *How cool is that?* I love the idea of kids being there. Those buildings *need* kids. The Home has always been there. I hope it will be there forever."

Even in the final years, the familiar Home rituals carried on, aimed at giving students a sense of place and purpose.

(Although much of its land was leased to local farmers for corn and soybean production, the Home still maintained its farm. Children working there now earned academic credit for their labor, the dairy herd continued to be one of the best in the state, and the greenhouse and gardens were famous throughout the area.)

One student who took advantage of all Woodrow Wilson had to offer was Leon Charles Wilson, who came to the Ohio Veterans Children's Home during his junior year in high school. He became captain of the football team, editor of the *Home Review*, and president of his senior class. In the summer between his junior and senior years, Wilson attended Buckeye Boys State and described his experience in the *Home Review*.

"I boarded a bus with approximately sixty or seventy guys I've never before seen in my life," he recalled in an article published in the *Home Review*. "The only thing I knew was we were going to Bowling Green State University to set up a mock government and to run for political offices . . . . When I figured out what was going on, I went to work immediately campaigning. I organized a group of ten guys to help me . . . . We had to have eight signatures from each county by noon of the following day. Upon the completion of this task, I had to raise seven hundred dollars to run for governor and extra money for various campaign expenses . . . . The rest of the day was to be spent promoting yourself (who you are, what office you are running for, your platform). . . . The next day it was announced that I had been elected as the 1987 American Legion Buckeye Boys State Governor."

Wilson graduated from the Home with the rank of major in ROTC and made plans to enter the army.

"With all the honors, positions and awards credited to Charles," observed the *Home Review*, "he has set a good example for other students. He has been an honor citizen almost the entire time he has lived here . . . . He's well on his way."

Traditional Ties

Of all the education programs, none was more deeply rooted in the Home's past than military science. The flags changed over the years, as did uniforms and weapons—probably some drills, too—but the Home continued to award academic credit in armed forces training and instill the children with a sense of the institution's long and proud military tradition. Here's how Veterans Day was celebrated in 1988, as reported in the *Home Review*:

The activities began at 9:00 AM with a battalion formation in the armory. From

Ever since the prime of J.R. Rooney, theatrical productions—of several different kinds—were a Home staple. Witness these high-steppers of the mid-1980s.

there they marched to the auditorium for an assembly. The Boys Drill Team stood in line at the door as the guests and battalion arrived. . . . Chaplain Wilson gave a moving speech about our freedoms and how many soldiers had died at war to protect our freedoms. The presentation ended with the Cadet firing squad consisting of Tim Casteel and the Boys Drill Team giving a 21-gun salute. Andy Dobie played taps . . . .

A week later, veterans of the Grand Voiture of the 40 & 8 made their annual fall visit.

The visit began at lunch with the posting of the colors. . . . After lunch, the boys and girls drill teams performed. In conjunction with Woodrow Wilson's open house, many of our guests were taken on a tour of the school facilities. The [Association of Ex-Pupils] Museum was also open. The students spent an enjoyable afternoon taking the famous Forty et Eight boxcar ride. Later in the afternoon, the Den was opened. Many

students watched football and played games.

Some of the most memorable events in the lives of children continued to be the traditional holiday observances and celebrations. The Home's "Show Choir" kicked off the Thanksgiving-Christmas season in 1988, according to the following item in the *Home Review*:

The ever popular Woodrow Wilson Show Choir is in constant demand. On November 8, they traveled to the Dayton VA Hospital to perform for the women's auxiliary. . . . A very special performance was held on the evening of December 1, when the choir performed two selections at the Wright-Patterson Air Force Base Officers Club. Many of the top Air Force brass were present in the audience, including a four-star general. . . .

On December 15, a Winter Wonderland scene was displayed in the Orfenz Den

. . . . *Thursday evening the entire campus attended. Santa Claus was also in attendance to take pictures with the kids.*

On Saturday, December 17, the ex-pupils, employees, Women's American Legion Auxiliary and various veterans groups were in charge of wrapping all of the students' Christmas gifts that various posts donated.

And then there was the big dance.

Tony Wortham, the activities director at the Ohio Veterans Children's Home, arranged a Snowball Dance on December 21 for the main campus student body. . . . [Wortham] invited 'Zawaap,' a band, which played music the last hour and a half of the dance.

The holiday season culminated in the annual Christmas celebration.

First it started with carolers caroling through the main building and the children's

The Home basketball team of 1984-1985, presided over by 6-10 coach ; Jim Cunningham (at right), includes (front row) Earl Woods, Curtis Proffitt, Aaron Brown, and Larry Walton. In back is assistant coach Robert Butler, Gene Cogswell, Scott Bateman, Frank Arbogast, Mike Shepard, Elbert Allison, and Shannon Welch.

dining room. Each caroler had a candle and a partner. They walked around the children's dining room twice singing the Home's Christmas Carol. . . . After the band played, the Home choir sang. Breakfast was served, which was followed by the Christmas church services.

The Home's athletic trophies were now on display in the new Museum of the Association of Ex-Pupils, located in what was formerly the Memorial Library. The hardware filled not one, but two large floor-to-ceiling cabinets, much of it from an earlier time when the teams of George Woerlein and Warren "Mousie" Eisenhut won multiple league titles as well as district and state championships. After Eisenhut retired in 1972, the Home divided his coaching responsibilities among several individuals, who did their best to cope with declining numbers of eligible young men and women. Woodrow Wilson struggled on the football field during the Eighties, only able to suit up with twenty to thirty players most seasons in a league with 50- and 60-man squads. And one might say that the track and field teams, once the most successful of the Home's athletic teams, fell off the pace

John Davis
Coach, teacher, principal, counselor

"Growing up, I knew that if something happened to me, one relative or another would take care of me. When I arrived at the Home in the summer of 1968, I couldn't comprehend that there were kids with absolutely no one. Your education never prepares you for what you faced there.

"So we tried to create all the normal activities, from holidays to the homecoming dance, everything as normal as we could make it. And one of the first things you understood was that no matter how terribly they had been treated, you could never take them completely away from their family. And you didn't really want to. The kids always held that someone would visit, or take them, or come to see them on whatever holiday. That carrot was always out in front of them.

"During football season, we took the kids to Saturday games, but some of them would say someone was coming to visit, parent, or uncle, someone. What the relative had really said was that he or she *might* visit this weekend or next. Rarely did anyone show up. The kids'd be waiting forever. So we just made the events mandatory. Afterward, the kids said, 'I'm glad you took us; my relatives probably wouldn't have showed up anyway…'

"My job was to lead them toward goals, steer them into a vocation, whether it was army, trade school, or college. A couple of coworkers and I, we generated summer vacations for kids who would otherwise have never had one. Our first vacation was a trip to Gettysburg. We spent part of the summer studying Gettysburg, then we got on the bus and drove there. Most of our kids had never been out of Ohio.

We camped out, spent four or five days there, then came back.

"I always thought of the Home as a big country club, a place that was missing nothing but the parents. And that was our job. The kids needed someone to latch onto, whether that person was a houseparent, secretary, teacher, or farm worker. I thought that the job of *everybody* employed there was to help the students. I didn't care *what* your job was, mowing the grass, fixing the plumbing, everything else was secondary.

"The first fifteen years I was there, the staff was hugely responsive to the kids. I was guidance counselor, taught, and was an assistant football coach. I became head coach in 1971, and in 1972 I had the Home's last undefeated team. It was something of a throwback to the unscored-on teams of '37 and '41. Well, according to Mike Ford, there *was* one score in 1937: the B team scored on the varsity in practice. Mike said that night after supper, the varsity went over to where the B players were and just beat the hell out of them. It was a real donnybrook. All because they'd managed to score against the varsity in practice.

"So my 1972 boys were a bit like that. We played a tough schedule, teams that were a lot bigger, but I had Ernie Sheeler, who went to Iowa on a Big Ten scholarship, and the two Davidson brothers who played at Capital University, and I had the Thomas brothers, Ricky, Dwayne, and Robert. Dwayne was a guard, so quick I had to instruct the referees because they'd think he was offsides. 'Watch Dwayne's hands and the ball,' I'd tell 'em. 'He's never offsides; you just *think* he is.'

"We were playing Trenton Edgewood, Ernie Sheeler breaks a 72-yard play and, sure enough, they think Dwayne's

That's Earl Woods, a mid-1980s Home player, scoring for the Cadets, who even with diminished numbers were never really out of their games.

offsides. So we run the play again. This time, Ernie goes 78 yards. Two plays back-to-back, 150 yards.

"They were all good kids, good athletes. We put in a new offense, the wishbone. We had quick kids, and the most coachable ones I ever had. Everything came together, and we went 9-0.

"Now here's a thing about Home kids: the coaches always had to start from scratch because the boys didn't usually have any experience. They hadn't come up through pee-wee ball and these other leagues. We even had to show some of them how to put on their pads. But the Home boys prided themselves on being a little tougher than whoever they played. Their backgrounds made them this way. What was tougher than what most of them had come out of? We might be smaller, or up against a stronger, better team, but the whole time I coached there, we never got beat *physically*.

"There were some real culture clashes, too. Once, we went down to play Cincinnati Country Day, upper class kids who played real good football, and our rag-tag kids get off the bus and the first thing they see is some kids sitting in a Rolls Royce watching a football game.

"Something else about our kids, and as time passed this hurt us: there was never a gate when anyone played us. We had no crowd. No one was watching. We were always playing in front of other people's crowds, *their* friends and parents. So as time passed, no one wanted to play us. First, we didn't bring a crowd. And, second, we might beat you, no matter how small we were.

"Gradually, things began to change. As the kids admitted into the Home became more delinquent, the staff drew back. I became principal in the mid-1980s, and the job wasn't much fun. It was difficult to find good staff, our salaries were not competitive with the local schools, and there was always that pressure to get the budget approved by the state. It was like a school system faced with passing a levy every two years.

"The 1980s was a kind of a finger-in-the-dike operation. It was as if we were saying, 'Well, let's not ask for much, cut what we can, and not make too much noise.' But you can't operate that way. Your facilities disintegrate,

programs go downhill, and so do you.

"More and more of our kids were troubled. I'd ask myself, *How in the world can we work in these conditions?* I remember the first time I walked down a hallway and smelled marijuana. Some student was smoking marijuana in the bathroom. Oh, my. Our staff wasn't trained for this population. We were constantly under a microscope, scrutinized by this agency and that agency. Finally, I went back to being a guidance counselor. I was sure I could do more for the kids as a counselor. That's where I was when the Home closed.

"I knew the Home couldn't survive, but I thought if we could change our focus and get back on track, well, guidance counselors are by nature optimistic people, and it was my pipe dream. Up until the mid-1970s, I had the best job in the world. I loved coming to work everyday. I thought someone would come up and retrain us to deal with this new population of kids, and let us put our energies toward helping *them*. I thought we were doing a super job with what we had to work with, but we were just getting kicked in the teeth.

"One day in the 1990s, I was leading some legislators on a tour around the Home and they were saying what a beautiful campus and this and that, and I said, 'Yeah, it'd make a damned good place for a children's home.' They just clammed up after that. Nobody said anything. They followed me around for a few more minutes, and that was the tour.

"I put twenty-nine years in there, and for the most part, it was a great, positive experience. Great kids, great memories. I couldn't get over the spirit the kids had. Normal kids faced with what our kids had been through, well, I don't know if they'd done nearly as well. And there's no way a foster home could do for our kids what we did for them. Absolutely no way."

as fewer and fewer children apparently had the time or volition to continue the program's winning tradition.

Three Woodrow Wilson girls' basketball teams did manage to beat the odds in three respective seasons, finishing with records of 19-2, 17-1, and a perfect 18-0. A story from the *Home Review* in 1988 recounts what must have been the Lady Cadets' most lop-sided victory:

They traveled to Greenville on Saturday, January 24. . . . Greenville's team looked pretty good before the game with tall, aggressive players making plenty of baskets. Mrs. Matos had her team begin with a tight press. Practice can be deceiving. . . . At the end of the second quarter we were ahead 50-0.

Mrs. Matos apparently didn't have much to say during the halftime pep talk. She did, however, call off the press. The final score was 92-1.

A Series of Exits

Before stepping down as superintendent in the fall of 1979, Colonel Freakley urged the board to adopt a new "Table of Organization" that divided the functions of the Home into four sections—Support Services, Direct Services, Schools, and Business Management—each with its own administrator. The trustees approved the reorganization plan and hired Dr. James W. Battoclette as Freakley's successor.

Battoclette was a practicing counselor—just the man for the job, or so it seemed, as the Home began its new mission as a "residential care facility." One of his first tasks was to implement a special education program. The board would seek permission from the state to accept children with learning disabilities, emotional disabilities or other learning handicaps, and make applications to the Ohio Department of Education to fund the program. In December of 1980—"with the intent of increasing enrollment" at the Home—the trustees also agreed to seek a legal opinion as to whether the institution could accept children still under the legal custody of their parents; traditionally, custody of children at the Home had been held by a local court or, in some cases, by the Home itself.

But by early 1981, it was apparent, both to trustees and the new superintendent, that efforts thus far to re-invent the Home had fallen short of expectations. The two parties reached a settlement, with Dr. Battoclette resigning in April. His immediate successor was Assistant Superintendent James York. York had been at the Home for some time and had a good working relationship with both the staff and the children. And while he agreed with the comments made by the board president— "there is a lot of work to be done with respect to recruitment, public relations, the administrative situation and the school situation"—James York faced a more pressing problem.

Since March of 1981, after legislative budget hearings, Home officials had been concerned about the future of the Home's farm. By May, when it became clear that funding for the farm would not be included in the Home's next biennial budget, attempts were made to retain farm employees in other positions at the Home. Most, however, eventually would be laid off, bringing to an end an operation that not only had provided food and training to generations of children at the Home but also afforded the institution the luxury of self-sustainability that, once lost, would be difficult to regain.

Superintendent York worked with staff and students over the summer of 1981 to coordinate the Home's current programs with the new programs for children with learning disabilities. In September, he reported that he was impressed "with the enthusiasm of the teachers, the interest displayed by the students and the overall atmosphere of learning that seemed to prevail." Meanwhile, York and the board struggled to find ways to make ends meet and recruit new children. As a state-run facility, the Home received most of its funding from Columbus. But it also received regular donations from veterans organizations, former pupils, and friends of the institution. Most of these donations had been deposited in banks for use as the board and the superintendent determined. In the fall of 1983, the board agreed to "establish an endowment fund for all donated monies and other financial gifts received, for the purpose of investing such funds for maximum return. This fund is to be used for the programs and services directly related to, and for the students of the Home."

The Home dealt with the departure of two long-serving employees, Emlyn Whilding and Mildred Blair, in January of 1984. Whilding, who arrived in 1951 as a teacher and was promoted to principal of the academic school in 1959, was replaced by instructor John Davis as principal. Blair retired after thirty-nine and one-half years of service. As the social services director, she was responsible for screening children who applied for admission to the Home. "We are not a correctional facility and we are not a mental hospital," she said, looking back on her time at the Home. "What we have is a place for youngsters who really get along better in group situations. Some have been hurt so much they do not trust the family situation. We reflect what happens in society, good or bad. Most of what we used to do was try to determine whether they (children's families) were financially destitute. That's not where we come from now. Somewhere along the line it occurred to everybody that a lot of people needed help whether they had the money or not."

In June, after submitting a plan to the board to increase the Home's residential population to 300 by the end of 1984 and letting contracts totaling more than $59,000 to remove asbestos from the McKinley Gymnasium, Superintendent York announced that he, too, would be leaving, informing the trustees of his intention to resign in October. York was a veteran, like each of his predecessors dating back to the founding of the Home more than one hundred years earlier, but as the board began its search for a new leader, the trustees asked that the clause "must have served honorably in one of the branches of the armed services" be removed from all postings and advertisements. During the search that summer, the board received an unexpected but much appreciated gift—$316,842.33 from the estate of Lawrence Fink. It was the largest private bequest ever made to the institution, and it would provide a solid base for loan, scholarship and other student assistance programs not funded by state agency funds.

In October, the board appointed a member of the Home's staff, Charles R. Adams, to serve as the new superintendent. Adams set to work immediately. When not dealing with the day-to-day problems, he found time to tackle issues that would affect the Home over the longer term. One of these issues stemmed from the Fair Labor Standards Act, which required employers to provide minimum wage and overtime pay. In a recent case—*Garcia vs. San Antonio Metropolitan Transit Authority*—the U.S. Supreme Court held that Congress had the power to extend the federal "Wages and Hours" law, as it was known, to state and local governments. The Home, therefore, would have to employ its "houseparents" for eight-hour shifts because it simply could not afford to compensate them for the overtime hours they worked by living in the cottages, as had been the long-standing practice of the institution. This would be a major change.

The "house parent" system had been one of the great strengths of the Home. Children often considered their house parents temporary and sometimes lengthy substitutes for the parents they never had or had left behind. Now, their cottages would feel less like a "home" and more like an institution—not what anyone wanted, but the law was the law.

Despite all of the Home's recruitment efforts, the average enrollment by late 1985 had fallen below 200 children. There was debate through the 1980s as to how children at the Home should be counted. Many state agencies relied on a daily attendance count. But Home officials preferred to count the total number of children served in a given period—not daily—because many children only stayed on campus for a few months. In any case, there were far too few of them.

For much of 1986, the board and administration worked to find a balance between the Home's traditional programs and the new treatment regimens being offered by the institution. It was not always easy. In August, the trustees received the staff's monthly Social Service Report, which revealed that a large number of the children had several "out of home" placements that didn't work out. "This information," the board noted, "could go far in refuting some notions that foster care is the panacea for 'out of home' placements. . . . Lengthy discussion was entered into regarding methods that could be utilized to interest students in remaining in the Home versus the continuous barrage [from] parents and agencies to return [them] to the natural home. The consensus was that the sooner we entered into additional social, athletic, and extracurricular skill programs, the more quickly students would become interested and involved in their environment."

A few months later the board considered the possibility of operating a "younger child abuse program" in the Home's "ready-made" (and under-utilized) facility for younger children—the Peter Pan Cottages. The cottages, however, were deteriorating due to a lack of regular maintenance and the trustees were unable to secure funds to upgrade the units and implement the program.

By all accounts, Charles Adams had done a very good job managing the affairs of the Home during his tenure as superintendent from the fall of 1984 through the winter of 1987. But after his son had been involved in a serious automobile accident, Adams no longer was able to give his full attention to his duties. He submitted his resignation to the board in March so that he could spend more time assisting in his son's long and painful recovery. Adams was the fourth superintendent to leave the Ohio Veterans Children's Home since the retirement of Colonel S.I. Stephan in 1976. This time, the board hoped to find someone who might be able to stay a little while longer. In D. Leon Huff, the trustees believed they had found their man.

Leon Huff had been with the Home since 1985 and as assistant superintendent was aware of its problems and possibilities. Married with three children, he came to Xenia after serving for eight years as the executive director of a children's home in Wisconsin. After several months in his new job, Huff suggested that the board of trustees and members of the administrative staff hold a spring retreat to expand the vision of the Home. He also recommended closing the Peter Pan units due to safety issues associated with postponed maintenance. Shortly thereafter, administrator John Davis presented a report on the Home's educational programming needs.

While an entire family, such as this one, might have been placed in different outside facilities, the Home tried to unite them.

Davis cited the specific need for learning disability units and an educational mentally handicapped program. He warned, though, that the EMH program "should be of as short duration as possible, since this is not the direction the Home would like to take."

Superintendent Huff had been at the Home long enough to recognize the need for a few changes in how things were done from day to day—changes that might make a big difference in the quality of life for the children. In a report to the board in early 1988, he shared his agenda with the trustees:

1. *Set up an on-campus clothing store*
2. *Establish family-style eating at the evening meal*
3. *Reform the Home band*
4. *Open the Orfenz Den as a snack shop*
5. *Undertake an Adopt-a-Senior program*

In the fall of '88, the board agreed to ban smoking by employees, students and visitors anywhere on the grounds of the Home. Trustees also expressed their ongoing concern "regarding our discharging more youngsters than are coming in" and asked that specific attention be given to "the large numbers that are leaving that have been here six months or less." It seemed that finding a way to increase the number of children at the Home was a problem that defied a solution. Even with the closing of the farm, the closing of unused buildings, and reductions in staff through attrition and layoffs, the Home was still a large institution with a very small population. A low point had been reached in 1985 with only 135 children on a campus where 900 children once resided. The population had increased somewhat over the succeeding years, but it was still quite low.

In 1989, critics in the General Assembly of the high cost of caring for a child at the Home—as much as $26,000 per year by one estimate—proposed a change in the management of the institution. The legislators' proposal lacked support, but was a warning to Home officials that something needed to be done to increase the numbers of residents and thereby reduce the cost per child. That "something," as it were, would be Senate Bill 89, which established a system by which local authorities could direct children to a location that would meet their needs—a location like the Ohio Veterans Children's Home, or so the board and the staff hoped would be the case. Superintendent Huff proposed a self-study of the institution, identifying possible changes to the operational structure that would allow the Home to fully participate in the child care system of the state. In September the board approved the self-study "to respond to the concerns . . . as to whether we fit into the child caring continuum."

The Home Study Committee, chaired by former superintendent Colonel S.I. Stephan of Xenia, met regularly in 1990, gathering materials and interviewing children, staff and other interested parties. Superintendent Huff, meanwhile, continued his own efforts to try to make the Home a better place to live and work. He noted that while support by veterans groups remained strong, there were no real guidelines for what constituted proper gifts and when gifts should be given. Huff proposed that guidelines be established similar to those used by the Indiana Children's Home. In March, the Home hosted the first meeting of a "Veterans Council" with representatives of the major veterans organizations to explain Huff's proposal. Huff also sought a change in the rules governing the Julian Rooney Fund. At the time, scholarship decisions were made by the superintendent, four staff members and three members of the Association of Ex-Pupils. Huff recommended that the Association make all of the decisions regarding Rooney Fund disbursements.

In May of 1990, the superintendent told the board that he had been contacted by Greene County Children's Services regarding a number of allegations of child abuse at the Home. Huff explained what he thought the situation to be and said he expected to hear from Children's Services after the agency completed its investigation. The board instructed him to seek that decision weekly until it was received. Huff followed up this bad news with some good news, reporting that the Home was currently admitting a larger number of younger children as well as a higher percentage of the children of veterans. He also said he was looking at the possibility of moving at least some of the younger girls to one of the open cottages in the Peter Pan complex and possibly re-opening the Junior Campus dining room if funds could be found to do so.

The superintendent had more good news to report at the board's monthly meeting in September, informing trustees that the Home's 501(c)(3) tax-exempt status was forthcoming and that the staff felt the Home was in "good shape" for the upcoming biannual review by the State Department of Education. The Home Study Committee presented its findings after a year-long look at the institution, identifying the need for fundamental change in "the philosophy of leadership, to include cooperation, trust and dedication," as well as change in "the program, to meet the special needs of the present and future occupants of the Home." The panel had concluded, however, that the 121-year-old institution was well worth the effort needed to solve its problems.

A Downward Spiral—The Home from 1990 to 1995

On December 14, the Woodrow Wilson High School choir presented its Christmas musical, "Winter Magic." Those in attendance, including Superintendent Huff, had good reason to feel optimistic about the future. Enrollment was holding steady for the first time in years. Staff morale seemed to be better than it had been for some time. The Study Committee had been critical of the leadership and program, but the panel also had set forth achievable goals and objectives. The Home had its critics, but the children and staff could still count on the support of veterans groups and the Association of Ex-Pupils. And with Governor-elect George Voinovich set to take office, there would be new opportunities to make the Home's case in Columbus.

The next day, though, the world started falling apart. A grand jury indicted two staff members on various criminal charges. More indictments would follow. In all, seven people would be charged with crimes ranging from rape and theft to obstruction of justice. At a special meeting of the board on March 28, 1991, the trustees asked for and accepted Huff's resignation. "Mr. Huff did a lot of good

The Home boys (1985 version) dwindled in number but as Coach Davis liked to point out, they were never physically beaten.

things during the time he was superintendent at the Ohio Veterans Children's Home," commented one board member, "and it was unfortunate to have to ask for his resignation, which had to happen."

Colonel Stephan and Lieutenant Ralph Fusner, a member of the staff, served four months and three months respectively as interim superintendents as the Home now operated under a dark cloud of suspicion. To make matters worse, the Legislative Office of Education Oversight had issued a report about alleged inadequacies in the Home's education program. Some members of the Ohio General Assembly were saying the Home should be closed.

Governor Voinovich and Lieutenant Governor Mike DeWine, a Greene County native, decided to appoint a task force before taking any action. The OVCH Task Force, consisting of state agency administrators, local educators, social service professionals, and civic leaders, met for the first time on April 29, 1991. One month later they delivered their report, with eighteen pages of recommendations, to Voinovich and DeWine. After considering three questions—1) Should OVCH

be closed or should the Home remain open? 2) If the Home remains open in the 1990s and beyond, what unique role can it play in the state system of the delivery of services to children? and 3) What specific types of children should the Home serve and what programs will be necessary to help them?—the committee unanimously recommended that the Home remain open as a residential center for troubled adolescents. "A state-run residential facility should exist to provide worthwhile treatment services to children who have 'fallen through the cracks' of the present child welfare system," the task force asserted in its report. "A state-run facility can also provide much needed structure, stability and discipline in the lives of young people who have been shuffled around from foster home to foster home."

One recommendation immediately implemented was the expansion of the Home's board of trustees from five to nine members. After the existing board approved a Plan of Compliance to address the alleged inadequacies in the Home's education program and bring it up to state standards, the new board met for the first time in August and formed committees of Finance, Admission, and Education to move forward with the other recommendations by the OVCH Task Force. At their next monthly meeting, the trustees also hired a new superintendent, Ramon "Ray" Priestino, formerly community services administrator for the Franklin County Court in Columbus. Priestino held a Ph.D. from Ohio State, had served in academic and administrative positions with both traditional and community-based adult and juvenile correction programs, and was married with six children.

In January of 1993, two and a half years after it began looking into allegations of child abuse at the Home, Greene County Children's Services reported its findings in a letter to Governor Voinovich. The local agency did not mince words, describing the situation at the Xenia institution as "potentially explosive" with possible "serious outcomes" to children and staff. The Home's board of trustees, however, was already on top of the matter, persuading Voinovich and DeWine to appoint yet another task force to address safety and security at the institution as well as other issues.

In February, the board appointed a woman, Sheridan Jackson, to replace Superintendent Priestino, who had resigned after just sixteen months in the position, citing a deteriorating arthritic condition. Jackson had worked with children's services organizations in New York and Columbus since 1974. More importantly, she came to the Home from the Ohio Department of Human Services, whose staff, along with employees of the Department of Youth Services, had contributed more than 1,200 hours to the second task force report. It recommended that the Home be governed by a new "Board of Control," that the existing board act only in an advisory capacity, and that the Xenia institution be licensed by the Department of Human Services—recommendations which the state implemented.

Sheridan Jackson became a dedicated and hard working advocate for the Home, attempting to do what was necessary to keep it open. Apparently not everyone, however, appreciated the superintendent's management style and persistence. Not long after submitting a "reform plan" to better manage the Home, she met with the board of control on November 16, 1994, and was dismissed. According to a newspaper account at the time, "The board praised Jackson's commitment to children, but cited poor management skills as the reason for her ouster." The newspaper also noted, ominously, that "the fate of the home's state funding remains in doubt."

At its regular meeting on January 31, 1995, the new board of control convened in Columbus and announced the "phase-out" of operations at the Ohio Veterans Children's Home, set to begin in September, with the children placed in other centers as needed. A joint committee would study future uses of the facilities in Xenia.

This was the school building that went up in the early 1940s, when the original building came down. In its time, it accommodated as many as 700 students.

Over the spring and summer, a number of veterans groups, local organizations, and students and staff of the Home tried to convince the Voinovich Administration and the state legislature to reconsider. Their appeals, while persuasive and poignant, were to no avail. The problems were perceived to be too great, the political opposition too strong, the possibility of success too remote. It seemed more than a few people in Columbus were saying it was simply time to move on.

The final days

George Oliver was the acting superintendent of the Home in its final days. He had worked for the Ohio Department of Youth Services (DYS) and spent a lot of time at the Home as a consultant for the state during Sheridan Jackson's term as superintendent.

"My [former] boss said, 'George, the place is floundering. If we don't save it, it's going to go under.' . . . So I went down there, working four and five days a week, ten, twelve, sixteen hours a day, writing policies and procedures for those folks and sticking my nose into every little nook and cranny," recalled Oliver in his lengthy and candid reminiscence. "They took me in because I came from a system that worked with kids. The kind of kids we had were the criminal element," he said, referring to his Youth Services experience. "We had kids locked up, supervised twenty-four hours a day, seven days a week. Everything I had ever heard about the Home was contrary to what we did. It was a glorified story—all true, it turned out—about these kids who played football, had a champion herd of cattle, great bands, and one of the first schools in the state to do vocational education."

Oliver made some "strange" discoveries upon "sticking his nose," as he put it, into the Home's business.

"They didn't follow state policies and procedures. They didn't bid projects out the way they should. They had several staff members drawing two paychecks, maybe even three, in an era when the only people who could draw two from the State of Ohio were teachers because their union contract allowed them to have supplemental contracts to coach, or teach drama. They had a manager who, as I recall, had maxed out his state pay scale, so the board decided, 'Well, we'll just give him a couple hundred hours of overtime a year, but he doesn't have to work to get it.' That certainly wouldn't pass the scrutiny of the state auditor."

As one might imagine, the state's consultant didn't make a lot of friends at the Home—at least not in the beginning.

"We wrote policies simply on how to account for people's time and how to schedule time off. We wrote policies on how kids would get clothing from the storeroom. We took a system that was working informally and made a formal process out of it, to satisfy the bean counters. A lot of what we did was replicate Department of Youth Services policy, especially in terms of youth rights. We wrote policy for what happened when a kid was forcibly dealt with. There was no authorized paddling, nothing like that, but kids got in fights and you had to separate them. The process should protect the staff member from being accused of mishandling a situation. So, first thing, you have it investigated. You need more than one staff person involved because kids will turn on you. . . . Those were the kind of policies we wrote: how to handle this, who to report it to, and by God, you *will* report it. People thought it wasn't necessary. They thought we weren't being supportive of them by reporting those incidents. . . . The staff felt we were selling them down the river."

There were investigations.

"Investigation," said Oliver, "always made people nervous. But I don't think I ever had to fire anybody for abuse. The two people who probably had the most reports to Children's Services would have been our Phys. Ed. teachers. One was the sweetest person you will ever meet, but when girls got overheated and frustrated in

The Home Christmas was another tradition that remained unchanged and one always foremost in the minds of the ex-pupils.

gym class, they'd get into fisticuffs and, by God, she'd wade into the middle of it. Then both the Highway Patrol and Children's Services came in and investigated. By the sheer number of reports, people could draw the conclusion that the teacher was an abuser of the girls. No, she wasn't. Neither the Children's Services investigator at the time nor the plainclothes highway patrolman ever pointed a finger at her."

Oliver disagreed—vehemently—with the state's decision to close the Home.

"It was a place that cared for kids. Even staff people with whom I didn't get along, I can't say they didn't care about kids. It was an unfortunate mix of kids, though. This is only an opinion that I have: That place started out as an orphanage for kids who couldn't take care of themselves. We were in the business of killing people from the Civil War on, always involved in a damn war, so there were kids left unattended.

"There had to be a place like OVCH. Then about the time of the Vietnam War, the social structure of the country began to change. We started shutting down mental health hospitals and turning these people out on the streets, so to speak. People were

In the Home traditions, there was a remarkable continuity. Maybe because of its very nature, Memorial Day was always and forever connected to the past. Home superintendent Charles Adams is in foreground.

looking for simple solutions that cost less than what it cost to run OVCH."

Sadly, in Oliver's opinion, the Home ultimately became a convenient alternative for judges seeking someplace other than a correctional facility to send delinquent children. "We went from true orphans," he said, "to juvenile court judges saying to themselves, 'I don't have to send them to the juvenile correctional facilities, but maybe I need to get them away from mom, or uncle, or whoever the caretaker is, and I can send them to OVCH, and it is free.' Underscore that—FREE—because when we closed [the Home] down, some of us were trying to change state policy. 'Let us charge back,' like the Department of Youth Services. 'Let us charge the juvenile courts.' But the powers that be, from the governor's office on down, said, 'No way, Jose. We are not doing it.' Was there a conspiracy? Were there groups who just didn't want the Home to survive? Yeah. I couldn't prove it, but there were people who did not want us to do anything that would help support the place and keep it going."

The "death blow," said Oliver, were the admissions.

"We started taking kids who didn't belong there. It was not that we didn't have some bad kids [throughout the Home's history], but they weren't sent there by the courts. The state started sending too wide of a variety of kids to the place, and the Home's original mission was lost. Too many people wanted to send kids there because it was free. It cost the Department of Youth Services something like $38 a day to house a kid. It was costing us $90-plus a day at the Home.

"But we provided so much more. We provided a quality education to kids who, for the most part, wanted it. We had the General Barnett Vocational School, where any kid could learn a trade. The DYS wasn't providing that, and it didn't cost as much to keep a kid behind bars as it did to keep the same kid at the Home. Those costs were a driving force with legislators who didn't give anymore of a damn about those kids than the man in the moon. What *they* cared about was votes and telling people, 'I'm worried about your tax dollars.' Closing that place was a travesty. I liked George Voinovich, but the most bone-headed decision he ever made was deciding to listen to those who were saying it was bad public policy to keep that place afloat."

George Oliver's reminiscence revealed the strong emotions stirred by the decision to shut down the Home.

"Legislators wanted to say they saved the taxpayer a few dollars. It cost too much money to run that home—$90 for a kid in the Home vs. $38 for a kid behind bars. The fact that our kids got better service, and that most of our kids turned out to be useful citizens . . . well, nobody wanted to hear about the success of Jack Werthlin, first attorney for the Cincinnati Bengals and a Home graduate, or Bob Impson, who became superintendent of Greene County Schools. No one wanted to hear about what great educations or what great care they got at the Home. The only thing that seemed to register was the cash register, and it said $90 vs. $38.

"When we closed," continued the former superintendent, "there were about 150 kids at the Home. A lot of the kids went back with whatever family they had, which played badly in my mind. Some of them came to the Home *because* of the family environment. . . . God, I remember the day we put kids in cars and sent them out. It was a tear-jerking day. You don't love every kid there, because there were always certain troublemakers, but on that day you felt bad even for them. It was their home, and now we were putting them in a damn car and sending them off . . . to what? I watched them hugging each other . . . and it was . . . it was just disgusting. They should have made every freaking legislator in this state come down and watch that process.

"Closing the Home was one of the poorest decisions ever made," said Oliver. "Institutionally speaking, it was one of the few places in this state that was right for kids. They were secure, and they had a home. I would imagine kids coming there for the first year were nervous and unsure of themselves, but they were *safe*. They had people who looked out for their interests, and these people actually gave a damn about them. It was the best job I ever had and I started out in this racket, May of 1968. I never had a job with the DYS that was as fulfilling, nor one in which I felt as positive about myself and the people I was working with as I did about the people down there. The worst thing about it was that the people let it run down. The state didn't want to compete with local farmers and dairy industry. We're going to close it down because we're competing with the dairy industry? Give me a break. What a travesty. They let it go to hell in a handbag, and nobody will ever convince me it shouldn't have been maintained. Whether you were a cottage parent or a schoolteacher, or whether you had the privilege of running it, it was a *good* place."

When a Home student was enrolling at the University of Dayton, one of the Dayton students asked, "Where did you say you were from?" And the Home student said, "Well, I went to a private military school." John Davis, who was helping the Home student move in, liked that response. "I'm not touching that," he said, admiring the Home girl's thinking, for she had deflected any possible stigma of being from an orphanage, and she had still told the truth.

An Ending and a Beginning

Many of the children still living at the Home in the summer of 1995 had been shuttled from one foster home to another, one institution to another, one home to another, for much of their young lives. Now, all of them would be on the move again. By September, they were all gone. For the first time since 1870, there were no boys and girls on Poverty Knoll. All that remained were the grounds and buildings, largely still and silent. About two dozen staff members stayed on, helping to maintain and secure the buildings for the winter. Linda Powers, secretary to the superintendent, and John Davis of the academic staff, spent months sorting through the Home's records and files. Davis personally reviewed the files of each of the 13,000 children who had passed through the Home—files that would be turned over to the Ohio Department of Education.

"We had all of the school records to go through," he recalled. "We had to

A bittersweet moment in May of 1995, celebrated by Jon Bradshaw and Stacey Pattee at the Home's last prom. As midnight came, the disc jockey played, fittingly, "End of the Road" by Boyz II Men.

combine them with all of the medical records and all of the social records so that [each] kid would have a profile sent to Columbus. During that time, I would be asked, 'Are you working on these files or are you reading these files?' I would go through practically every file. I was pulling out stuff—a kid whose father was at Andersonville Prison, who fought in such and such a battle. I'm a history major. I was reading this stuff and I couldn't believe it. We pulled a kid out of a cave in Jackson County and she got a degree from Wilberforce. There is unbelievable stuff hidden in these records."

It was a "horrendous chore," said George Oliver, describing the closing of the 125-year-old institution. "We accounted for everything. I think I've still got seven computer paper boxes full of the final inventory of that place. . . . A lot of stuff went to the Department of Youth Services. . . . We've still got beds from the Ohio Veterans Children's Home out at one of our institutions called the Freedom Center." The remaining equipment and supplies were offered to state agencies, local governments and other non-profit institutions. Some of the historical artifacts, including the two cannons by the Home's front gate, were entrusted to the Association of Ex-Pupils.

A number of groups expressed interest in the grounds and buildings, first and foremost the Greene County Commissioners, who wanted the state to give them the site. Greene County Administrator Steven Stapleton suggested that it could become the home of the Greene County Educational Service Center, formerly the Greene County Board of Education. Superintendent Oliver also revealed that local religious leaders and an international children's service organization called Basic Life Principles were interested in the Home, as well as a number of juvenile court judges who saw the institution as a possible place to house non-felon juvenile offenders.

The state, however, was not inclined to give away a valuable asset, not after Greene County, itself, had recently appraised the more than forty buildings and 400 acres on "Poverty" Knoll at $15 million. A subsequent state appraisal put the price tag at $4.9 million—a valuation even further reduced by the projected costs of required asbestos removal. Meanwhile, officials in the Voinovich Administration and the Ohio General Assembly hoped at least $1 million of the proceeds from the future sale of the Home would be allocated to an Ohio Veterans Plaza scheduled for construction on the east side of Capitol Square in Columbus.

In the end, Greene County acquired the Ohio Veterans Children's Home in June, 1997, with passage of Senate Bill 7 authorizing the sale of the property for $1.3 million. The *Dayton Daily News* editorialized, "The state got a closed facility off its back, the county government got a complex that it had its heart on recycling, and the citizens keep a place with a serene, tree dotted ambience that should never go out of style." But it was not quite that simple for secretary Linda Powers, who remembered her emotional last day. "We had to turn [in] the keys. George Oliver . . . and I got to be pretty good friends. He was supposed to go down and officially turn [over] the keys. I said, 'George, you have to do that,' and he said, 'No, I'm not doing that.' So I went down and I turned [over] the keys and I drove back up the hill. I thought, 'I can't go back in.' George was outside and I said, 'I can't stay here.' We had shredded the last bit of everything. Everything was cleaned up. There was really nothing left for us to do. I just left."

The Greene County Commissioners also discovered that maintaining a site as large as the Home was costly. Simple repair, security, and roof replacement exceeded $200,000 over the next two years. The commissioners appointed a twenty-nine-member task force to come up with some possible uses for the buildings and grounds, and among the ideas discussed was a school, a senior center, arts facility, and a domestic violence shelter. By January of 1998, Administrator Stapleton estimated at least fifteen different organizations had approached the county with site proposals, including the Dayton Christian School System, whose school in Xenia operated out of a remodeled skating rink.

"We drove on [the] campus," recalled Reverend Claude "Bud" E. Schindler, Jr., founder and superintendent of the Dayton Christian Schools, "and it had been vacated. There was nothing going on. Very quickly we all felt . . . three buildings—the school, the gymnasium and the auditorium—would be wonderful for our needs. We went to [Greene] County and put in a bid—just those three buildings, on twenty acres of land, for $1.2 million. The county came back to us and said, rightfully so, that we first had to go through public bidding because it was public property. They also said, 'We don't want to parcel it out. We want to maintain the integrity of what it was used for. So if you are going to bid on it—it's all or nothing—not three buildings and twenty acres but forty-four buildings and 253 acres.' We began to say to ourselves, 'This is going to be more than a Christian school.' We looked at the [site's] potential. . . . We spent a lot of time with the Association of Ex-Pupils. We wanted them to feel comfortable with us because we felt this was their home. The county had established a committee to review the uses of this facility. We spent time with them [and] with the government officials.

"The state had made an assumption that the buildings were full of asbestos. . . . We brought in our own environmental engineer and took over 100 samples. There was not as much asbestos as everyone had thought. Because the assumption turned out not to be totally correct, I really believe it scared off some people who might

Here's another poignant scene, this one from the Home's graduation in 1991, in which Angela Bubeck embraces a classmate.

have been interested in bidding on the property. As it turned out, two organizations made formal bids. [The other group] could not come up with any of the money it was necessary to put down, so we were awarded the contract.

"[But] the story does not stop there," said Schindler "because we had no money. . . . We had to sell property on Lower Bellbrook Road, and of course that took time. We had three different closing dates [on the Home]. We didn't have the money on the first two, but it wasn't our fault. Came the third time and we had the money to buy the property. We took title on July 1, 1999. During part of that time, we got the county to allow us to come in and remodel the school building. It was a risk on our part. We needed to do that to open school on September 1."

The school system had more buildings and grounds than it needed, so officials went looking for partners. They found one in Wendell Deyo, who had moved his global sports ministry, Athletes in Action, from California to southwest Ohio. Deyo toured the property with Bob Hartenstein, a member of the board of Legacy Ministries International, the new umbrella organization created to manage the recently acquired Home. According to press reports, Deyo said he returned for several days in a row and prayed for guidance about his decision. "On a Sunday afternoon, (Hartenstein) saw me walking the property. I said, 'Based on what I heard you say, God wants you to build a ministry mall here. This may be a bit presumptuous on our part, but I believe God wants us to be your anchor store.'"

Deyo accepted Legacy's offer, converting seven buildings into the World Training and Resource Center for Athletes in Action. With the help of a $12 million anonymous gift, Athletes in Action refurbished four dormitories and a conference and retreat center, and built a sixty-acre sports complex that includes two soccer fields, two softball fields, a baseball stadium, a synthetic turf football field, an all-weather track, and a volleyball court. Soon thereafter, two Christian radio stations, WFCJ-FM and WEEC-FM, began broadcasting from one of the small buildings on campus, the educational consultants of International School Project remodeled part of the Barnett Vocational Education Building, and several ministries opened offices, including Heart to Honduras and evangelist Franklin Graham's Samaritan's Purse. Another ministry collects wheelchair parts and sends them to prisons, where inmates use the parts to build wheelchairs that are sent around the world. "These are things that were not in my mind," concedes Schindler, recalling the Dayton Christian School System's initial plans for the site, "but we did want to show the world that Christians can work together."

In the future, Legacy Ministries would like to open a "Christian vocational school," said Schindler, as well as a school for the deaf. He also has made a

"As a child, the Home just seemed to have an emergent property of its own. It looked...how big it was...the buildings... how *old* they were. As a child, it had an Oliver Twist aura to it. It was beautiful, and there were so many tunnels and hiding places. It just had this intrinsic property of being misplaced, like the boy Oliver himself.

"It seemed that even in the town there were townspeople you'd meet who had lived in Xenia their entire lives and they knew about the place but they never knew what it was. It just seemed like a misfit kind of place. People right outside the gates didn't know what they did up there.

"It was a self-sustaining place with its own power plant, water tower, church, farm, and hospital. The need to even go off campus was just...I mean the only time we went off was if you were one of the athletes and the team went off to play another school. Other than that, there were kids who hardly ever left the Home at all. There were privileges where you could go into town but in my era, most students didn't do a lot of that. We were content with being on campus. Other than a handful of times a year, I never left the campus.

"It's possible that I was the last student there who met the original criteria of the Home—whose parents were both deceased and one had been a veteran. I don't know of any other after me. It's odd, looking back on it, but there wasn't any structured orientation. The students seemed just plucked out of life and displaced there. The curiosity of 'Where did you come from? Why are you here?' was merely part of the child's curiosity, which was the way I met Mark, my new sidekick, who showed me the routines.

"There was, of course, the whistle, the cue of your day. It denoted when you got up, when you left for school, eating times. It was loud, and there were people I spoke with later from the town who heard it every day of their lives and never knew exactly where it came from or what it did. Which wasn't good for a town that had a history of tornadoes.

"A lot of the students were plucked from numerous school systems, dysfunctional backgrounds. It was a complicated thing for the Home to encompass all that. There were students doing well, and students who were not, so to fit everybody in, the bar had to be lowered. No educational system could easily develop a curriculum encompassing all those circumstances.

"The demise of the Home was because of the caliber of the kids coming in, of more violent backgrounds and delinquency, more dramatic dysfunctions at home, kids that had been abused. The Home just wasn't equipped for that. It didn't have the physical barriers or counselors to deal with kids of a harsher mindset.

"It's terrible to see the Home close because it was larger than life. It was a very positive place, a safe haven, sort of like a womb of the earth place. The life of the Home unfolded along a natural course, especially in the yesterdays of the orphans. It was genuine. It wasn't founded by someone to make money, or as a business. It emerged out of necessity, which I think gave it a noble kind of sincerity.

"The Home saw people come, go, live, and die. It always went on. How long it had nurtured the orphans of the world. It took the place of our parents, and the Home became our permanence. It said to us, 'Here's the other permanent thing.' Growing up, you had the impression that the Home always was, is, and will be. As a young kid walking onto the campus, you see this building that was built in the 1800s, and in the child's perspective, it's like, well, that's as long as there was ever buildings.

"It's a very powerful force for a child to experience that. It's something the average person doesn't experience. Kids grow up, move two or three times, their parents get divorced or separated. So kids, especially these days, don't have any kind of permanent thing. That was part of the heartbreak of seeing the Home close. It's hard for me to articulate but to this day I go back there often. I go down and stay there because you're able to rent rooms. And sometimes, in the middle of the night, I go out and walk around for hours.

"How do I say it? It's perhaps like when you are a child and entertained by the idea of a ghost. You hate hearing later the explanation of how it *wasn't* a ghost, it was this phenomenon, completely rational, and it strips you of that euphoric wonder of entertaining things larger than you are.

"There was a life that breathed inside that place. And yet it's esoteric, as well. I'll give an example: At a reunion, right before I left, I was in the museum talking to ex-pupils who had been there in the 1960s and 1970s. We were talking and I found myself saying that I would not change anything about the way my life was, being at the Home. But to go there, I had to lose both parents. I would never say that out in public because I would be labeled crazy. Do you mean you want your parents to die so that you can become a ward of the state? But I knew that everyone in the room understood me. It doesn't mean you wish something bad to happen to your parents, of course, but I could not imagine growing up without that place."

Former Home kids return to their old haunts in 1991. Jacqueline Smith Robinson, Janet Smith Bagdazian, and Robert Smith in front, and George, Hoyt, and Don Smith in rear.

commitment to the Association of Ex-Pupils to one day re-open one of the cottages on campus as an orphanage for children from the United States and abroad. "We are very evangelical in our approach to what we want to see happen. We are not done here."

Always a Home

In its last years, the Ohio Veterans Children's Home had a lot of problems, as George Oliver and others articulated.

Changes in leadership—seven different superintendents in ten years.

Staff turnover, as limited budgets led to layoffs.

A dwindling resident population, with seldom more than 200 children under roof at any given time.

Shorter stays—some children only in residence a few months before being sent back to their families or transferred to another institution.

Children with severe mental, emotional or behavioral problems requiring a higher level of uniformed security on the grounds.

The list of challenges was a long one. . . .

Yet despite the inevitability of its fate, the Home continued to operate, in many ways, as it had operated throughout its long and remarkable history. The schools, as always, offered pupils a comprehensive academic and vocational education. (In the spring of 1994, the *Home Review* reported that 100 percent of the graduates that year—albeit, a small class—had passed Ohio's high school proficiency tests.) The Home carried on its military tradition, conducting regular drills and training that culminated in the annual inspection by officers from the United States Army, and holding the annual 40 & 8 Field Day, drill competitions, and military ball. The state's many veterans organizations remained unwavering in their support. A Veterans Shelter House was christened and dedicated during a ceremony at the Home in 1990. An item in a 1993 edition of the *Home Review* indicated that the Sons of the AMVETS pledged to provide the basketball team that year with a camcorder for videotaping games, sports bags for the boys and girls teams, team chairs, a public address system for the OVCH gymnasium, basketballs, water bottles, and a scorebook. "Veterans groups have been gracious to OVCH children during the year, sponsoring on campus events, along with several off-campus trips to sporting events and recreational activities. Whether it was a trip for seniors to Kings Island, a bus trip to a Cincinnati Reds game, or a picnic on a northern Ohio lake, behind the scenes making it possible were Ohio's veterans." Holidays were observed in typical fashion, including Christmas, when staff and friends of the institution sat down to breakfast as the children sang the Home's traditional Christmas carol.

And as they had for more than a century, the Association of Ex-Pupils continued to return to the Home for their annual reunion over the Fourth of July weekend. Even now well into a new century and a new millennium they still do. As long as there is a Home, they probably always will. And as long as they continue to care, there will always be a Home.

"The saddest thing that ever happened was when the Home closed. It was a sad, sad day for me. The new people going in there have been great, but they knocked off 'OSSO Home' etched onto the main building. Just chiseled it off and now it's flat. It's just like my home and somebody coming in and taking things off. It was like, 'What are you doing to my house?'"—Sam Pfeffer, Class of 1980

Ron LaCour, sixth grade teacher and assistant coach, engages his Home classroom.

Places to call

Home *(the orphanage in America)*

Past, present, future

It has been a long journey for the Home. From the time it was founded as the Ohio Soldiers and Sailors Orphans Home in 1869 until the time of its closing as the Ohio Veterans Children's Home in 1995, the Home provided more than 125 years of service to the people of the State of Ohio and the more than 13,000 children who passed through its doors.

In some ways the Home was a product of its time. It was born of the spirit that moved Nineteenth Century America to take the people most in need in a community and put them where they could be helped. Some of those places literally saved the lives of the people who lived in them.

Others sometimes harmed people more than helped them. Most of the treatment facilities for the blind and the deaf and mentally ill and the infirm provided at least some assistance to the people they served. But a number of these places— especially local poorhouses and asylums—were not all that much mourned in their passing.

The Home was different. It was one of the truly good places that came out of the institutionalization of America. Across most of its history, the Home was usually— and sometimes significantly ahead of its time.

This was a time when most institutions were large, foreboding buildings constructed in the style of brick, slate and gingerbread that we today call "Victorian" architecture. The Ohio State Hospital on a west side hilltop in Columbus, Ohio, for instance, was the largest building under one roof in America until the Pentagon was built.

The Home built one big building—for its administrators and teachers. And it built cottages that were really slightly adapted single family homes for its children. The twelve to twenty children who lived in these original cottages had adults who lived with them, worked with them, and often became the closest thing to parents many of them would ever have.

As late as the 1920s, orphanages and other institutions were "discovering" the cottage system and claiming to have been the first place in America to do so. They weren't. For that matter, neither was the Home. But then the Home never claimed to be first in cottage living for children in America. It just claimed to be the best.

And in many ways it was.

The Home was ahead of its time in other ways as well.

Built to be its own world in its own way, the Home quickly recognized that there would have to be a school on the site. But it was a school like few others in America at the time. Understanding that the children in the Home had little in the way of family support, the founders of the Home—from its earliest days—stressed both the practical as well as the academic. Few had tried to offer both kinds of education to young children. And even fewer succeeded.

Complementing the progressive familial and educational structure of the Home was a social structure like few places in America in its time. We tend to forget that until well into the twentieth century, most schools offered classes for a few hours a day and not much else. The Home provided the widest variety of athletic, social, and cultural opportunities.

One administrator at the Home in the years after World War II observed that the place almost seemed like a boarding school with its indoor and outdoor swimming pools, a fine auditorium, and riding trails in the fields beyond the barns.

The comparison was apt. The Home in many ways *was* a boarding school—for a very special group of people.

And over much of its history, that is what set it apart from other similar institutions in America.

The Ohio Soldiers and Sailors Orphans Home was an orphanage at its very best.

Part of the reason the Home did so well for so long was that it was not as isolated from the world as many believed.

When disaster came to nearby Xenia, most memorably in the great flood of 1886 and the devastating tornado of 1974, the people of the Home provided aid and comfort to the stricken community. Doing so was not requested. It did not need to be. Xenia had helped the Home often enough in times of epidemic disease, fire, and unexpected accident to earn the confidence and trust of the people on Poverty Knoll. The Home may have been outside the city, but it was never far away. And neither was the Home that far away from the rest of the country.

For more than a century, the battalion and band of the Ohio Soldiers and Sailors Orphans Home was a regular participant in the state and national meetings of virtually every major veterans organization in America. With additional appearances at the state fair and local events of every variety, the Home was showing the people of Ohio—and America—that their support had made a difference. The children of the Home were saying "Thanks" in the best way they knew.

Orphanages: A look back

Orphanages have had a long and circuitous history in America. Like the European counterparts from which they were derived, orphanages were few and far between in early America. And the ones that were around were not all that friendly.

The age of the orphanage in its modern form began with the Industrial Revolution. The extraordinary dislocations caused by the movement of many people away from the farm and from Europe to America, led to large numbers of homeless children on the streets of America's cities. As states like New York tried to empty their towns of orphans by putting them on "Orphan Trains" to the Midwest, states like Ohio responded by mandating children's homes in every county in the state.

Responding to the growth of orphanages by mostly Protestant legislatures, Catholic and Jewish orphanages soon were founded as well. In fact these new institutions—founded by new denominations—soon were the most numerous in America.

There were people who saw aerial photographs of the Home and asked, "But which one is the Home?" And the kids attendant would say proudly, "ALL of it is the Home."

Because so many children ended up in orphanages—68,000 by 1890—these places became the stuff of myth and legend. And like most myths and legends in our country, the stories were both larger than life and often contradictory.

To a generation that idolized English author Charles Dickens and devoured his novels as they were issued in serial form in monthly magazines, the dominant image of the orphan became poor little Oliver Twist seeking an extra bowl of gruel from the heartless master of his orphanage. We tend to forget that compared to the life he had left on the street, Oliver's experience at the orphanage was not all that bad. But the idea of orphanages as bad places lingered for most of the 1800s. It only began to be dispelled a bit by the early twentieth century. A new generation began looking at the street youth of urban America as less of a challenge and more of an opportunity. Beginning as volunteers in the settlement houses in the cities of industrial America, the new profession of social work began to train and send forth people who came to be called "professional altruists."

Social workers and their friends protested fiercely against the employment of 9-year-old children in spinning mills and coal mines and fought hard for child labor laws and mandatory public schools. And so by 1900, the orphanage had a mixed history, abhorred by some and liked by others. The irony of American social work is that just as social workers brought energy, talent and dedication to the management of orphanages—places like the legendary Boys Town in Nebraska— they would also soon be advocating the demolition of the places they served so well.

The evidence was sketchy at first but soon became inescapable. Some orphanage managers were not very nice people and some orphanages were very badly managed. Believing that the best home for any child was a home with one's parents, the militant and best informed began to advocate foster care over institutions— especially after President Theodore Roosevelt endorsed the idea at his first White House Conference on Youth in 1909.

Over the course of the next century, orphanages became less and less popular in America. It is not hard to see why. As the costs of food, fuel, and supplies continued to rise, the numbers of people applying for assistance began to decline. This meant the cost of care for each child began to rise. The decline in numbers happened for several reasons. The economic collapse that came to be called The Great Depression and the Second World War that followed caused a sharp decline in birth rates as families postponed parenthood. Many others had children but were without means to care for them. To these people, Aid to Families with Dependent Children was a lifesaver. It literally kept many families together and away from places like the Home.

The final nudge came from the social workers assigned to advise families in need of their options. Many if not most social workers believed as an article of faith that orphanages simply were not good and that children— in lieu of their own parents— should be in a foster home. Many social workers, with a passionate intensity, still believe this.

And it is a belief that is not as defensible as one might think. . . .

In the face of the simple fact that virtually every country in the world to this day maintains not just one but a large number of public and private orphanages, advocates of foster care or other forms of family placement still maintain that their approach is correct and the rest of the world— including many places in our own country—simply have not caught up to preferred best practices.

And this belief is contentious at best.

It is debatable on the basis of the theory and research underlying its promotion. It is debatable on the basis of historical and contemporary practice. And it is debatable on the basis of the unique experience of places like the Home.

Theories and Thoughts about Practical Child Raising

As he was often wont to do, New York Mayor Fiorello LaGuardia summed up the thoughts of many Americans about the role of children's institutions in Depression Era America when he said, "The worst mother is better than the best institution."

But to the consternation of the newly emerging profession of social work, America was not apparently listening to the advice of the man who came to be called the "Little Flower."

For more than a generation, social work professionals and supporters of groups working to improve the lives of America's poor had been arguing that family life was preferable to impersonal institutions. Yet the number of orphanages or other children's care facilities did not decline. The number of such places had actually increased in the years after The White House Conference in 1909.

In 1910, there were 837 orphanages in America and there were 1,151 children's services institutions in the country. A little more than twenty years later, in 1933, the number of orphanages had risen to 1,320 and the number of children's services organizations to 2,280. Even with the rapid rise in the number of foster care organizations, 58 percent of children living outside their biological families were living in institutions.

A growing number of people in professional social work, health care, the judiciary and education began to lobby state and local governments for more support for foster care and adoption—the two terms were often used interchangeably—and less for support for traditional orphanages.

To support these appeals, researchers began to produce studies that compared the psychological, emotional, and intellectual development of children in a variety of living arrangements. Prodded by contemporary psychological thinking that deprivation of a mother's attention was harmful—and sociological assumptions that institutions in their nature were cold and distant—many of these studies not surprisingly lent support to political arguments against institutions and for foster care.

It was only several decades later that a new generation of scholars began to look at some of these earlier studies more closely and noted several problems with them. In many cases the samples studied were opportunistic—that is, they were not random samples from the population but often consisted of the children available for study. Second, the numbers of children studied were often quite small. And finally, the results obtained were not always clear.

In 1999, one critical review of the earlier studies reached the following conclusions:

1. Theories about the detrimental effect of maternal deprivation receive highly tenuous, indirect support at best from orphanage research. Where psychological deterioration in infants was found, it is not clear whether the mother's absence or simple physical and social neglect was the essential cause. Neither was there any evidence that such neglect was a widespread practice.

2. Some teenagers and young adults with orphanage experience show deficits in language development, intellect, personality, and social skills. It is far from clear, however, that these were caused by their orphanage care. Orphanage care per se was almost never directly observed or manipulated in these studies.

3. Most of the research suffers from the overuse of small, opportunistic samples, and there is a general failure to describe population sources and methods of selection. These limitations make it impossible to generalize findings based on isolated samples to all orphans or orphanages.

4. Most orphanage research is limited to narrowly focused, clinical search for psychological damage. Very little of it deals with the effects of age or gender groupings, the role of work, moral training and a host of other practical issues in orphanage care.

5. Critics of orphanage care seem overzealous to produce negative evidence and then generalize their findings to all orphans or orphanages. More consideration should be given to positive orphanage experiences and ways of assessing their effects . . . .

This same review noted that one of the few really large studies was undertaken by clinical psychologists comparing the intelligence of several thousand home raised and orphaned children. Comparable results were found for both groups. The study was done in 1929 and no comparable study has been done since that time.

Perhaps the lesson that one takes away from the longstanding struggle among those who favor orphanages and those who don't is one not unique to this issue. People often bring a variety of accepted points of view, arguments, and opinions to the social questions of the day. These ideas are reinforced by studies that seem to fit these preconceptions and then used as part of the political argument for a particular point of view. This is not to say that such studies are somehow wrong or deceptive—though some might be. It is simply to say that a small study of a few people is just that—no more and no less.

The political arguments for and against orphanages are only limited by the imagination of the people making them. And any number of studies—scholarly or otherwise—will continue to be made as well to reinforce these points of view. Although it is fair to point out that comparative analyses of people in orphanages and outside them are harder to do in America since the number of orphanages continues to decline. The most recent detailed published studies examining the effects of orphanage life on young people was reported by a team working in Romania. Like many other former Communist countries, Romania has a lot of orphanages.

At one time, there were more than a dozen state-sponsored institutions like the Ohio Soldiers and Sailors Orphans Home. In 2009, due to the economic problems induced by the greatest economic downturn since the Great Depression, two of the last remaining homes of their kind, in Pennsylvania and Indiana, closed for the last time.

Perhaps a better way to understand the place of the orphanage in America is to look a little more closely not at what might or should have been done. We should evaluate more closely what actually happened.

The American Orphanage in Practice

For much of the twentieth century, the orphanage had few defenders. The dominant image of the orphanage in most people's mind was that formed by the popular literature and cinema of the day. Orphanages were dark, dreary, dangerous places, little better than the prisons they sometimes resembled. And perhaps some of them were. But it has become increasingly clear over the past couple of decades that most orphanages were not all that bad. And many of them were actually quite good at what they did.

The turn in the road of American political opinion can be traced back to comments that then House Speaker Newt Gingrich made in 1994 in which he said that bringing back orphanages might not be such a bad idea. This immediately launched a firestorm of controversy with Hillary Clinton, the wife of the then President, accusing the Speaker of trying to use America's children to advance a political agenda. From there, the conversation went downhill rapidly.

Leaving the politics of 1994 in the past, it is still fair to say that the renewed public attention to the issue stimulated a modicum of public interest in orphanages and led to both research and publication of a new series of books of various length and complexity about the history of the orphanage in America.

And while no one book rediscovered the orphanage in America, a number of books in recent years have made it a much more acceptable topic for discussion. A brief review of a few of the most important of them will indicate why that is the case.

In 1990, Gary Edward Polster set out to tell the story of one orphanage in one town. *Inside Looking Out: The Cleveland Jewish Orphan Asylum, 1868-1924*, gives the reader an excellent understanding of both the origins and operation of a religiously based orphanage brought into being by the industrial revolution. Founded largely to help the children of recent Eastern European Jewish immigrants, the Asylum moved to a more suburban location in 1929 and still is in operation as a non-sectarian residential treatment facility for emotionally troubled young people.

Many of the residents of the Asylum were not true orphans and still had at least one parent living, although that parent was not in a position to raise the child. But orphans or not, the children of the asylum received food, shelter and an education unavailable to them otherwise. And most of them went on to successful lives and careers. Polster makes no apologies in describing a lifestyle that was hard at best. But it was also a lifestyle that made successful Americans out of the sons and daughters of recent immigrants.

Kenneth Cmiel saw his work about a Midwestern orphanage published a few years later in 1993. *A Home of another Kind: One Chicago Orphanage and the Tangle of Child Welfare.* Cmiel traces the history of the Chicago Nursery and Half-Orphan Asylum from 1860 to 1984. Founded as means to religiously uplift the poor and needy children of one Chicago neighborhood, the institution was operated and overseen by a number of wealthy Chicago women.

Over its long history, the organization came to be known as Chapin Hall. It also grew in size and the volunteer staff turned over its operation to professionals. Eventually public money subsidized Chapin Hall and the institution became a treatment facility for troubled children. Telling a good story as well as tracing an administrative history, Cmiel points out that the people of Chapin Hall were motivated largely by a desire to help the children in their care in every way possible. He places their work in context with other similar agencies of city and state government and against the background of change in America after the Civil War and changing American attitudes about childcare.

A similar point is made in Nurith Zmora's study of orphanage life in Baltimore. *Orphanages Reconsidered: Child Care Institutions in Progressive Era Baltimore* is a study not simply of one orphanage but of the way orphanages worked in Baltimore for several decades about a century ago. In contrast to the rather nebulous ideas put forth by many Progressive Era reformers at the turn of the century, the managers and staff of Baltimore's orphanages succeeded in making the city's orphanages work quite well. They worked so well, in fact, that Zmora argues that the physical, medical, and educational environment was superior to the one the same children would have experienced had they *not* been in the orphanage.

The experience described in these three cities over the years between the end of the Civil War and the outbreak of WWI suggest that orphanages worked far better for far longer than many people had previously believed.

It would only be a matter of time before someone would take a fresh look at the orphanage experience in America in general in the same years. "Someone" would actually be two different men working on quite different books but intellectually moving toward the same sorts of conclusions.

In 1998, Matthew Crenson published *Building the Invisible Orphanage: A Prehistory of the American Welfare System.* His major point was that the system of welfare that dominated most of twentieth century social policy had its origins in the orphanage system of the previous century. The system of centralized and federalized assistance to children in need through payments to their parents had its origin in the failings of the previous system.

He does not argue that orphanages were necessarily bad. In fact, many of them were quite good. But they were expensive. Many were private and many simply would not or could not adapt to an increasingly centralized federal control of the welfare system. Crenson's arguments are not without their critics. Other historians and social researchers argue that other factors were in play as well. But Crenson's central idea—in their time many orphanages worked and worked quite well—was shared by other historians as well.

Most important among them was Timothy Hacsi. His book, *Second Home: Orphan Asylums and Poor Families*, was also published in 1998 and argued, too, that orphanages worked well. But rather than looking at specific cities, towns, or even states, Hacsi examined the totality of the orphanage experience in the United States from 1800 to the Great Depression. His most important point is that orphanages were not trying to reform the children in their care. They were trying to protect them and prepare them for life. They were making a "second home." He also argues that the answer to the problems of children in need lies not in orphanages or the lack of them but in curing the causes of the poverty that led to the need for them.

Few would dispute that a world without poverty is a world worth seeking. But few would also dispute the fact that such a world will not be with us soon. In the meantime, it might be well to consider where the orphanage might fit in the world we have with us today. In the view of more than a few, it might fit quite well. One of the most passionate advocates of that view is Richard B. McKenzie. As a child who grew up in an orphanage, McKenzie brings both personal experience and genuine feeling to his advocacy.

In his 1999 volume of edited essays, *Rethinking Orphanages for the 21st Century*, McKenzie argues that orphanages are not for everyone. But then they never were. His contributors also point out the inadequacies of the present system of "reformed" welfare and an increasingly challenged system of foster care and adoption.

McKenzie wonders why it is considered acceptable to send wealthy children to boarding schools but wrong to send children from homes that are unsafe, abusive, or incapacitated to similar institutions. He notes that if orphanages never worked too well, why have most of their graduates succeeded and why do those same graduates credit that success to the orphanages they left behind. McKenzie knows they do because he asked a large number of them and reports their opinions.

At the end of his work, McKenzie makes a few proposals that could lead to the revival of his preferred approach—a privately owned and operated system of orphanages dedicated to the long term care, protection, and preparation of the people in their charge.

A few of McKenzie's ideas include some proposals to deal with a foster care system that he believes is broken and seriously in need of repair.

1. Elevate the importance of "permanence" in child welfare policies.
"Clearly we must make subjecting the child to the fewest possible substitute-care placements a top priority."
2. Narrow the range of cases in which reasonable efforts must be made to reunify children with their abusive and neglectful families.
3. Assign the initial investigation of cases of substantial abuse and neglect to the police and the criminal justice system.
Establish a reasonable presumption of unfitness in the child welfare system.
4. Shorten the timetable for the initial hearings on the termination of parental rights.
5. Speed up the notification of judicial authorities of cases of parental rights termination. Establish guidelines for the permanent placement of children.
Place responsibility for rehabilitation on parents.
6. What is best for children should be made the central issue in case of termination of parental rights.
Require concurrent case planning for both reunification and termination of parental rights.
Evaluate parents' fitness to be parents at the beginning of child neglect and abuse cases.
7. Use public funds to encourage child care innovations.

Turning to residential care facilities, McKenzie offers the following suggestions "to afford homes greater flexibility in their programs . . ."

1. Lessen the burden on child care institutions.
"There must be a broad liberalization of state licensure statutes and regulations applicable to residential educational institutions, the goals of which are to lower the costs of care facing current and would be operators of such facilities and to promote innovation and entrepreneurial efforts."
2. Expand work opportunities in child care institutions.
"Many state laws allow parents to assign the children in their care a broad range of work responsibilities in the home, on family farms and in businesses. Child care institutions should be afforded the same rights to assign work responsibilities to the children in their care."

3. Convert public child welfare funds to block grants.

"A portion, if not all, of federal child welfare funds that are now allocated to foster care should be distributed to the states as block grants, allowing states maximum flexibility in the placement of disadvantaged children in existing permanent institutional settings . . . and in the development, monitoring and evaluation of new options for the permanent individual placement of children."

Richard McKenzie"s ideas spring to some extent from his own experiences and the status of the public child care system in America today. The general operating assumptions for most of the past several decades has been that many foster care and other placements are made by court order because one or more of a child's parents or guardians are unfit to care for the child.

But there was a time not all that long ago when people brought their children willingly to an orphanage or other residential facility. And in some parts of the world and indeed in some parts of this country they still do, hoping for a better life in the new place than they possibly could provide themselves.

And that brings us to the Home.

An Orphanage at Its Best

In its time and in its way, the Ohio Soldiers and Sailors Orphans Home was quite simply one of the best places of its kind.

And it is important to remember what exactly that meant.

It was an "orphans home" and one of the best in the nation.

It was also a school and one of the best of its unique kind in the nation.

It was a working farm and one of the best in the country of its kind as well.

It was a place of enormous talent, skill and innovation throughout its history.

And it was home to more than 13,000 children over 125 years— to those still living, it still is—fifteen years after it closed.

As this lengthy look at this place so many people called Home comes to a close, it is important to remember some of the things that made this place so special and still does. First and foremost in the hearts of the people who were here for so many years, coming to the Home was never a matter of charity.

The Home was a matter of right. Founded in the wake of the deadliest war in American history by the Grand Army of the Republic, the Home was created to meet the challenge set forth by President Lincoln in his Second Inaugural Address to care for the widows and orphans of the men who fought for the Union in the Civil War.

So children coming to the Home did not come here because they were poor, or because their Home life was painful, or because they were troublesome souls who fit in nowhere else. They came because they had a *right* to be there. The Home was partial compensation for a debt that could never be repaid.

Because of that reason for being, the Home in Xenia and several Homes like it across the country were never the last resort for many of the children who came here. It was the place where a surviving parent or guardian wanted them to be. And after a time it was where they themselves wanted to be. It was a place they left for occasional holidays or vacations. But it was a place they returned to until they were discharged. And even after that they would return. And they still do.

Because the Home was not a last resort but a *first* choice, it was well accepted by the people within it and the people who looked at it from outside.

There is an important lesson here about institutions that survive and prosper.

Simply put, they are places of hope, confidence and trust.

The Home prospered because it was well supported through most of its long career. The Grand Army of the Republic—arguably one of the most powerful organizations in America—was especially strong in Ohio. And the Home was a special concern of the Ohio GAR. That meant when the Home became a state agency in 1870, it became a special concern of the Ohio General Assembly as well. For most of its history the Home was not just well-funded—it was *very* well-funded. But the support of the GAR went further. On special days—Memorial Day and Christmas to name just two of many—the aging veterans came to the Home and for a moment became one with the children of their comrades.

That network did not die with the original generation of veterans or with the passing of the GAR. Subsequent veterans of subsequent wars followed in the long tradition and supported the Home—the Home of the children of their comrades as well. This broad network of support extended beyond the veterans organizations to the rest of the community and beyond as many people came to believe in the Home and its purpose. The most important of those groups were the people of the Home itself through their Association of Ex-Pupils.

There is a lesson here as well. Funding and strong public support are critical to success. And the two go hand in hand.

What then did this purpose and its support bring into being?

The Home was a school. But it was a school like few others. Long before "vocational education" was even a phrase, the school of the Home was practicing it. The founders of the Home recognized that many of the children came from humble origins and could not rely on family to support them after they left the Home. And while a sound academic education was important so too was a trade one could follow to support oneself.

In time the Home developed one of the most sophisticated vocational education programs in the country offering each of its graduates not only a diploma but the promise of a secure future. Other schools adopted vocational as well as academic education and many of them copied their programs from the successful ones at the Home.

The Home was a military training center. The Home ran by the whistle. The whistle woke one up and sent one to bed. It sounded when classes changed and mealtimes were at hand. For many years, the students at the Home marched to class—and everywhere else—in uniform. And on Sunday, the band played and the battalion of the Home marched on the parade ground.

This should not be all that surprising. In the 1860's, people in every state institution from the Ohio Penitentiary to the Lunatic Asylum wore uniforms and marched to work to the signal bell or signal whistle. Eventually most other places stopped wearing uniforms. The Home continued the tradition for some time. They were the children of veterans after all. Even after the Home became less military in its day to day operation, the tradition remained.

The Home was a religious place. The chapel was one of the earliest buildings to be erected at the Home. It has been in regular use ever since. Since attending services in the chapel was mandatory for most of the history of the Home, special efforts were made to make in non-denominational—something not all that common at the time. After a time, arrangements were made for the transport of any pupil who desired it to services in a church of their choice. For some time, the chapel was the Home's auditorium and assembly center as well. And behind it is the cemetery where a number of the pupils and a few of their teachers are buried as well.

The Home was a farm. The farm at the Home grew much of the food consumed by the people who lived here. It also provided a farm life experience to every child who lived at the Home—something even many boarding schools cannot say. And it was not just any farm. The dairy cattle of the Home were a prize-winning herd with a national reputation.

The Home was a social institution. The Home was not simply a school and dormitory with a military edge. It was also a self-contained community in its own right. The Home produced its own paper, made its own clothes and shoes, cooked it own food, and operated its own hospital. It even had its own fire department. In addition, the children of the Home participated in an extensive sports program, attended summer camp, belonged to the Scouts and the 4H, took part in drama, and even had their own rifle team and a social center in the Orfenz Den. The sports program included interscholastic competition in several sports and multiple state championships in several of them. When the pupils of the home did things, they usually did them quite well.

The Home was a way of life. Being part of the Home meant one was part of something much greater than oneself. The Home was not just a place to live and work and play. It was how one looked and acted and conducted oneself. The lessons of dress, deportment, and discipline were learned at a very young age and once instilled were never really lost. The people of the Home became quickly accustomed to the life of the whistle and the work that went by a well- planned schedule in each well-planned day. This did not mean that there was no time for laughter, play, and the simple silence of a quiet time in a quiet place. Because there was always time for that as well.

No Other Place

Some people remember the Home best through the memory of its special times—the frivolity and chill of a New Year, the candy and embarrassment of Valentines Day, the songs and worship on Easter Sunday, the excitement of drill on Field Day, the quiet in the cemetery on Memorial Day, the return of the Ex-Pupils on the Fourth of July, and Halloween and Thanksgiving and Christmas.

Always Christmas—with the Ex-Pupils coming into the Dining Room singing the Home Christmas Carol. For many people at the Home, there is no other Christmas but this.

For many people of the Home, there is no other place but this place. This was the place where they grew up running through the rooms of Peter Pan, and learned to sing and march and learned a trade. This was the place where they found friends and enemies and learned to live with both. This was the place called Home— because it was Home and it always would be.

And this is the last and greatest lesson of the Home: One can call a place an orphans' home, a children's home, or a residential center and it might try to be any of them. But if it is not well and truly a Home, it will really be none of them. The Home learned all of these lessons over a long memorable history, which is still unfolding.

Places like the Home worked once and in some places they still do.

They can work again.

And they will.

"In certain weather, in the morning, I go outside and the smell of the grass, the air, sends me back. I was not thinking of The Home at all, then I see it in the sunlight. It is summer, a nice day. I see The Home again, and I get a feeling of well-being. I'm 10 years old again, at The Home. My home..."
—Bill Chavanne, Class of 1955

In 1968, Cottages 10 and 21 held
a reunion, featuring Bells, Greens,
Mayberrys, Clifford Anderson and
others, depicted in these photos,
before and after. In bottom
photograph of Cottage 21,
that's Jack Mayberry, Happy
Green, Joe Green, David Green,
and Art Dyamond sitting on
the steps, and Myron Bell, Paul Green, Harry
Dyamond, and James Hill standing behind them. In top
photograph taken at the mini-reunion in 1968, front row: Jack Mayberry,
Myron Bell, Dale Mayberry, and Clifford Anderson. Middle row: Jeanne
Mayberry, Betty Jefferson, Vivian Gant, Thurlow Jefferson. Back row:
Gladys Reid, Helen Bell, unknown, Charles Strauder, Bill Strauder,
and David Anderson.

Acknowledgments

Like most rather large books, *A Home of Their Own* received a lot of help from a lot of people. First, a number of people at each of the following libraries were most helpful over a period of months and sometimes years in the gathering of material and helping make sense of what was discovered. A list of all of the people who helped at all of these places would probably run to several pages. My thanks to all of you.

Archives, Library Division, Ohio Historical Society, Columbus, Ohio
Columbus Metropolitan Library, Columbus Ohio.
Greene County Public Library, Xenia, Ohio
Leon A. Beeghly Library, Ohio Wesleyan University, Delaware, Ohio
Library of Congress, Washington D.C.
National Archives and Records Administration, Washington D.C.
Paul Laurence Dunbar Library, Wright State University, Dayton, Ohio
Rutherford B. Hayes Presidential Center Library, Fremont, Ohio
State Library of Ohio, Columbus, Ohio.
William Oxley Thompson Library, The Ohio State University, Columbus, Ohio

Then there are the organizations that provided assistance as well. Several newspapers were quite helpful in making available materials from their files. These included the *Columbus Dispatch*, the *Dayton Daily News* and the *Xenia Gazette*. In Xenia, a number of people at Greene County Historical Society and the Greene County Clerk of Courts were sources of helpful information. In Columbus, the Ohio Historical Society, the Columbus Historical Society and the Columbus Landmarks Foundation all provided help of one sort or another at one time or another.

There are also some thanks due to the Association of Ex-Pupils. This book would not have been possible without the materials they brought to the project. These include both the exhibited material and archival collections of the Association Museum in the former Memorial Library at the Home. In addition, more than eighty former pupils provided their reminiscences and observation in written or oral form—and sometimes both. Association President Larry Tolle was particularly helpful with his laborious scanning of the files of the *Home Review*. The Museum is a unique place and some of its many treasures can be seen in this book.

Then there is the Rooney Fund. Established as a memorial to longtime Home teacher J. Robert Rooney, the Fund provided the resources and direction to make this book possible. Rooney Fund Board members Lester Anderson, William H. Chavanne, and Robert Impson guided this book through every step of its research, writing and publication. My thanks to them as well.
A special thank you is extended to Michael Curtin for his advice as the project proceeded and his thoughtful review of the manuscript. The people at Orange Frazer Press all need to be thanked as well. John Baskin, Marcy Hawley and others took the modest effort of this writer and gatherer of pictures and actually made a book out of it. This book owes a lot as well to my wife Andrea, without whose help and support its completion would not have been possible.

Finally, there are the more than 13,000 young people who passed through the Home on its long journey. Hopefully, this will only be the first of many books by many people about all of you who came here seeking a Home—and found one. If this book belongs to anybody, it belongs to you.

In the course of writing this book, any errors made as to fact were certainly unintentional and are regretted. The interpretations of what all of this means may be shared by others but are mine and mine alone.

Notes

CHAPTER ONE: A place called Poverty Knoll (circa 1870)

Several books have been especially helpful in the preparation of *A Home of Their Own.*

Most important is *The Pride of Ohio: The History of the Ohio Soldiers' and Sailors' Orphans' Home at Xenia, Ohio 1868-1963* (Xenia: AXP, 1963) by Edward Wakefield Hughes and William Clyde McCracken with later editorial assistance by a number of other people associated with the Home. It is an invaluable resource about all aspects of the history of the Home. On the general subject of children in America, the definitive early work of Grace Abbott in the two volume, *The Child and the State* (Chicago: Univ. of Chicago Press, 1938) is complemented by the later multivolume work edited by Robert Bremner and others and entitled *Children and Youth in America*, (Cambridge: Harvard University Press, 1970 et seq.). On orphanages in America, two books were particularly helpful. They were Matthew A. Crenson's *Building the Invisible Orphanage: A Prehistory of the American Welfare System* (Cambridge: Harvard University Press, 1998) and Timothy Hacsi's, *Second Home: Orphan Asylums and Poor Families in America* (Cambridge: Harvard University Press, 1997). Also useful is Michael Katz' *In the Shadow of the Poorhouse: A Social History of Welfare in America* (New York: Basic Books, 1986, 1996). On the poor laws of Ohio, the best single source is still Aileen Kennedy's, *The Ohio Poor Law and Its Administration*, (Chicago: University of Chicago Press, 1938). For the general history of Ohio, the standard modern source is George Knepper's, *Ohio and Its People* (Kent: Kent State University Press, 1989). And for the history of Xenia, Ohio, the thoughtful memoir *Ohio Town* (Columbus: Ohio State University Press, 1962) by Helen Hooven Santemyer is a good place to start.

CHAPTER TWO: Building the Home (1870-1900)

As is the case with many institutions, early records of the Ohio Soldiers and Sailors Orphans Home are not all that easy to find. The surviving minutes of the Board of Trustees begin in 1893—twenty-five years after the Home was founded.

No single institution—including the Home itself—has a complete set of its annual reports. The most complete set can be found at the State Library of Ohio with significant collections at The Ohio State University and the Ohio Historical Society. Only scattered issues of the *Home Weekly* newspaper can be found until well into the twentieth century. Other than newspapers like the *Xenia Gazette*, the best single source for this period is *The Pride of Ohio* (op.cit). Information about the back ground and subsequent careers of the Superintendents and other staff was obtained from local histories, obituaries and other secondary sources. Many of the fires, floods and other disasters were well documented in the newspapers of the era.

CHAPTER THREE: These orphans are a select class (1900-1930)

This chapter owes a lot to the meticulously detailed annual reports of the Home which—while not all in one place—tell a remarkable story when they are reviewed as a whole. A lot of important and useful material was also found in *The Pride of Ohio* (op.cit.). But in addition to these materials, some other important sources begin to become available as well. There is no complete set of the *Home Weekly* newspaper extant in public hands. But a significant collection of the publication beginning in the 1920's can be found in the Museum of the Association of Ex-Pupils in Xenia. The minutes of the Board from 1893 on can be found at the Ohio Historical Society Archives/Library in Columbus, Ohio. A lengthy series of interviews was conducted in 2006 of several ex-pupils of the Home as well as several former administrators. Most of the people interviewed were from more recent years. But a few of the oldest living ex-pupils were interviewed as well. Written reminiscences were also requested and collected. Some of their stories are in this chapter. The interviews and written accounts are the property of the Rooney Fund. The interviews have not been published but have been transcribed. The interviews and written recollections are an invaluable resource and will be referred to hereafter as the Rooney Fund Home History Project. Information about the previous experience and subsequent careers of the Superintendents and other staff was obtained from local histories, local newspapers, and obituaries.

CHAPTER FOUR: A good American home (1930-1940)

This chapter owes a great deal to *The Pride of Ohio* (op.cit). The *Home Weekly* ceased publication as a weekly newspaper in 1933 and became the monthly *Home Review*. Because it was published less frequently, many of its articles tend to be longer and more detailed than was the case with the weekly. While no one site has a complete set of the *Home Weekly*, complete sets of the *Home Review* can be found at a few large libraries and at the Xenia Museum of the Association of Ex-Pupils. The minutes of the Board for the decade of the 1930's can be found at the Ohio Historical Society. By the 1930's the minutes were typed and are considerably easier to read than the handwritten minutes from the early years. And once again the oral history interviews conducted with ex-pupils and written materials submitted by them in 2006 under the auspices of the Rooney Fund were used extensively and are quoted in this chapter. Biographical information about the staff of the Home and other public figures was obtained from obituaries, biographies and newspaper accounts.

CHAPTER FIVE: A fine place and a real home (1940-1963)

More so than any other part of this book, this chapter relied heavily on the oral history interviews and written materials collected by the Rooney Fund in 2006. Much of the reason for this is that many of the people contributing material lived at the Home in the period covered in this chapter. As has been the case in the past, heavy use was also made of *The Pride of Ohio* (op.cit.) and the *Home Review* monthly publication of the Home. Articles in the *Home Review* tended to become shorter and more concise with the passage of time and long descriptive articles, like those in the 1930's editions, become harder to find. Nevertheless, the *Home Review* and its predecessor *Home Weekly* remain good sources of information on day to day life at the Home. The best single source for annual reports of the Board of Trustees is the State Library of Ohio. The minutes of the Board are held by the Ohio Historical Society. The Society holds the papers of several of Ohio's recent governors. The papers of Governors Bricker, Lausche, Herbert, O'Neill, and Rhodes at the Ohio Historical Society are useful, particularly with reference to issues related to budget, board appointments and policy issues about the Home directed to the governor's attention. Biographical information about the Board and staff of the Home was obtained from obituaries, biographies and newspaper accounts.

CHAPTER SIX: Transition comes to the Home (1963-1978)

This chapter relies to a great extent on oral history accounts and written materials collected by the Rooney Fund in 2006 for the Rooney Fund Home History Project. Again a large number of people are quoted directly, especially about their memories of life at the Home. The primary sources of information for this chapter were the minutes of Board at the Ohio Historical Society, the annual reports of the Home at the State Library of Ohio, and the collected editions of the *Home Review* at the Xenia Museum. The papers of Governor Rhodes and Gilligan were also helpful and can be found at the Ohio Historical Society in Columbus. Biographical information about the Board and staff was gathered from obituaries, biographies and newspaper accounts. The *Home Review* also provided background information about many of the more prominent people mentioned in the story of the Home.

CHAPTER SEVEN: So much permanent good (1978-1995)

As was the case previously, this chapter relies to some extent on the oral history accounts and written materials collected by the Rooney Fund in 2006. There were fewer interviews conducted with people from the last years of the Home. The interviews conducted with former teachers, staff and administrators were particularly useful. The primary sources of information for this chapter were the minutes of Board at the Ohio Historical Society and the collected editions of the *Home Review* at the Xenia Museum. The papers of Governor Richard Celeste and Lieutenant Governor Michael DeWine were also helpful and can be found at the Ohio Historical Society in Columbus. The papers of Governor George Voinovich are located in the Center for Archives and Special Collections of the Ohio University Libraries in Athens, Ohio. Background information about the Home and its people was gathered from obituaries, biographies and newspaper accounts. The *Home Review* also provided background information about many of the more prominent people mentioned in the story of the Home. The *Home Review* for many of the later years of the Home's history has only survived as scattered issues.

CHAPTER EIGHT: Places to call Home (the orphanage in America)

This chapter also uses the oral history accounts and written materials collected by the Rooney Fund in 2006 as part of the Rooney Fund Home History Project. New interviews were conducted by the author in 2009 as well. Primary sources of information for this chapter included the collected editions of the *Home Review* at the Xenia Museum and newspaper accounts from the period. Claude "Bud" Schindler, the President of Legacy Ministries International was particularly helpful in providing information about the recent history of the place which is now its home. Other information about the Home was obtained from obituaries, biographies, newspaper accounts as well as the books specifically mentioned in the chapter. The *Home Review* also provided background information about many of the people mentioned in the story of the Home. Issues of the *Home Review* for many of the later years of the Home's history have not been retained by local libraries or other repositories.

The conclusions are those of the author.

Index

(A page number in **bold italics** indicates a picture.)

These ladies of the Home served at the 1950 reunion.
The prayer at mealtime had been revised a bit and
like skirts, it had grown a bit shorter:
"We offer thanks to thee, O Lord,
For this our daily food,
May we in thought, deed and word
Show forth our gratitude. Amen."

Ed Lentz holds degrees in history from Princeton University
and The Ohio State University, and he has been teaching, writing, and
exploring the history of central Ohio for the past forty years
or so. When not doing that sort of thing, he teaches history, political
science, and other subjects at various local colleges and universities.
He is the author of several books about the history of Ohio
in general and central Ohio in particular.
He has been known to write for local newspapers, consult in history
and historic preservation, and keep company with his wife, three
cats, and occasionally resident two children.
If the best life is a busy one he has no reason to complain.